W9-BSD-724

THIS
AFRICAN-
AMERICAN
LIFE

ALSO BY HUGH B. PRICE

Achievement Matters: Getting Your Child the Best Education Possible

Strugglers Into Strivers: What the Military Can Teach Us About How Young People Learn and Grow

Mobilizing the Community to Help Students Succeed

Destination: The American Dream

THIS
AFRICAN-
AMERICAN
LIFE

HUGH B. PRICE

John F. Blair
Publisher
1406 Plaza Drive
Winston-Salem, North Carolina 27103

Copyright © 2017 by Hugh B. Price

All rights reserved. No part of this book may be reproduced in any form or by any electronic or mechanical means, including information storage and retrieval systems, without permission in writing from the publisher, except by a reviewer, who may quote brief passages in a review. For information, address John F. Blair, Publisher, Subsidiary Rights Department, 1406 Plaza Drive, Winston-Salem, North Carolina 27103.

Library of Congress Cataloging-in-Publication Data is available upon request.

Library of Congress Cataloging in Publication Control Number: 2017004144

All photographs are from Hugh B. Price's personal collection, unless otherwise noted.

ISBN 978-0-89587-691-1

Printed in the United States of America

10 9 8 7 6 5 4 3 2 1

Design by The Roberts Group Editorial & Design

Cover design by Anna B. Sutton

Cover photographs: *From left to right:* Price's mother & father on wedding day 1935; Price as little boy playing in his back yard; Price and Marilyn Lloyd on their wedding day in 1963; Price giving keynote address at National Urban League annual conference in 1994

CONTENTS

PROLOGUE

I harbor no illusions about the advantages bestowed upon me from the beginning. I was blessed with an intact family, loving parents and a brother who cheered me on, a comfortably middle-class upbringing, and the safety of a stable neighborhood.

Some discoveries during adolescence can be fleeting and inconsequential. Others border on epiphanies, illuminating the world as it really is, like it or not. They even can tellingly influence the arc of one's professional career.

I endured such a life-changing experience in high school. In the summer of 1958, between the eleventh and twelfth grades, I was selected for an internship with a U.S. Defense Department subcontractor known as the Operations Research Office (ORO). Those who were chosen excelled in math and science. I made the cut. In fact, I was the first black student ever selected for this prestigious opportunity.

As our task that summer, we estimated the damage that thermonuclear bombs of varying megatons would inflict if an enemy such as the Soviet Union dropped one on Washington, D.C., or another major American city. The idea was to project what scale of investment in civil defense was required in order to limit the loss of human life and physical devastation.

Today, we harbor anxieties about terrorist attacks, dirty bombs, weapons of mass destruction, and slaughters even in public schools. My generation grew up scared of outright annihilation. The news media bombarded us with coverage of the brutal Soviet dictator and America's archenemy, Joseph Stalin, who we feared would launch a preemptive strike against the U.S. mainland. Of course, the nation's capital stood as a prime target.

The busybodies at ORO, who were white, took it upon themselves to administer a battery of tests designed to gauge our potential. If memory serves, the tests resembled an SAT exam or IQ assessment. I was puzzled why they even bothered. To my mind, the interns had demonstrated already that we were strong students with bright futures. We would not have been selected otherwise. My preliminary SAT scores, grades, and class ranking were plenty strong enough to qualify me for admission to Ivy League universities and their small-college equivalents.

I shall never forget the prognosis the ORO staffers handed me when they debriefed me individually on the test results. "You probably will go to college," they said encouragingly, "but you shouldn't count on getting into graduate or professional school."

I walked, silent and fuming, out of the room. Fortunately, I possessed enough self-confidence to keep their equivocal assessment from rattling me. I reported the episode to my parents, who told me to pay it no heed. Even so, the encounter triggered a kaleidoscope of emotions. It confused, embarrassed, and humiliated me.

Many reasons may explain the lukewarm assessment by ORO. Perhaps, perish the thought, it was an accurate reflection of my intellectual ability and potential. I didn't buy that then, and I do not now. It is possible, of course, that it was an aberration, that I simply had a bad test day. Since I mangled the law school entrance exam a half-decade later, an off day was not out of the question. Even so, sharing a so-so prognosis about a youngster's future based on only one exam bordered on child abuse.

For the first time in my life, adults had called my scholastic ability, intelligence, and potential into question. I had set my sights on applying to top colleges and universities. Was I naively overreaching? Should I lower my sights for college and beyond?

The assessment left me wondering if I had suffered an early encounter with institutional racism. I refer to those barely discernible, seemingly innocent decisions by gatekeepers that are designed to stifle hope, hold people of color back, deny us deserved opportunities to advance, and sow doubt about our potential and our rightful place in the American mainstream.

I discovered as an adolescent that racism isn't always blatant. It can be subtle, as if written with invisible ink. But the net effect—denial of equality, opportunity, and upward mobility—is the same. Youngsters of all races and socioeconomic groups can be "misunderestimated" by tests and teachers. I have listened to titans of industry and creative geniuses complain bitterly of being dismissed as dyslexic, only to soar later to the pinnacle of their professions. I know of influential lawmakers who earned unimpressive scores on the SAT or were shunted off to special education, only to ascend to the heights of power and influence in public life.

I am neither anti-intellectual nor anti-test. But my experience with ORO left me deeply mistrustful of the reliability and predictive power of such assessment devices. Imagine how dangerous these tools can be in the hands of those who are skeptical of one's potential or who consciously—or even subconsciously—mean harm.

The lesson I derived from ORO's test taught me volumes about the way the world works. It underscored the need to set my personal radar to detect any signs of racism or hypocrisy. In retrospect, I realize it helped chart the course of much of my career, with its recurring focus on cultivating youngsters' academic and social development, recognizing their undetected or underestimated potential, affording them second chances to straighten out their lives, and guiding them onto constructive paths.

The experience also underscored how indispensable caring adults are in the lives of kids. I was blessed to have loving parents who understood how the world worked, who knew me intimately, and who therefore blew off ORO's assessment. They shepherded me through this adolescent crisis of confidence so my ego and future emerged intact and on track.

ORO's devaluation of my potential helped fuel my determination to fight for the rights of my people, and especially young people, to enjoy equality, opportunity, upward mobility, and access to the American mainstream.

This early equivocal prognosis about my life prospects remains deeply etched in my memory. I remembered it when I earned a BA from Amherst, one of America's preeminent liberal arts colleges, and later a law degree from Yale, arguably the best law school in the world. I remembered it when I received the Award of Merit from Yale Law School, a highly coveted award also bestowed on the likes of President Bill Clinton. I recalled what ORO predicted when I subsequently earned honorary degrees from Amherst, Yale, and Northeastern, among other institutions, and when I was inducted into the American Philosophical Society and the American Academy of Arts and Sciences.

On behalf of the "misunderestimated" of the world, enough said.

CHAPTER I

THE VILLAGE THAT RAISED ME

Historians who should know say Africa is "the cradle of civilization." I say the cradle is closer to home—namely, Howard University, the historically black citadel of higher learning smack in the heart of the village that raised me in Washington, D.C.

Howard served as the de facto intellectual and geographical hub of Washington's black community when I was growing up. This was the era before integration. The era before talented and ambitious blacks began dispersing in droves to far-flung, newly integrated neighborhoods and suburbs rimming D.C., not to mention to the campuses of historically white colleges and universities across the country. The era, prior to the 1960s, before waves of highly educated black public servants gravitated to Washington to assume leadership and administrative positions in the federal government as well as the law firms, lobbying outfits, and trade associations that orbit it.

Mom and Dad met at Howard. A native of D.C., my father, Kline A. Price Sr., was a first-year medical student there. Charlotte Schuster, my mom, hailed from West Haven, Connecticut. In a scene straight from a romantic movie, she was eating in Miner Hall, the freshman dining hall, when a dashingly handsome medical student spotted her. Evidently, the med students used to come to the dining hall and stand in the balcony, surveying the incoming crop of coeds. Their eyes met. Dad made his move, and the rest, after the requisite courtship, was history. Howard molded the lives of most of my loved ones and many of the friends who've been closest to me over the years.

On November 22, 1941, I entered this world on Howard's campus—at Freedmen's Hospital, to be exact. Back then, it served as the medical school's teaching hospital, as well as one of two hospital ports of entry for newborn Negro babies in our segregated city. My older brother, Kline Jr., had preceded me at Freedmen's by five and a half years.

A mere fifteen-minute walk north of Howard University lies my old neighborhood—and my family's first house, at 3505 New Hampshire Avenue NW, near the intersection with Park Road. When we lived there, the community consisted primarily of African-American families. Whites lived mostly north of us and west of Fourteenth Street. Number 3505 was—and remains—a sturdy, unimposing brick row house that probably could withstand a severe earthquake. Today, it's doubtless called a townhouse. My parents paid about $10,000 for it in 1940. In 2013, the house sold for $459,000, an affirmation of Washington's startling metamorphosis from a mostly black city into a robustly gentrified one. When we lived there, our neighborhood did not have a chic name. Today, it goes by Columbia Heights.

The curse and constraints of segregation aside, ours truly was a community straight out of a postwar Hollywood script. Every house on our block featured a front porch. On sweltering summer evenings in that era long before home air conditioning, TV, and the internet, my buddies and I prowled our tiny front yards, snaring lightning bugs in glass jars with air holes punched in the tops. We competed to see who could count the most station wagons whizzing by along New Hampshire Avenue. With one eye on us, our parents rocked lazily on those indestructible cast-iron

Mom, Kline, and me on summer vacation in Oak Bluffs, Massachusetts

gliders with Naugahyde-covered cushions. Neighbors chatted across the railings of their porches, sipping cold beer and swapping hot gossip. Since crime seldom intruded in our lives, families routinely left their doors unlocked during the day, so the children could dash in and out for snacks and naps. Neighbors wandered freely in and out as well. No one called ahead or needed an appointment to drop by for iced tea or beer.

One of Dad's favorite rituals was to cook up a batch of crabs or chitterlings, spread some newspapers across the kitchen table, and invite neighbors over for an impromptu feast. Crabs I could stomach. But when Dad started cleaning and cooking those "chitlins" that smelled like an outhouse, I cleared out as fast as I could. My brother, Kline, claims I missed out on some good eating, but I never felt deprived.

My best buddies lived nearby. Billy Lindsay was right next door. His dad drove a cab, and his older sister, Sylvia, sometimes babysat me.

She was really pretty. In fact, I had a crush on her. Billy's little brother, Lawrence, hung around almost everywhere we went.

Alonzo Smith resided across the street. His father was the first African-American to receive national board certification as a pediatrician, and his mother, Marie, was one of Mom's dearest friends. Alonzo, who grew up to be a historian at the Smithsonian Institution, possessed a wacky sense of humor and a cackling giggle. He would do almost anything for a laugh. Once, we were riding down Georgia Avenue in a streetcar. Alonzo reached out the rear window and yanked the cord connected to the pantograph. It in turn was attached to the overhead electrical lines, which provided the power. The streetcar stopped dead in its tracks. Instead of looking about innocently as though he hadn't a clue what

With my indulgent kitty

happened, Alonzo burst into an ear-splitting laugh that drew every eye our way. Fortunately, the conductor let us off with a warning.

Though my buddies and I had mischievous streaks, we were basically goody-two-shoes types who performed well in school and would never dream of doing anything really bad.

One fall day when we were about ten, we cooked up a harebrained scheme to shatter that image. The hottest toy at the time was a Duncan yo-yo with specks of embedded glass meant to mimic diamonds. It sold for about thirty-five cents.

The five-and-dime around the corner on Georgia Avenue was a cornucopia of alluring trinkets, including those glitzy yo-yos we coveted. Alonzo, Billy, and I hatched a heist from the store. Naturally, Lawrence tagged along. We entered the five-and-dime one day after school and fanned out across the aisles. We three amateur thieves surreptitiously stuffed assorted items into our pockets, including plenty of Duncan yo-yos. Mind you, this was decades before metal detectors and barcodes. We then sashayed through the doors and dashed back to our houses with the haul.

Apprehension and shame gripped me almost immediately. I tossed my stash way under the oil tank in the basement. Petrified of detection and dishonor, I never retrieved and enjoyed my ill-gotten gains.

My brother Kline and his wife Bebe

I remained in this state of guilt and anxiety for about a week, although it felt like forever. Then, one afternoon when I returned home from school, Mom gravely summoned me into the living room. She said she had received a call from the police station, Precinct 10, which was a mere half-block from our house, on Park Road between New Hampshire and Georgia Avenues. My heart sank all the way to my black high-top Keds. Why? Because I walked by the Precinct 10 station house almost daily. The cops knew where I lived and went to school. Worse still, they knew my parents. You see, they, too, belonged to "the village," even though they were mostly white.

Mom said the desk sergeant who called told her the five-and-dime had reported a shoplifting incident, and that my buddies and I had been fingered as the thieves. He instructed her to bring me to the precinct for questioning. Terrified beyond belief, I asked Mom what

Mom and Dad in downtown D.C. in the 1950s

this meant. She speculated that I might have to stay overnight in jail at Precinct 10. She sternly told me to go upstairs, take a bath, put on my Sunday suit, and pack enough underwear for two nights behind bars. Mind you, I was ten years old. Oblivious to my legal rights, I dutifully complied. No way would I disobey her and appeal to the highest authority in the land—my dad.

When I'd done as I was told, I came back downstairs and sat on the sofa, trembling in fear. Mom then revealed that in fact she hadn't received a call from the cops. Instead, she said, it was Mrs. Lindsay, Billy's mother, who called her. It turns out Billy's little brother,

Mom and Dad on their wedding day in front of St. Philips Episcopal Church in Harlem, June 3, 1935

Lawrence, had gotten cold feet and ratted on us. Mrs. Lindsay then contacted my mother and Mrs. Smith, and the three of them concocted this scheme to scare their wayward sons half to death.

Did it ever work! In the most humiliating episode of my life, they made us round up the contraband and return it to the store with a sheepish apology. Mom punished me for a month. She made me come home immediately after school and head straight to my room, where I remained all afternoon and evening except for dinner. I don't know if Dr. Spock would have approved, but Mom's home remedy for misbehavior worked on me.

In 1996, roughly forty-five years later, I returned to Coolidge High School, my alma mater in D.C., for a school assembly to launch a new initiative of the National Urban League, which I then headed. Afterward, a familiar-looking man approached me. He said he was a science teacher at Coolidge and that his name—you guessed it—was Lawrence

Playing in our tiny backyard

Lindsay. As we shook hands, I blurted out, "Do you remember . . . ?" He completed the sentence before I could, laughingly recalling how he had told his mother on us. Praise the Lord for mothers and, I grudgingly admit, little brothers. Both obviously are card-carrying members of the village it takes to raise a child.

In the late 1940s, my parents joined All Souls Unitarian Church. Having weathered many a wrenching neighborhood change over the years, it's located to this day at Sixteenth and Harvard Streets NW, a leisurely fifteen-minute stroll from our old house. The setting of the church's moral compass suited my parents perfectly. When they joined, All Souls was led by its crusading senior minister, the Reverend A. Powell Davies, who gained national recognition for his progressive views and staunch opposition to segregation. Over the years, All Souls remained true to its tradition of civil rights activism. In January 1962, my brother married Bebe Drew at the church. She's the eldest daughter of the legendary Dr. Charles Drew, the head of the surgery department at Freedmen's, who gained international renown during World War II for developing the process that preserves blood plasma. The church's young associate minister, the Reverend James Reeb, presided. Four years later, Reeb joined the freedom struggle in Selma, Alabama, where he was beaten to death by racist white thugs. The murder became a cause célèbre of the civil rights movement and was graphically depicted in the soul-stirring film *Selma*.

The Sunday trek from our house to All Souls took me across Fourteenth Street, which served as a de facto dividing line between black and white Washington. En route, I would stroll past the Tivoli Theatre, at Fourteenth and Park Road, which stubbornly barred blacks from entering. I recall asking the ticket clerk when colored kids would be admitted. "One day, son," she replied ruefully. "One day."

On the way home from All Souls, I routinely stopped at a sprawling outdoor newsstand to stock up on sports magazines such as the *Sporting News, Street & Smith's Baseball Annual, Sport, Complete Baseball,* and *Baseball Digest*. I read them cover to cover more than once. Mom begged me to read classic books, but I would have none of it. I tried to assuage her by reading *Classic Comics*.

Fourteenth Street up our way was a bustling commercial corridor in the 1940s and 1950s. Its segregated theaters represented the tip of the iceberg of racial discrimination in D.C. in those days. Prior to the Supreme Court's landmark *Brown v. Board of Education* decision in 1954, Washington's public schools were rigidly segregated. I attended Blanche Kelso Bruce School, an elementary school for black children named after an ex-slave who, during the heyday of Reconstruction in 1875, was elected to the U.S. Senate representing the state of Mississippi.

Bruce typified black schools back then. It truly was a neighborhood school. My parents knew many of my teachers from church, civic clubs, and social events. In fact, my father and several of my teachers—or their siblings or spouses—were contemporaries and had even been classmates two generations earlier, at Mott Elementary School, Dunbar High School, or Howard. As a physician and surgeon, Dad ministered to the health needs of my teachers and their families. In fact, he operated on my fifth-grade teacher's father, who was also the grandfather of my future wife. Thus, even if I had tried, there was no escaping the network linking those who reared me with those who educated me.

A welcome neighbor next to Howard's campus was the Wonder Bread factory, whose heavenly aromas wafted across the whole area. The smell was intoxicating. It addicted me to the squishy bread that makes for scrumptious peanut butter and jelly sandwiches.

Howard abutted black Washington's unofficial downtown, which stretched north and south along Georgia Avenue and Seventh Street, as well as east and west along Florida Avenue and then U Street. Jim Crow barred blacks from virtually all restaurants and cinemas in the official downtown, so we were obliged to patronize this part of town for entertainment. U Street, the spine of our downtown, was home to a dense concentration of black-owned jazz clubs, restaurants, shops, and fraternal and religious institutions. The saucy entertainer Pearl Bailey dubbed U Street "the Black Broadway." This area actually predated Harlem as the cultural mecca for black people. A PBS documentary anointed it Duke Ellington's neighborhood, since he was born in the adjoining Shaw District.

As a youngster, I loved cowboy movies. One curious anomaly of segregation back then was that the black movie houses along U Street, such as the Lincoln and the Republic, showed second-string cowboy stars—Hoot Gibson, Lash Larue, Kevin Maynard, and such. I got to see first-stringers Roy Rogers and Gene Autry only when I traveled north to Connecticut to visit relatives and went to integrated cinemas.

Farther west stood a versatile entertainment venue of my youth— tiny Turner's Arena, near Fourteenth and W Streets. It seated a mere two thousand fans. Trumpet virtuoso Dizzy Gillespie and his orchestra performed there. In 1946, Turner's hosted the first Central Intercollegiate Athletic Association (CIAA) basketball tournament, which showcased black hoop stars at historically black colleges and universities. Black fraternities also fielded talented basketball teams that competed fiercely at Turner's for bragging rights in the frat world. The arena hosted boxing matches as well.

Accompanied by my father, I saw many a pro wrestling match at Turner's. The names were outrageous even then. Gorgeous George pranced around the ring swishing his golden locks. Iron Mike Magurski had the mien of a mobster, while the French Angel resembled a gargoyle on Notre Dame in Paris. The "sport" probably was bogus way back then, too, but all the grunts, ketchup-like gore, and body slams made me cringe even so.

As with many other central-city neighborhoods, the U Street area had been mostly white and middle class in the late 1800s. Blacks then predominated as segregation tightened its grip in the early twentieth century. Thanks to robust gentrification, the Greater U Street Historic District of today is an ethnic kaleidoscope where residents and tourists frequent trendy new eateries and nightclubs.

This was the village where I grew up, the village it took to raise me in the 1940s and early 1950s. It was neither a figment of my imagination nor an idealized black version of *Ozzie and Harriet*.

Looking back on my village, I realize I took the intact family life, mores, support, safety, stability, economic security, and communal networks for granted. Segregation notwithstanding, I considered the climate normal, free of trauma and anxiety. What a blessed upbringing! My village contrasts sharply with the prevalent image of inner-city communities today, riven with poverty, crime, and dysfunction. Mine wasn't an illusion glimpsed through a rose-colored rearview mirror or remembered through a haze of early-onset Alzheimer's. Villages like mine were not rarities, especially in cities, North and South, of any size. Nor are they today in stable middle-class urban neighborhoods and nearby suburbs.

But regrettably, villages like mine do not exist for millions of African-American youngsters today. The connections and cohesion, the socioeconomic diversity within black neighborhoods that helped propel children in the right direction, dissolved long ago, thanks to integration, the erosion of factory-based inner-city economies, and the exodus of black middle-class families, leaving poor youngsters stranded without strong support systems and readily accessible role models. With rare exceptions, gentrification won't recreate village life of this caliber for youngsters at risk of being left behind. The unanswered—but hopefully not unanswerable—question is whether or not the village of my youth can be reconceived in the twenty-first century in order to embrace the children most in need of nurturing by family and community.

CHAPTER 2

AN UNCOMMON MAN
WITH RESILIENT ROOTS

My father, Kline Armond Price Sr., was a native and lifelong Washingtonian.

His great-great-grandfather was a mulatto named Robert Gunnell, a farmer who lived in Langley, Virginia, just across the Potomac River from D.C. According to family accounts, Robert Gunnell purchased his freedom from his slave masters in the mid-1830s. Soon after registering as a free man, he bought a six-acre farm in Langley, along with farm animals, equipment, and furniture. His property was situated on what is now Old Georgetown Pike in McLean (a.k.a. Langley), just up the road from what generations later became the sprawling estate of Robert and Ethel Kennedy, within walking distance of CIA headquarters, erected in the late 1950s.

After marrying a mulatto slave named Harriet Lee, Robert had eight children. He registered them and two other adults as his personal slaves to prevent them from being seized or sold in other Southern states. At some point, Robert, Harriet, and their brood moved to D.C. The impetus is unknown. Perhaps Robert shrewdly anticipated that Congress would soon enact a law freeing slaves within the Washington city limits and compensating their former owners. This it did in 1862. That same year, Robert was paid $2,168.10 for the liberation of his slaves. The individual valuations ranged from $438.00 to $21.90.

Around 1866, blacks began to conduct religious services at Robert's house, according to the great-great-grandson of his former owner. This apparently was the first place they could worship in Fairfax

County, which encompasses Langley. The Gunnells subsequently built the first Negro schoolhouse in the area on their land. In 1879, they donated a half-acre parcel for the site of a church. Two decades later, construction commenced on what came to be known as Gunnell's Chapel Methodist Church.

Robert and Harriet Gunnell's daughter Mary married a man named Thomas Payne. Their son Richard Payne in turn married a brown-skinned woman named Roberta, nicknamed "Birdie." They had two daughters—Irene, who like my father was brown skinned, and Mary, the fair-skinned mother of Frank Jones. Richard Payne, who worked in a quarry, could pass for white. In fact, Dad occasionally accompanied his grandfather Payne on trips to the white neighborhoods and farmers' market in Washington, where he sold his produce. Black farmers were barred from the market. As they approached, Richard would instruct his brown-skinned grandson to hide under the buckboard of the wagon so his cover wouldn't be blown. Dad would recount this indignity with a tinge of bitterness but also with some tolerance for his grandfather's determination to do whatever he must in order to support his family.

Dad's mother, Irene Payne Price, also a native Washingtonian, trained at Miner Teachers College, a preparatory institution for aspiring black schoolteachers. Unable to find a teaching position in Washington upon graduation, she accepted an offer in Charles County, Maryland, roughly forty

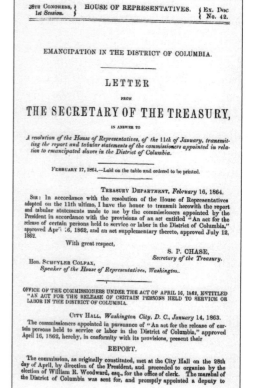

Cover page of the House of Representatives bill emancipating the slaves in the District of Columbia, enacted on February 17, 1864

miles south of the city. There, she met and married an enterprising local farmer named William Bernard Price, whose farm was located in Hill Top. William and Irene eventually moved to Washington. My father, their second son, was born in D.C. on May 7, 1907. Tragically, his father contracted a respiratory illness and died in 1910, when Dad was two years old.

A formidable and resilient woman, Irene supported her young children by toiling as a handmaiden to wealthy white women, most notably the actress Nora Bayes. A multitalented singer, comedian, and composer, Bayes was a flamboyant vaudeville star in the early twentieth century and was considered one of the first mega-celebrities in the United States. One of her favorite performance venues was the Chase Vaudeville Theater in D.C., home of "polite vaudeville." She also starred in the Ziegfeld Follies on Broadway. With her husband, Jack Norworth, Bayes cowrote the hit song "Shine On, Harvest Moon."

Nora Bayes occasionally journeyed to Europe to perform in London and France. According to family lore, she and my grandmother were due to sail to Europe on the *Lusitania*, a Cunard ocean liner

Listing of my African-American ancestor Robert Gunnell and his slaves, who were freed by the House of Representatives

owned by Great Britain, Germany's avowed enemy. Supposedly, they decided to cancel when the Germans issued a public warning that their U-boats would torpedo the ship. Their caution paid off, as the Germans carried through on the threat, sinking the *Lusitania* on May 7, 1915. Fortunately, Dad was spared the tragedy of losing his other parent on his eighth birthday.

Since his mother traveled frequently, my father lived from age two until sixteen with her sister Mary and her husband, Samuel Jones, on Third and T Streets NW in LeDroit Park, a short stroll from Howard. His roommate through these years was their son and his first cousin, Frank Jones. Ten years older than Dad, "Uncle Frank," as we called him, subsequently became his professional mentor and preceptor. Early playmates recalled my father as a quiet, gentle, well-mannered, and purposeful child. Often left to his own devices, he grew up highly self-reliant, like his mother, yet something of a loner.

Interestingly, the paternal branch of Frank Jones's family enjoyed some renown. His father's sister, also named Irene, married a celebrated minstrel named James Bland, who composed such staples as "Down

Irene Payne Price— Dad's mother   *William Price— Dad's father*

by the Old Mill Stream" and "Carry Me Back to Old Virginny," the official state song of Virginia.

When Dad rejoined his mother, her second husband, Austin Broadnick, and his older brother Roland, the family lived in Georgetown, which for years has been a chic upper-crust neighborhood. I doubt many Washingtonians today realize that Georgetown was predominantly black during the early twentieth century.

Grandmother Price belonged to Georgetown's Mount Zion United Methodist Church, home of the oldest black congregation in D.C. She and my grandfather married there on November 26, 1901. Known for her dramatic presence and flair, Irene ran the church's theatrical productions and directed many plays there. The engrossing book *Black Georgetown Remembered* contains vintage 1920s photos of my grandmother, one of her productions, titled *The Story of the Star*, and an overflow audience for a performance at the church.

My father attended the renowned, yet segregated, Dunbar High School at First and N Streets NW, where he received a superb education from its first-rate faculty, many of whom held PhDs but were

Roberta Payne—
Dad's grandmother/Irene's mother

Richard Payne—
Dad's grandfather/Irene's father

unable to land teaching jobs at mainstream colleges and universities. Following Dunbar, he enrolled at Howard. Dad yearned to teach French at the college level, but economic necessity steered many a black undergraduate like him into fields where they could earn a decent living and where they would encounter the least racial discrimination. Graduating with a BA in 1928, he opted to become a physician.

Howard Medical School was a struggle. Not academically, mind you, but financially. With scant help from his family, Dad supported himself during his undergraduate and medical school years by working lengthy hours as an elevator operator at the old Methodist Building. He persuaded congressmen who lived in the apartment building to secure books from the Library of Congress for his required reading. He prepared his assignments during lulls in elevator activity. Dad finished medical school in 1933. Traditional family life for him began soon after in 1935 with his marriage to my mother, Charlotte Schuster.

Dr. R. Frank Jones, my father's first cousin, was the first black physician to earn certification from the American Board of Urology. My father decided to follow his cousin into urology by joining his practice. By 1943, my father felt primed enough to seek American Board certification. He journeyed alone to Chicago to take the test. One white examiner tried to foil him by asking him to provide a diagnosis based on an x-ray so faint that it could barely be read. Fortunately, a supervisor interceded and instructed the examiner to give Dad a more legible x-ray.

My father passed the grueling exam and became only the second African-American certified by the American Board of Urology. This was truly historic, although as a two-year-old at the time I hardly appreciated his accomplishment. Nor was I aware, until my brother brought it to my attention at the time of John Wayne Bobbitt's high-profile operation in 1993 to reconnect his penis after it was sliced off by his enraged wife, that Dad had successfully performed a similar operation many years earlier. In fact, it was a first. More important, the procedure was successful or, as his proud cousin and mentor characterized it at the time, "physiologically satisfactory." My father published an article on the operation, entitled "Accidental transection of all corpora of the penis: Repair with good results," in the September 1952 issue of the *Journal of Urology*, the preeminent publication in his specialty. The mere thought of it still makes me grimace.

A medical scholar as well as a meticulous surgeon, Dad wrote and coauthored with his cousin Frank Jones numerous articles on urology and venereal disease. Since he also maintained a full-time medical practice, was an active surgeon, taught part-time in the medical school, and regularly logged pro bono time at Freedmen's free clinic for poor patients, I cannot to this day figure out how he carved out time to write journal articles.

After practicing medicine with Frank Jones, my father was eager to venture out from his cousin's shadow. In 1950, he launched a solo practice in an office on Rhode Island Avenue. He conducted an old-fashioned "country-style" practice. He and his nurse enjoyed chatting with patients about life, children, and travel. He made house calls, occasionally accompanied by my brother or me.

Throughout their thirty-eight years of marriage, my parents were an extraordinarily devoted couple. My father wasn't much of a talker, but our household always felt his presence. His unswerving devotion to Mom and our family shone through in the way he interacted with her and us. He made it abundantly clear that my brother and I were never to raise our voices against her in anger, a line neither of us ever approached, let alone crossed. If Kline or I did something bad, the disappointment and disapproval in Dad's eyes smarted more than any spanking, which he seldom, if ever, administered.

Dad's love of nature and simplicity sustained him—a residue, perhaps, of spending summers on his father's ancestral farm in Charles County, Maryland, and of growing up a loner. Many a weekend, he reached back to his own father's roots by taking us to the farm in Hill Top, where his father had lived at the turn of the twentieth century. Before that, the property was that of his grandfather Robert Price.

Robert and his wife, Julia, belonged to the remarkably resilient generation of ex-slaves who purchased farms and became self-reliant following the Civil War. Contrary to the image in 1920s movies of blacks as servants and slackers, black folk strove for independence immediately after the Emancipation Proclamation by acquiring farms and thereby enabling themselves to provide for their families. Robert bought fifty-six acres in 1893, and Julia acquired three adjacent acres.

Two sisters survived Grandpa Price, including Clara Price Marbury, who resided with her husband on the farm adjoining Grandpa's. Clara, affectionately known as "Pinkie," married Joseph "Teenie" Marbury, a farmer and country preacher whose modest whitewashed church sat in nearby Pisgah.

As a child, my father spent summers on the Price family farm, staying with aunts and uncles. The farm lay fallow for years after his father's death. Dad decided in the late 1940s that it would be the perfect weekend retreat from the rigors of his medical practice. So we restored the farmhouse for use by our family. Mind you, I'm not talking about a designer renovation job worthy of *Architectural Digest*. Armed with sledgehammers and crowbars, we tore out the old walls and pulled off the wood slats. There was construction dust and debris galore. I got a kick out of making a colossal mess—with my parents' permission.

Childhood is the season of life for imagined adventure and vivid dreams. The farm fulfilled my every youthful fantasy and served as a versatile playground. There were open fields perfect for baseball and football. Down the hill from our house flowed a stream with high banks on both sides. Next to the stream stood some tall trees with sturdy vines hanging from the branches. We emulated Tarzan and swung across the stream, howling just like him.

Having spent summers on the farm when he was young, Dad grew up enjoying country life. This included hunting. The nearby woods were filled with assorted animals, especially squirrels. In the fall, Kline and I went hunting with Dad. We entered the woods well before dawn, each armed with a shotgun. To avoid alerting our prey, Dad taught us how to walk silently on the fallen leaves by placing our toes down first, then our heels. We silently took up a perch on a tree stump and waited until we spotted some vigorous rustling of branches and leaves. This was a surefire giveaway that our prey was up there. Then we would take aim and fire. I enjoyed these macho outings with my father until one day I blew a squirrel to smithereens with a twelve-gauge shotgun. I soon began to wonder what the point was.

Besides, actually eating squirrels was revolting. My country cousins swore these rodents tasted like chicken, which was close to true. But we had filled their little bodies so full of buckshot that each place setting at the dinner table included a small plate for the pellets we chomped on as we chewed the meat. By the end of the meal, enough buckshot was piled on these plates to fill the muskets of a small army.

One summer, an offbeat entrepreneurial bug bit my father and several of his physician friends. It must have been the latent farmer genes in their blood. They all decided to raise and sell Poland China pigs.

One Saturday, Kline and I joined Dad in picking up the half-dozen pigs he had purchased. He rented a pickup truck to haul them to the farm. Once loaded, we headed down the two-lane road, only to spot up ahead a small bridge with a sign. It said the bridge had a load limit of three thousand pounds. Worried we would cause the bridge to collapse, we stopped by the side of the road and tried to guesstimate the weight of the cargo plus the vehicle. We suspected we exceeded the load limit by several thousand pounds. But there was no turning back. After all, the pigs were now ours. They certainly weren't welcome in the nation's capital.

Dad backed up the truck, gunned the engine, and raced across the bridge, which of course didn't even creak under the load. When we reached the farm, we attached an off-ramp to the back of the truck. I climbed up and removed the gate. Those pigs barreled down the ramp and broke free of our grasp. Everyone chased them until they grew bored, after which we herded them into their pens.

Bill was my main pig. I visited him every time we came to the farm. I rode him, flopped happily in the mud with him, and generally got away with games that mortified my fastidious mother. Then, one day, I arrived to discover that Bill was missing. I learned he had gone the way of all pork—to market, like all the other piggies. I was crushed to lose my porcine buddy.

My primary pet was Flash, our dog with the effervescent personality. We got Flash, a combination Spitz and who knew what else, in the city but decided he'd be happier in the country. Flash would spot our car and come bounding up to us before we turned onto the dirt road to the house. He was the quintessential child's dog—always there, always cheerful, always ready to play whatever game we wanted. One summer, Flash vanished, never to reappear. My folks told me he had run off. Years later, they revealed he had actually been hit and killed by a car, but that they could not bring themselves to break the news to me when I was young.

Deep in the woods next to our country house stood the skeleton of another farmhouse covered with vines and brush—our own "Blair Witch" haunted house. It must have been my grandfather's. Although we played all sorts of games outside, we never mustered the nerve to venture in.

A holiday ritual etched forever in my mind is the festive Thanksgiving and Christmas dinners that alternated between our house and the Marburys'. Dinners at their place were more fun by far. Pinkie would peel and wash the vegetables in her tiny, sweltering kitchen, heated by a wood stove. Meanwhile, Teenie headed for the chicken coop to grab the main course. To my horror and fascination, I watched as he chopped off its head. The bird would then dash haphazardly about the yard until it bled to death. I saw what the elders meant when they said someone was "running around like a chicken with its head cut off."

Dinner lasted for hours, as Pinkie piled on course after delicious cholesterol-rich course. Without doubt, the highlight of dinner was the gossip. I listened with eyes wide while the adults talked openly about who "knew" whom in the biblical sense. The conversation really got interesting when they moved back in time and described how, thanks to illicit relationships between slave owners and their slaves on both sides of the family, I just might be a direct descendent of Robert E. Lee and—can you beat this?—the queen of England. Who knew if there was anything to it? Whatever the truth, such chatter made for a helluva yarn for an impressionable youngster.

To my everlasting shame, I was less enthusiastic when it was our turn to host holiday dinners. The Marburys embarrassed me, through no fault of their own. They were decent, warm, loving people—upstanding, religious, and self-reliant. Yet they also were "country." Teenie and Pinkie lacked the polish of city dwellers like my parents. They dressed unfashionably, to say the least. Teenie's sky-blue Oldsmobile coupe stood out like a sore thumb in front of our house. He walked with a farmer's shuffling gait. He split infinitives when he spoke. This all made me uncomfortable when they entered our space in Washington.

While writing this memoir, I was mortified to discover that I had completely misread Pinkie. Beyond expressing his love for her, my typically reticent father never talked much about his aunt. In a box of family memorabilia meticulously maintained by my late mother, I discovered that Pinkie wasn't only a farmer's wife. She taught for fifty-one years in the Pisgah, Middletown, and "Old Port Tobacco" schools in Charles County. She trained as a teacher at Bowie Normal School and pursued additional studies at Morgan College, Hampton Institute, Catholic University, and Howard University, as well as extension courses from New York University. She belonged to the National Education Association, the International Reading Association, the Southern Maryland Reading Council, and, for good measure, the NAACP. I learned a belated lesson about not judging a book by its unassuming cover.

Bless him, my father always kept his feet on the ground. His Charles County cousins loved "Doc" and took immense pride in his professional accomplishments. Dad reciprocated his cousins' love and respect without equivocation. These were good, simple people, the salt of the earth. They were the ancestral link to his father and to the original Price way of life. Washington always put my high-strung father on edge. He felt calm and secure in the country, in the company of his kinfolk. With the passage of time, my embarrassment has gradually given way to the realization that I was blessed to have known close relatives as loving and loyal as Pinkie and Teenie.

Dad reveled in family and close friends but definitely could have done without the socializing associated with big-city life. Mom was his soul mate in this regard, and they teamed up to pass those genes on to me. Dad never aspired to be someone else or somewhere else. Nor did he envy what others had. If ever the phase "comfortable in one's skin" applied to an individual, it fit my father. In my entire life, I've never heard anyone speak ill of him. Nary a soul. Not a pejorative word. In fact, old friends get wistful, bordering on reverential, when they speak of him. He was the real deal—no artifice and no guile.

Dad died suddenly in 1973, just shy of age sixty-six, of a combined heart attack and stroke, as he had long feared. He took such pride in my accomplishments that it grieves me still that he never saw me ascend to the national stage. Given, despite his reserved personality, to hooting for joy when I won an academic prize at a Bruce School assembly, he would have lost his cool entirely watching me deliver a keynote address before thousands of Urban Leaguers, appear on *Meet the Press*, speak before an audience including current and former U.S. presidents, or hear about my travels in the company of President Bill Clinton aboard Air Force One.

My father truly was an uncommon man who sought and achieved a delicate balance between civilization and nature. He offered the ultimate service of saving lives, while deriving sustenance from his family and solace from nature. Although never a public person, he touched and deeply influenced the lives of hundreds of men, women, and children. He was an uncompromising nonconformist who eschewed materialism and pomp and circumstance in favor of moderation, humility, and integrity. There was an authenticity, a purity of being, about him that I marvel at but could never emulate.

All sons should be reared by such a profoundly inspiring, yet utterly grounded, role model.

CHAPTER 3

AN ENERGIZER BUNNY WITH FASCINATING ORIGINS

The youngest of ten children of Alfred Ernest Schuster and Cora Hawley Schuster, my mother was born October 6, 1912, in New Haven, Connecticut. She grew up in nearby West Haven. In 1935, Mom married my father at historic St. Philip's Church in Harlem, whose rector, Shelton Hale Bishop, was her brother Gussie's brother-in-law. A traditionalist about the paramount role of the wife in the home during children's formative years, my father believed wives should not work if they could afford not to. My mother the activist acquiesced but got even by volunteering almost full-time each week with various civic causes devoted to integration, equal opportunity, and voting rights.

Once my brother and I were grown, Dad encouraged my mother to pursue a graduate degree and a professional career. At the age of fifty-eight, she transformed herself from activist to archivist by earning a master's degree in library science from Catholic University. This belated career move proved fateful and fortunate because my father died barely two years later. Thus, she was well equipped intellectually and professionally for widowhood at a comparatively young age.

Energetic and indefatigable, Mom lived for forty more years entirely on her own. She moved from Washington to Plymouth, Massachusetts, where, at the age of sixty-one, she launched a new career as an archivist at Pilgrim Hall, the historical society there.

22

She set up the archives and was curator of books and manuscripts for twelve years.

In 1975–76, the board appointed her acting executive director of Pilgrim Hall. This was the first full-time job she had held since her early twenties. The acclaimed "Remember the Ladies" exhibition, which celebrated the nation's first ladies, premiered at Pilgrim Hall on her watch.

Although Mom could have held the directorship on a permanent basis, she decided she had proven to herself that she could handle it. Also, she had finally mustered the emotional strength to move to the home she and my father had built years earlier in East Falmouth in anticipation of retiring on Cape Cod.

During her years in Falmouth and into her late eighties, she served as a librarian and archivist for various institutions on the Cape. She created the archives and served as first archivist at the Falmouth Historical Society and the Woods Hole Historical Museum. In addition, she provided archival assistance to the Wampanoag Native American tribe of Mashpee. Her work led to the publication of three guidebooks: *A Guide to the Manuscripts and Special Collections in the Archives of the Falmouth Historical Society* and two guides to the archives of Cape Cod Community College.

A lifelong fitness and health-food aficionado, Mom took great pride in being known as "the Walker." On Cape Cod, she routinely walked along the seaside path from Falmouth to Woods Hole and back, typically outpacing her sons and grandchildren. That's roughly six miles round-trip. My mother practiced yoga. When a cousin from St. Croix visited our home to meet her for the first time, he knocked on the door and was invited to come in. There, he encountered her standing on her head. Much to his astonishment, she conversed in this inverted position for a while before turning upright and continuing to chat.

Mom (on buckboard seat) at a League of Women Voters rally in Washington, D.C., in the 1950s
The Washington Star

She worked, drove, lived in her own home, shoveled snow from her driveway until she was nearly 90, and continued walking daily until her late 90s. In other words, Mom was the prototype for the Energizer Bunny. Blessed with longevity genes, she lived to 101. The combination of optimism and fitness accounted for her buoyant personality and eternally sunny disposition, which brightened the lives of family members and friends who were blessed to know her.

In my book, Mom's clan takes the prize as the all-American family. Generation after generation, they intersected up close and personal with significant episodes of U.S. history.

Her mother, Cora, was a Hawley from Connecticut. Nero Hawley, Cora's great-great-grandfather, lived in Trumbull, known back then as North Stratford. Born a slave in 1742, he was persuaded by the promise of freedom, plus a signing bonus, to enlist on April 20, 1777, in the Second Connecticut Regiment of the Continental Army. At the time, he belonged to a sawmill owner named Daniel Hawley.

A scout, Nero joined other starving, ragtag troops who camped at Valley Forge during the brutal winter of 1777–78 under General George Washington. He earned an honorable discharge in April 1781

George Latimer—Mom's grandfather/father of Margaret Latimer Hawley and Lewis Latimer

Alfred Schuster and Cora Hawley Schuster—Mom's parents

and was emancipated on November 4, 1782, by his master. He and his wife, Peg, remained in North Stratford, where they raised their seven children. Blessed with an entrepreneurial spirit, Nero bought some land laden with clay and set up shop manufacturing bricks. His property also included nearly forty acres of woodland, from which he cut timber to sell.

When I was growing up, genealogy held little interest for me. Mom often told us about Nero, but I used to joke that her real goal in ferreting out his story was to become the first black woman admitted to the Daughters of the American Revolution. It was amusing to contemplate the heartburn this was bound to cause the ladies of the DAR, since, in 1939, the organization had barred the renowned black soprano Marian Anderson from singing at Constitution Hall, the prestigious Washington concert venue it owned.

In February 1997, my wife, Marilyn, and I attended the opening reception at Glenn Horowitz Bookseller in New York City for an exhibition titled "Against the Tide: African Americana, 1711–1987." The intriguing collection ran the gamut from historical documents and manuscripts to first editions of novels written by African-Americans. Since Mom was a professional archivist, we purchased a copy of the thick catalog of the collection. I shipped the unopened book to her the following day. She called within hours of receiving it to ask if I realized what was in the collection. With great excitement, she told me it contained the description of an original document signed by Nero Hawley in 1782.

House in Trumbull, Connecticut, where Nero Hawley lived in the mid-1700s

At that instant, I silently vowed to obtain it for her. The next day, I called the gallery owner to inquire about the document. He replied that it was owned by a collector who surely would not part with it. But after several futile pleas, I finally acquired it.

A messenger arrived at my office a

couple of weeks later and handed me a manila envelope. There it was, encased in clear plastic. Slightly frayed, it nonetheless seemed in pretty decent condition for a slip of paper more than two centuries old. The document was a printed treasury note dated June 1, 1782, payable to Nero in the amount of thirteen pounds, two shillings, and five pence. It was partial compensation for his service in the Connecticut Line of the Continental Army. Nero had countersigned it with an *X*. I stared at the document as though it were a swath of skin peeled off of Nero way back when and meticulously preserved ever since. For nearly half an hour, I savored the surreal feeling of holding in my hand an item that had been touched, signed, and cashed by my ancestor 215 years before.

I called my mother and in a matter-of-fact tone said that I wanted to visit in a couple of weeks. When I entered her house, I betrayed not a hint of what I'd brought her. I sat with her at the breakfast table, as was my custom upon arrival. I handed over the package, which she opened casually, probably thinking it was the latest packet of press clips from the National Urban League. Mom gasped when she spotted the surprise inside, and again when I said I was giving it to her. Mom fingered the document gently with the practiced grip of a pro and said she would treasure it. Ever the archivist, she declared that the first thing she intended to do was deacidify it. Then it would last for centuries, as if two-hundred-plus years weren't testament enough to its durability.

In early 2002, I received a telephone call from Nancy Gibson, a curator with the Daughters of the American Revolution. She explained that the DAR planned to mount an exhibition heralding the contributions of blacks and Native Americans who had fought on behalf of America's independence in the Revolutionary War. Gibson had heard I was related to Nero Hawley and was delighted to learn about Nero's treasury note, since a signed original document from that era would greatly enrich the DAR exhibit. We granted permission to display it after receiving assurances about insurance coverage, security, and appropriate climate control in the exhibit hall.

The exhibition, entitled "Forgotten Patriots: African-American and American Indian Service in the Revolutionary War," opened October 18, 2002, in the DAR Museum's main gallery, adjoining Constitution Hall. It featured the original treasury note and described the role Mom and her sister, Violet Royster, had played in discovering the information about Nero. Although at ninety my mother traveled less than she used to, you'd better believe she made this trek to D.C. from her home on Cape Cod. I loved watching her swell with pride at the sight of the display devoted to Nero Hawley.

Today, Nero's grave site—located at Riverside Cemetery, just off Daniel's Farm Road in Trumbull—is a featured stop on the Connecticut Freedom Trail. The clapboard house at 49 Daniels Farm Road, where Nero lived with his master in the mid-1700s, still stands nearby. In fact, it is in sound condition and is currently occupied—very much so.

On a crystalline Saturday afternoon in the fall of 2007, I drove to Trumbull, a bucolic town north of Bridgeport, to see the house first-hand. I stood in the street at the edge of the lawn snapping photos of the house. When a car pulled into the driveway, the driver gave me a quizzical look. I introduced myself and explained my ancestral connection. Intrigued by my story and well aware of Nero, the owner, Bill Feller, invited me inside to look around.

He and his wife, Michele, lived there with her mother, Paulette Guion, whose family had owned the property since the 1920s. Bill led me through the two-story dwelling. The rooms on the first floor had the original exposed beams and low ceilings dating back to when people generally were much shorter. Cutlery hung from the ceilings. The furnishings suited the early-American origins of the house.

I asked Bill if he had heard any rumors about the ghost of Nero Hawley. As a youngster, my relatives used to regale us with such tales, which I dismissed as pure fantasy, designed to spook children. Not only did Bill know about Nero's ghost, he told me that on at least three

Treasury note payable to Nero Hawley in 1782

occasions he had seen a female ghost standing near the window in the master bedroom. His wife added a convincing note when she said that, while she hadn't spotted this ghost herself, she could vouch for her husband's agitated state each time he told her he had just seen it. He hadn't been able to discern its ethnicity or the vintage of its clothes, he said, because the overall image was hazy and shrouded in white.

My ancestor's story gives the lie to two troubling impulses in American race relations. For centuries, white racists have cast aspersions on the credentials of African-Americans as bona fide Americans. Meanwhile, some black leaders have occasionally espoused returning to Africa, whence we originally came.

Nero Hawley hailed from Trumbull, Connecticut, deep in the heart of New England. He fought for America's independence from England and risked his life so that Americans could exercise the very freedom of speech that emboldens racists to say we should be sent back to Africa. Let them return to their ancestral lands. Black folk long ago earned the right to stay put as full-fledged U.S. citizens. It's a hard-won entitlement we'll never relinquish.

A second branch of my family tree is even more intriguing. On October 4, 1842, my great-great-grandfather George W. Latimer and his wife, Rebecca, who was pregnant with Mom's grandmother Margaret, escaped slavery in Virginia and headed north. I marvel at his account of their daring journey, including a stretch when he, a fair-skinned man, and his darker-hued wife traveled as master and slave:

> I started in September from my home in Norfolk, Virginia. With my wife, also a slave, I secreted myself under the fore-peak of the vessel, we lying on stone ballast in the darkness for nine weary hours. As we lay concealed in the darkness we could peek through the cracks of the partition into the bar-room of the vessel, where men who would have gladly captured us were drinking. When we went aboard the vessel at Frenchtown a man stood in the gangway who was a wholesaler of liquors. He knew me, for my master kept a saloon and was his customer. But I pulled my Quaker hat over my eyes and passed him unrecognized. I had purchased a first-class passage and at once went into the cabin and stayed there. Fortunately he did not enter.
>
> From Baltimore to Philadelphia I traveled as a gentleman, with my wife as a servant. After that, it being a presumably free country, we traveled as man and wife. I was twenty-one when married.

Latimer was spotted in the Boston area by William Carpenter, a former employee of Latimer's slave owner, James Gray. Gray took out an ad in the local newspaper that read,

> Ranaway [sic] on Monday night last my Negro Man George, commonly called George Latimer. He is about 5 feet 3 or 4 inches high, about 22 years of age, his complexion a bright yellow, is of a compact, well made frame, and is rather silent and slow spoken—I suspect that he went North Tuesday, and will give Fifty Dollars reward and pay all necessary expenses, if taken out of the State. Twenty Five Dollars reward will be given for his apprehension within the State. His wife is also missing and I suspect that they went off together.

Gray posted a similar ad about Rebecca. He reached Boston on October 18 and arranged for Latimer's arrest on larceny charges and incarceration in the Leverett Street jail. Gray also initiated legal proceedings to force Latimer's return to Virginia. However, according to the late historian Asa J. Davis of Amherst College, on Sunday, October 30, "a tumultuous meeting took place in Faneuil Hall," the historic tourist attraction restored in the mid-1970s by visionary developer James Rouse. The impassioned meeting "not only excited the public mind in favor of Latimer, but also increased the determination of the abolitionists to demand new legislative measures to protect the fugitive slave."

Professor Davis maintained that Latimer was "the first fugitive slave whose emancipation guided and influenced the American abolitionists of the 1850s." According to Davis, "His flight to Boston, arrest, imprisonment, trial and emancipation, as well as the numerous public meetings held all over Massachusetts on his behalf, made his a cause célèbre. . . . His supporters called it a 'war on slavery.' "

The legendary Frederick Douglass and the noted abolitionist William Lloyd Garrison rallied publicly to Latimer's side. On November 11, 1842, several prominent and well-heeled supporters launched a newspaper called the *Latimer Journal and North Star* to help rescue George from custody and fight his recapture by Gray. The publication's circulation reached twenty thousand. Critics claimed that the journal "greatly excited and alarmed the credulous, vexed the irritable, inflamed the passionate, and exasperated those whose sympathies ran beyond their judgment." The saga even inspired John Greenleaf Whittier to write a poem about George's odyssey, entitled "From

Massachusetts to Virginia." Free blacks in Boston took up a vigil at the courthouse to prevent George from being spirited out of the city. After a flurry of legal wrangling and negotiations, an abolitionist minister offered to purchase George from his slave owner for four hundred dollars. The terms were accepted, and he was finally freed.

The episode solidified George Latimer's status as a celebrity. *The Liberator*, a local newspaper, carried this account of a Latimer sighting at an event:

> George Latimer, the lion himself, was present. His appearance caused a sensation among the audience. . . . At the close of the meeting, by the request of several present, Latimer stood in front of the rostrum, that those who wished might pass along and shake hands with him, as is the custom when the president and other distinguished men receive the attention and civilities of the sovereign people.

Gratified but not satisfied, abolitionists pressed for more sweeping changes in Massachusetts to prevent a recurrence. Their cause prevailed when the legislature enacted laws mandating that "all judges, justices of the peace, and officers of the commonwealth, are forbidden, under heavy penalties, to aid, or act in any manner in the arrest, detention, or delivery of any person claimed as a fugitive slave."

Sadly, George Latimer soon abandoned his family for reasons I have never ascertained. His disappearance left Rebecca to fend for herself and her young brood. William and young George were placed in a state institution called the Farm School, which was akin to an orphanage. Margaret was sent to live with a family friend, while Lewis remained with his mother. Then Rebecca went to sea as a stewardess, so it was off to the Farm School for Lewis as

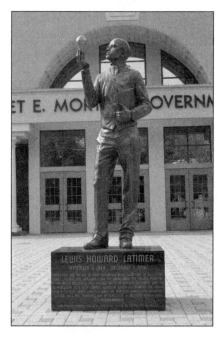

Statue of Lewis Latimer in Bridgeport, Connecticut

well. He and William managed to escape and, hiding out in railroad cars, rejoined Rebecca in Boston.

In 1864, sixteen-year-old Lewis fibbed about his age and enlisted in the navy. He received an honorable discharge when the Civil War ended, after which he sought work in Boston. He eventually secured a menial job with the patent law firm of Crosby and Gould. Through research, practice, and observation, Lewis taught himself mechanical drawing. Emboldened to demonstrate his skills to others in the firm, he won a promotion from office boy to draftsman.

Lewis Latimer became a noted inventor and a pivotal player in the stunning technological revolution at the end of the nineteenth century and the beginning of the twentieth. Alexander Graham Bell retained Lewis to perfect his patent application for the telephone so it could be filed first, barely a few hours before a rival inventor. As a mechanical draftsman for Hiram Maxim, the inventor who founded the U.S. Electrical Lighting Company in Brooklyn, Lewis drew on his knowledge of electric power and lighting to help Thomas Edison perfect the light bulb. He devised and patented the carbonized conductors for incandescent lamps that enabled them to stay lit significantly longer, thus revolutionizing electric light bulbs. By 1918, he had garnered such professional acclaim that he became a charter member—and the only black member—of the esteemed Edison Pioneers.

Lewis Latimer's impressive accomplishments illuminate another chapter in the African-American experience that isn't fully understood or appreciated—namely, the notable contributions of black inventors to America's growth and prosperity. As recently as 2014, PBS broadcast a documentary about Thomas Edison, yet it omitted any mention of Lewis Latimer. This represented a threefold deprivation for viewers. First, they learned nothing of Latimer's achievements, which impact their lives every day. Moreover, the film missed a golden opportunity to fill out the portrait of Edison, who a century ago displayed no hesitancy to include a black man on his team of pioneers. Finally, adding Latimer to the mix would have illuminated how mastery of the STEM disciplines (science, technology, engineering, and math) can propel minorities into the mainstream against great odds.

Lewis Latimer was yet another ancestor whose significance I scarcely appreciated growing up. One of Mom's most beloved cousins was Winifred Norman, Lewis's granddaughter. Winnie devoted much of her life to preserving Lewis's legacy and transforming his former home at 137–53 Holly Avenue in Flushing, Queens, into a museum at another site in the borough.

I remember that house, sort of. As a college student in the early 1960s, I sometimes drove up to New York City to visit a girlfriend who lived in the Midwood section of Brooklyn. Lewis's daughter Louise, who was Winnie's aunt, lived in the house and kindly let me stay there. I actually slept in his old bedroom.

Like so many oblivious and preoccupied young people, I wasn't terribly curious about my famous relative's claim to fame, much less his family connection or the fact that this house had been his. Aunt Louise would implore me to sit with her so she could tell me about Uncle Lew. Regrettably, that would have to wait, I replied. Right now, all I wanted to know was how to get from Flushing to Midwood. Which highway should I get on, and what exit should I take? I'd learn about Uncle Lew another time, I assured her.

Of course, I never did, squandering an opportunity to hear stories, see photos, check out papers, and fill in the gaping holes in my knowledge of Lewis, my great-grandmother Margaret, and her father, George. It was only decades later, when the house was transformed into a museum, that I appreciated the historic significance of the pad where I once crashed on weekends.

In late July 1994, I delivered my inaugural keynote address opening the annual conference of the National Urban League. C-SPAN covered the session. Since I was barely known to the Urban League and was largely unknown to the national audience, I used the occasion to trace my roots briefly. Among other family anecdotes, I mentioned George and Lewis Latimer.

Later that summer, I received a call at the office from a man who spoke with a deep Southern accent. "Mr. Price," he said, "I happened to catch you on C-SPAN the other night. I heard your story about these Latimers. Now, my name is Latimer, and I'm a white man from Georgia. But you know something? Growing up, I heard tell of a great-great-grandfather of mine named George Latimer. Nobody knew much about him, and nobody talked much about him. We heard he'd spent some time up there in Massachusetts. But I'll tell you something, Mr. Price. If I shaved all your hair off and stuck a straight-haired wig on you, you'd be a dead ringer for my uncle. Mr. Price, I bet we're kin."

This stranger's call out of the blue underscored the tensions and denial about race, from overt racism to ambiguous racial identity, that have thoroughly roiled American culture and society, our robust diversity notwithstanding. For generations, racial conventions and legal classifications were governed by the "one-drop rule," which proclaimed that anyone with so much as one forebear of sub-Saharan ancestry was deemed black—or Negro or colored or mulatto or Afro-American or African-American or, yes, the ultimate pejorative, nigger, depending on the era.

The human drama is so compelling that the subject of "passing" has long attracted scholars, novelists, memoirists, and even filmmakers. My ancestors' experiences never rivaled the notoriety of these tales of crossing over. Yet my mother's family especially endured abundant drama and trauma caused by straddling and traversing the color line.

George Latimer's son, George Jr., fought in the Civil War in the Twenty-ninth Connecticut Army Regiment, a.k.a. the Colored Army Volunteers. Augustus Hawley, the great-grandson of my Revolutionary

Augustus Hawley—Mom's grandfather/Margaret Latimer's husband/Nero Hawley's great-grandson

Margaret Latimer Hawley—Mom's grandmother/George Latimer's daughter

War ancestor Nero Hawley, may have served with him in the same unit. He probably met his future wife, Margaret, my great-grandmother, through her brother.

Margaret and Augustus lived in Bridgeport, Connecticut. They had one son and three daughters, including Cora, Mom's mother. Cora married Alfred Ernest Schuster, a native of St. Croix in what is now the U.S. Virgin Islands. His ancestry was mixed, a melding over the generations of the Crucian slaves who toiled on the sugarcane plantations and the Danes who colonized the island starting in the 1700s. Grandpa's father, Peter, born in St. Croix around 1823, was a mixed-race "free person of color" whose liberty was purchased a year after his birth. Cora and Alfred, a Pullman porter and shoemaker like his father, set up house in West Haven, Connecticut. Like clockwork, they had ten children over the course of twenty years. Mom was the baby of the brood.

At the risk of speaking ill of long-deceased ancestors, I'll note that my mother's parents harbored some biases about race and color—even as black folk—that were dysfunctional, though hardly uncommon back then. Alfred and Cora were so fair skinned that many contemporaries probably thought they were white. A check of the U.S. Census reveals that Grandpa Schuster was variously listed over the years as black, white, and Negro.

Like their parents, several of the early children were fair skinned. But things got complicated when, as genes are wont, swarthier sons and daughters started emerging from Grandma's womb. Three of Mom's siblings "crossed over" to live as white once they reached adulthood. I feel no need to "out" these relatives or their offspring because, to me, their isolation from biological family is punishment enough. Some of my "brown" aunts and uncles bitterly recalled how their

Peter Schuster—Mom's grandfather/Alfred Schuster's father

father would not deign to speak to or even acknowledge them if he encountered them on the streetcar in West Haven. This may be apocryphal, but there must have been some truth to the story for them to retain such angry memories generations later.

After my father and mother met at Howard, she left school following her freshman year and returned home to New Haven. When Dad began courting her, he would visit her at the Schuster home. Dad was a handsome brown-skinned man in pursuit of a medical degree. In other words, he was a prize catch for any young African-American woman.

No matter. Her parents were appalled that so brown-skinned a man was romancing their daughter. They treated Dad coldly. Though determined nonetheless to marry my mother because he loved her dearly, the experience left him permanently embittered toward her parents.

During World War II, long after Grandpa Schuster's death, Grandma would visit us in Washington. She usually started out planning to stay a week or so. But within a few days, the old tensions would resurface and turn everyone sour. Grandma would pack up and return early to her home in West Haven. Sometime in the 1950s, I believe, my grandmother moved in with a daughter and son-in-law who lived as white. Thus, I "lost" my only living grandparent, even though she lived a short drive from us for another dozen years to the age of ninety-six.

The "white" Schusters inflicted the ultimate pain on the rest of the family when Grandma Schuster died in September 1963. At the time, I resided in New Haven, where I had just started at Yale Law School. Aunt Vi also lived there with her family. Uncle Gussie was nearby in New York City, my folks were just down the road in D.C., and other siblings were a manageable drive or a short flight away.

The proximity did not faze my relatives. They brought Grandma's body back to New Haven, held a private internment service, and buried her before telling any of the "Negro" siblings that their mother had passed away. Mom was disconsolate. It was symptomatic of the lasting damage my grandparents inflicted on their children and the most callous treatment of one's own flesh and blood I have ever seen, before or since.

The emotional scars on my mother's generation of Schusters never healed completely. Nor has the chasm that separates members of my generation of first cousins ever been entirely bridged. To this day, I have little idea how many children or grandchildren my aunts and uncles who crossed over had. With the welcome exception of a long-lost first cousin who has reconnected in recent years, much to our mutual delight, I have never set eyes on any other first cousins who grew up as white.

America's anguish and confusion over race cost me the companionship, wisdom, and love of the only grandparent alive when I was born. I barely knew her and thus missed out entirely on the delights and quirks, the history lessons and folklore, and the tales about my mother as a child.

However, I harbor no bitterness—only a sense of emptiness—because these people virtually ceased to exist for me long ago, when I witnessed how much trauma the estrangement caused my mother. That's one burden of being black I declined to inherit.

While I wish America could move beyond the grief and pain caused to this day by racism and color consciousness, I do not foresee a color-blind society anytime soon. Too much of consequence—advancing quality education for all, squelching voter suppression, and combating the recurring outbreaks of police violence against blacks—hinges on keeping close tabs on how society treats African-Americans and other minorities of color. After so much progress, thanks in substantial part to affirmative action, universities and employers should not be allowed to regress toward tokenism in their admissions and hiring practices, whatever the Supreme Court may decree.

The key going forward isn't to deny the reality of race altogether or to de-escalate the crusades against injustice, inequality, and poverty bred of lingering racism. For all the headlines and surveys pointing to continuing schisms over race, I see glimmers of hope that young people are coming more honestly to terms with the subject and, given the growing phenomenon of intermarriage, understanding the complexity of ethnic classifications. They are "cool" about it, increasingly comfortable with diversity in broader society, as well as in their own genetic maps. Those who are the products of ethnic blending apologize less and less for their roots and appearance. They insist on being recognized and appreciated for who they are, instead of being circumscribed by who others want them to be. Megawatt celebrities who are biracial—Tiger Woods, Mariah Carey, Derek Jeter, Soledad O'Brien, Vin Diesel, Halle Berry, Wayne "the Rock" Johnson, and, of course, President Barack Obama—tell their legions of fans and society at large, "So what. Just deal with it."

Say amen, somebody.

CHAPTER 4

THE NATIONAL PASTIME, ALL THE TIME

doubt any boy ever worshiped baseball as passionately as I did. Our house on New Hampshire Avenue was a brisk fifteen-minute walk from Griffith Stadium. Bruce School, at Sherman Avenue and Kenyon Street, was even closer. The ballpark housed the Washington Senators of major-league baseball's American League and the Homestead Grays of the Negro League, as well as pro football's Washington Redskins. It stood at the juncture of Georgia and Florida Avenues on what is now the site of Howard University Hospital.

The proximity of the Senators to Howard was cruelly ironic because owner Clark Griffith steadfastly refused to integrate his team until the early 1950s. When big-league teams resorted to signing a white one-armed outfielder and a white one-legged pitcher instead of Negro League superstars including Josh Gibson, Satchel Paige, and Buck Leonard, who were in the prime of their careers, integrationists such as Sam Lacy, the crusading black sports reporter and our neighbor, turned up the heat on the major leagues to vanquish Jim Crow once and for all. Even though Griffith eventually capitulated, he still could not bring himself to sign an African-American. Instead, he broke the Senators' color barrier on September 6, 1954, with a marginally talented black Cuban named Carlos Paula. The outfielder lasted barely three seasons in the majors.

Clark Griffith's intransigence made me an even more devoted Brooklyn Dodgers and Cleveland Indians fan in the late 1940s, after Bill Veeck, owner of the Indians, followed Branch Rickey's lead by signing Larry Doby as the second black major leaguer. When the Indians came to town, black folk from miles around packed picnic lunches and drove to the stadium for the occasion. The adoration they showered on the players was infectious, fueling my dream of becoming a major leaguer.

Each year when spring training wound down, the Brooklyn Dodgers played exhibition games as they traveled north for Opening Day. Washington was a customary stop along the way. One spring day in 1952, Art Carter, our neighbor who was a sports editor for the *Washington Afro-American* newspaper, walked up on our front porch and casually asked if I wanted to meet Jackie Robinson, the fabled Dodger who had integrated big-league baseball. And would I like to have my picture taken with him?

I am not by nature a hero worshiper. Even so, three people stand atop my pantheon of heroes—Martin Luther King, Nelson Mandela, and Jackie Robinson. In fact, in my estimation, they border on deities, candidates for sainthood. Each displayed breathtaking bravery in the face of palpable risk to life and limb. Moreover, they bent the arc of human history irreversibly toward dignity, justice, and equality.

Jackie endured death threats and vile insults. In the early years, he sublimated his fiery disposition and natural instinct to retaliate and protect himself. He stood for much more than he accomplished on the field. After two years of civil behavior at the insistence of Dodgers general manager Branch Rickey, Jackie reverted to his combative self and stopped taking any crap from anyone. He energized our community and ignited our dreams that Jim Crow really would crumble in our lifetimes, not just in baseball but throughout society. Black folk young and

"Small Fry Meet Dodgers' Big Guy"—Jackie Robinson—in 1952
The Afro-American Newspapers

THE NATIONAL PASTIME, ALL THE TIME 39

old, male and female didn't merely root for Jackie in those heady days. We worshiped him.

I attended the Dodgers-Senators game with Art Carter and his son, Chip. We then headed to the clubhouse under the grandstand. In those days before ballplayers had seven-figure bank accounts, fans actually could go to the clubhouse, wait outside for the players to emerge, and then collect their autographs—free of charge—as they walked to the team bus or their cars. When Jackie came out, he recognized Art Carter right away and was friendlier than I would have expected of a megastar. Clearly, this offer of a photo op was real. His elegant wife, Rachel, joined us. A photographer from the *Afro* snapped our picture. It appeared in the April 15 issue with the headline "Small Fry Meet Dodgers' Big Guy." Hero worship didn't get any better than that.

A half-century later, I closed the circle. By then, I had become president of the National Urban League. In conjunction with the fiftieth anniversary of Jackie's breaking the color barrier in pro baseball, a colleague of mine at the Urban League, Lee Daniels, collaborated with Mrs. Robinson in writing a sumptuously illustrated biography of his life. I met her at a book-signing party at the New York Public Library. When I described our initial encounter, she requested a copy of the newspaper photo, which of course I sent forthwith.

Better yet, the Jackie Robinson Foundation invited me to present an award at its annual dinner. The highlight of the evening was mingling with Hall of Famers including Hank Aaron and Frank Robinson. Since the ballplayers of the 1940s and 1950s were, literally and figuratively, towering figures to a devout fan such as me, I was surprised to see that these stars were mere mortals in height and weight. No Jolly Green Giants like those sluggers of the 1990s, such as Mark McGuire and Frank Thomas. At six-two and a shade over two hundred pounds (when my eating habits behave), I was the physical match of these older All Stars of my youth. Or so I thought. But once I saw their broad shoulders up close and felt the vicelike grip of their handshakes, I understood anew that pro athletes are a different species of human being.

If memory serves—and it may not sixty-plus years later—I took in about fifty games a year. That may be an exaggeration. Many an afternoon, I sprinted down Georgia Avenue after Bruce School let out. In just over ten minutes, I'd be planted in the left-field bleachers, which suited me fine, even though the seats were made of concrete.

The lowly Senators sorely tried Washingtonians' loyalty in those days. I could not bring myself to root for them. For starters, they stunk. They had some solid players, but Clark Griffith was a cheapskate. He never acquired enough talent to field a competitive team.

If you attend enough ball games, you're bound to see baseball history, even with an awful team such as the old Senators. On April 17, 1953, I witnessed what was considered the second-longest homer ever hit in the majors. In the fifth inning of the Yankees-Senators game, slugger Mickey Mantle came up against left-hander Chuck Stobbs. The immortal Red Sox hitter Ted Williams once observed that when Mantle connected, the crack of the bat was like an explosion.

That afternoon, I was perched in the bleachers per usual. Mantle tore into a Stobbs pitch and walloped a liner that rocketed past the 400-foot sign in left-center, up over the bleachers, clear over the back wall, out of the park, and onto the street. Baseball statisticians back then said the ball traveled 565 feet. Supposedly, only Babe Ruth ever hit one farther—just over 600 feet. We bleacherites knew we had seen one for the books. When Mickey jogged back to center field, we cheered wildly. He acknowledged us by rolling up his right sleeve and flexing his bicep. Witnessing this spectacle fueled my boyhood dream of becoming a big-league slugger, just like Mickey.

During summer vacation, we played ball all day long, from right after breakfast until sunset. We interrupted the marathon game only for lunch and, if the afternoon heat became unbearable, the occasional double feature at the York Theatre on Georgia Avenue just below New Hampshire. As neighborhood demographics shifted, the York desegregated in order to survive. The Little Tavern hamburger joint stood nearby. We could order takeout but not eat inside. Such were the anomalies of segregation in those days.

In an early stab at micro-enterprise, I financed my bleacher seats, movie tickets, and "Popsicle Pete" habit by rolling my red Radio Flyer wagon through the alley in back of our house and rounding up discarded soda bottles. I exchanged them at the local grocery store to collect the deposits in hard currency. The refunds on ten bottles paid for the baseball ticket, another ten bought a hot dog and soda, and a popsicle ran a nickel. So one trip through the alley usually covered my out-of-pocket expenses and generated a modest surplus. Who says recycling is a modern, politically correct phenomenon?

At the York, we watched an endless supply of cowboy movies. Yet I remember the Flash Gordon serials most vividly, with their futuristic depictions of life in space. In those days after World War II and the onset of the Cold War, the Movietone News narrators reported breathlessly on how the Allied forces had vanquished the Axis powers and were divvying up supervision of what was left of Germany and Austria. When we weren't playing baseball, my playmates and I, inspired by the success of America's troops, dressed up in military costumes and carried out pint-sized war games in the neighborhood alleys and, best of all, in the sprawling parkland adjoining nearby Soldiers' Home, the ideal "battlefield" for make-believe combat.

But mostly, my buddies and I played baseball wherever we had access to a field—and a fence to hit home runs over. We played in the tiny, grassy triangle at the intersection of several streets diagonally across from our house. We dodged cars to track down singles and fly balls that escaped the park. We played in the alley behind my house, smacking rubber balls into our neighbors' yards and, heaven forbid, smashing the windows of their houses. Our greatest fear was getting caught by grumpy, old Mr. Wormley while retrieving an errant ball from his yard. Or encountering a dog with a nasty disposition.

We played in the yard at Bruce School during lunch breaks. The challenge there was to blast a homer over the fence onto Kenyon Street without hitting the school wall or, worse still, launching one through a classroom window. Fortunately, it was warm most days when we played there, and the windows were open wide.

Our primary ball field was the playground at Raymond Elementary School, just a few blocks from home. Oddly enough, the school was segregated by day—open only to white students—but the playground was fully integrated after school. Go figure. On sweltering August days when both the temperature and humidity crowded a hundred, we migrated from the baseball diamond to the tennis court, where we played a low-energy variant of the sandlot game. The batter was positioned at one baseline. The pitcher stood where the tennis net would have been. No one ran the bases, for fear of heat prostration. A ground ball hit between the net posts that the pitcher couldn't snare counted as a single. A fly ball over his head that the solo fielder couldn't catch in the air was a double. A fly ball that hit the fence behind the opposite baseline was a triple. Needless to say, a mini-blast clearing the fence counted as a homer.

Every season, I broke Babe Ruth's single-season record of sixty homers by a mile. This was long before anyone had heard of Roger Maris, Mark McGuire, or Barry Bonds, not to mention minor-league sluggers such as Dick "Dr. Strangeglove" Stuart or rotund Steve Bilko, the minor-league Sultan of Swat. One summer, I smote something like 175 homers. I think that's accurate. It might even have been 275. I generally was good for three or four round-trippers, game after game. Anyway, I hit so many that I used a notebook to keep the tally. Who needed steroids when you could bulk up with popsicles and Creamsicles?

I avidly collected baseball cards and even assembled a complete 1952 Topps set, which, had it not vanished mysteriously, would today be worth a small fortune. Still, those cards were merely pictures on pasteboard. I possessed a more memorable and meaningful connection to ballplayers—namely, their actual autographs. I didn't amass them the easy way, at autograph shows. I earned them by waiting outside the team clubhouse after games. We actually could do that back in the forties and fifties, when most ballplayers relished contact with their fans.

Immediately after games at Griffith Stadium, I would dash to the clubhouse and wait along with the other autograph hounds. As the players emerged, we tried to spot the established stars and high-profile rookies whose signatures we coveted, then lined up and waited our turns. During lulls between the prize catches, we deigned to seek the autographs of obscure benchwarmers and washed-up pitchers.

Since I never rooted for the Senators, I concentrated on the visiting teams. In the spring, I focused on spring training games with the exotic National League clubs the Senators never played during the regular season, as this was prior to the advent of interleague play.

My autographs would rival almost any collection from that era. They included such Hall of Famers as Jackie Robinson, Roy Campanella, Robin Roberts, Mickey Mantle, Yogi Berra, Bob Feller, and Bob Lemon. Ted Williams was a trip. A dashing figure at six foot three, he would stride out of the clubhouse, seemingly oblivious to the horde of autograph hounds clamoring for his signature. As we crowded around him, he would insist we line up. Then he'd pick the last kid in the queue. To Ted's credit, he made sure to sign everyone's autograph book before leaving.

One evening in 1951, I witnessed the fabled Joe DiMaggio aura up close. It was his final season in the majors. After a routine Yankee bashing of the Senators, I headed to the visitors' clubhouse to see if I could grab his signature after years of trying. Eventually, Joe came out, dressed as though he had just stepped out of a Brooks Brothers storefront window. He hopped into a waiting limousine, the only car allowed inside the stadium. I initially gave up hope, but then spotted him as he rolled down his window and started signing autographs. I muscled some smaller kids aside, shoved my book through the window, and got back a barely legible signature. Next to Jackie's, Joe's is the autograph I treasure most.

Every few years, I glance through my dilapidated autograph book to see if the signatures conjure up grainy images of the players themselves. To this day, I remember what the majority of them looked like back then. I cross-check my memory by looking at my dog-eared copy of *Sports Photo Album*, published in 1951. I cover up the names and stare only at the photos. My success rate is two-thirds or more. Oddly enough, if you assembled a photo album, say, of donors who contributed heavily to the National Urban League during my tenure, I probably could identify only a small fraction by name. I mean these steadfast supporters no insult. That's just the weird way my brain works. This illustrates, if not explains, the mystical hold the national pastime had on the dreams of American boys of my era.

The first thirteen years of my baseball "career" played out within the village surrounding Howard University. Starting around 1954, integration gradually took hold inside D.C., if not Maryland and Virginia. That May, the Supreme Court issued its landmark decision outlawing segregated public schools. Black families on our block began moving to predominantly white neighborhoods that used to be off-limits. Billy Lindsay was the first of my friends to leave, when his family moved uptown to D.C.'s Gold Coast. How wonderfully ironic that my best buddy was now a neighbor of reviled Senators owner Clark Griffith!

Our family headed for the so-called Silver Coast in northeast D.C., near Taft Junior High School. Although we were farther from Griffith Stadium, the move proved a bonanza for me, though I doubt the real-estate agents promoted what was to me the most significant feature of our new neighborhood.

Just across the Maryland line in Mount Ranier stood the Kaywood Gardens apartment complex. It was nothing remarkable to look at. What was distinctive about Kaywood in those days was that most of the Washington Senators lived there during the season. A mere ten-minute bike ride from my house, it was almost enough to transform me into a Senators fan.

I used to pedal over to Kaywood and stroll among the stores. In the supermarket, I would spot Roy Sievers, the American League home-run champ. In the pharmacy, I'd walk up to Frank "Spec" Shea, the burly pitcher, and brashly inquire, "How'd it go today, Spec?"

Even closer to our house, just inside the D.C. line, was a private home where veteran Senators outfielder Clyde Vollmer rented a room. Some afternoons, my friends and I would ride our bikes over and stage Clyde Vollmer watches, waiting for him to come out. Imagine, a big-leaguer just a few blocks away!

Occasionally, after cleaning up on autographs from the visiting team, we dashed over to the Senators clubhouse and hitched a ride home with Eddie Yost, "the Walking Man," who played third base. He would drop us off at Michigan Avenue and Nineteenth Street on his way to Kaywood. This beat baseball cards any day. These encounters with pro ballplayers, from collecting their autographs to hitching rides home, stoked my determination to follow them into the major leagues someday.

Our new neighborhood proved a bonanza for another reason, too. It was replete with new friends who shared my passion for playing baseball. Every summer, we competed in a recreational league under the tutelage of a coach named Mr. Brooks. We practiced each morning and traveled all over the city, playing games in the afternoon. In the evenings, we organized a pickup league at the Franciscan monastery a couple of blocks from my house. The complex featured a basketball court along with a baseball field that was close to major-league dimensions. According to our crude calculations, it was 325 feet down the left-field line, from home plate to the edge of the basketball court. The fence in right field was farther away—about 345 feet, based on walking off the distance.

To access the field, located adjacent to South Dakota Avenue, we scaled an eight-foot picket fence. The Holy Name fathers seemed not to mind, since they spotted us out there almost every night and even joined in. Several "brothers" were seriously into hoops, which we played there year-round. A number of them really "had game," as youngsters today would say, and weren't above throwing their weight and unholy elbows around on the court.

By fourteen, I had matured into a power hitter, provided the pitch was a fastball. Trouble was, some teenage hurlers had learned to throw a curveball. I couldn't hit a sharp-breaking bender with a shovel or a prayer. For years, I attributed my failure to make the major leagues to the fact that I became nearsighted in my early teens and started wearing glasses. To be honest, this was a lame excuse masking the fact that when a curveball came spinning toward my head, I bailed out of the batter's box long before it broke over the plate for a strike.

Still, a curveball was enough of a rarity at this age that it didn't prevent me from starring in the summer recreation league. One humid August night, we played for the league title at Turkey Thicket, the playground on Michigan Avenue. For the championship game, Coach Brooks issued the first full-dress uniforms my teammates and I had ever worn. I thrilled to the sight of myself in "official" baseball dress, though the uniforms were a thick, prickly flannel that made my skin crawl. It was the last thing we wanted to wear on a muggy D.C. night. Even so, our team prevailed.

Reality intruded the following year when I tried out for the Coolidge High School baseball team. I didn't make it. I blamed the eyeglasses. I blamed the white coach at the newly integrated school, who, I told myself, did not want blacks on the squad. Only later did I affix the fault squarely where it belonged—on my fear and futility when confronted by a curveball.

Disappointed but undeterred, I kept trying out for the team. Finally, in my senior year, I made the roster as first substitute outfielder. By then, I had come to terms with my shortcomings. Fortunately, I had heeded my mother's advice about academics and was doing extremely well in school. So I viewed making the varsity squad as a treat, rather than as a step to the majors.

Coolidge fared well that season. I contributed an occasional pinch hit and got a kick out of traveling all over the city for games. The uniforms weren't nearly as uncomfortable as those scratchy sandlot suits. Our team finished high enough in the standings to compete for the city-wide high-school championship, which was played, of all places, in Griffith Stadium.

On June 8, 1959, we entered the field through the visiting team's dugout. I pranced, pawed the dirt, scratched my groin, and spat, just like a big-leaguer. If you think major-league parks look cavernous from the bleachers, they feel like the Grand Canyon from the batter's box. The infield dirt was as smooth as a hardwood floor, the outfield grass emerald green.

Since Dad was at the office, Mom came out alone to watch the pre-game warmups. I patrolled center field during batting practice. One of our guys smacked a long fly ball to center. I took off after it and made an over-the-shoulder grab, reminiscent of New York Giants great Willie Mays's stirring catch against Vic Wertz of the Indians in the first game of the 1954 World Series. Mom and the handful of other loyal relatives in the stands jumped up to applaud.

I watched the actual game against archrival Wilson High School from the dugout. We were dominated by its crafty lefty, Sammy Swindells. By the seventh inning, our team was trailing something like 7–0. We loaded the bases, and Coach Reynolds called my number. He actually wanted me to pinch-hit, with the bases loaded, in a big-league park, with sportswriters, parents, classmates—and girls—watching.

I decided to go for the fences. We obviously had no chance of winning if we tried to chip away at Wilson's lead. Besides, I rather selfishly reasoned, baseball historians would never remember a single or a bunt. What kind of headline would it garner in next morning's *Washington Post*?

I was emboldened by the recollection that when Coolidge had played Spingarn High School for the championship at Griffith two years earlier, our second baseman, Jimmy Dameron, all six-four and two-hundred-plus pounds of him, actually hit an authentic home run. Over the fence—not one of those inside-the-park jobs. Jimmy was all over the news the next day.

As I strode to the plate, I set my mind on smashing a grand-slam home run. While I dug my cleats into the batter's box, I gazed out to the left-field fence. I replayed the memories of sitting in those bleachers as a kid, watching Mickey Mantle's 565-foot homer soar majestically out of the park.

Dreams are wonderful, but they lack real-world depth perception.

My brief career as a catcher

As I gazed out from home plate, the fence appeared to be three miles away. The bleachers suddenly looked two-dimensional instead of three-, looming like a twenty-story wall. How was I going to clear that fence?

I swung mightily at the first pitch and missed.

As the pitcher and I fidgeted, I began thinking about the newspaper coverage my grand slam would generate the next day. I recalled that Dameron had been the lead story on the sports pages of the *Washington Post* and the *Washington Star*. Surely, my grand slam would top that.

While daydreaming about the press coverage, I let the second pitch whiz by for a strike.

Between pitches, I rehearsed my comments to the TV and radio reporters who would interview me after the game. I imagined what I'd look like on the evening news, how I would cock my hat and grasp my bat, exactly the way big-league sluggers did for their Topps baseball-card portraits.

Swindells, the devil incarnate, unleashed a curveball. I waved my bat and missed by a wide margin. The crowd groaned as I trudged disconsolately back to the dugout.

But you know something? To this day, I can describe to the commas and periods all the press coverage my grand slam generated. I can tell you how big the headlines were and how the sportscasters told the story of my historic homer on the evening television news.

I admit it was utterly selfish to swing for the fences. I knew the odds of connecting were one out of infinity. But succeed or fail, I had to keep my date with destiny. After all, how many shots do amateurs get to go for it in a big-league park? Besides, a grand slam worth four runs would have put us right back in the game. The baseball texts say that's the job of power-hitting pinch-hitters, such as Dusty Rhodes, Johnny Mize—and me.

Fast-forward to the mid-1970s, when I experienced another vicarious baseball thrill. A consulting assignment took me to Tampa in early March. It was the peak of spring training for big-league clubs. Unbeknownst to me, the hotel the travel agent picked was owned by none other than George Steinbrenner, "the Boss" of the New York Yankees. Better yet, the Yankees were there while I was. At the coffee shop in the mornings, they would shuffle in, already dressed in Yankee pinstripes, for a quick breakfast before heading out to practice. Catfish

Hunter, Thurman Munson, and Yogi Berra, their iconic coach—they were all there. It was Kaywood all over again.

I was about thirty-five and reasonably trim from playing slow-pitch softball in the summer heat. Several youngsters spotted me around the hotel. They thought I was a Yankee and solicited my autograph. I didn't make them queue up the way Ted Williams had. But I admit it took longer than it should have for me to dispel the fantasy—theirs and mine—that I was a big-leaguer. It wasn't fair to waste space in their autograph books with a mysterious name they would never find in *Who's Who in Baseball* magazine.

In more recent years, to get away from it all, my wife and I frequently headed for the Berkshires in Massachusetts. A batting cage en route, in the town of Winsted, Connecticut, became a mandatory detour. The pitching machines were set at fifty, sixty, and eighty miles per hour. Up through my mid-sixties, sixty-miles-per-hour pitches remained a piece of cake. Of course, the balls came straight in. No nasty curves, sliders, or—the bane of modern batters' existence—cut fastballs.

Once I warmed up on a sixty-miles-per-hour machine, I would tackle eighty. In the beginning, I scarcely made contact. One day when I trudged back to the cashier in frustration, I complained how tough it was on someone my age. She sympathized and said most batters had trouble with this speed. Then she confided that a couple of seventy-year-olds in town could still handle eighty. This really ticked me off. So I bought twenty dollars more in tokens and strode back to the cage to do battle.

After a few sessions, the reflexes returned, and I started making solid contact even with eighty-miles-per-hour pitches. One time when I was really in a groove, an elderly fellow sidled up to the batting cage with a boy who looked like his grandson. "Watch him closely," Gramps instructed. "That's the way to stroke the bat." I continued the impromptu clinic for fifteen minutes more, much longer that my usual stint in the cage. The next morning, I couldn't bend over.

Beyond the thrill of making solid contact, I delighted in knowing that the occasional retired teenager like me, dressed in tattered jeans and armed with a dented no-name bat, could handle eighty, while many real-life teens, with their designer bats and hitting gloves, could not. I felt their frustration—and gloried in it. Score one for the geezers.

In 1998, I experienced severe chest pain akin to being hit with a sledgehammer. The diagnosis was a clogged artery, the treatment angioplasty. I was frightened as I approached my first hospitalization and first surgery ever. To calm my nerves during recuperation, I turned again to baseball and read *Bunts*, a collection of baseball writings by George F. Will. The conservative columnist and I are diametrically opposed ideologically. Yet I discovered a common passion and a shared humanity that saw me through the health crisis. I wrote Will and told him how grateful I was. His assistant sent a gracious reply expressing his pleasure that the book had such a therapeutic effect.

Baseball does that. Though imperfect, as are all institutions, it unites as it excites. Thanks to Jackie Robinson, Branch Rickey, Sam Lacy, and all who opened the doors, baseball endures as a melting pot, working wonders on the ball field, in the stands, and in the hearts of fans. That's what makes a pastime truly national, even as other sports today compete for youngsters' devotion and participation.

Lamentably, I'll never know if I could hit eighty-miles-per-hour pitches—or even fifty—in my seventies. In recent years, a herniated disk necessitating back surgery brought my sixty-five-year career as a ballplayer to a premature end. No victory tours. Just vivid memories of cherished dreams lived to the fullest, if never quite fulfilled.

CHAPTER 5

ONE GIANT LEAP FOR INTEGRATION

As a native New Englander, my mother could not stomach segregation. Dad was the provider in the household, Mom the politico. She sought out causes and organizations devoted to eradicating racial discrimination.

Segregation prevailed by law and practice in the nation's capital. The exclusively white neighborhoods in Washington west of Sixteenth Street and Rock Creek Park might as well have been in Mississippi, for all the exposure we had to them. And forget about venturing into the nearby suburbs of Maryland or Virginia unless we knew someone who lived there. On Kalorama Road, just off Sixteenth Street NW, we could skate at the roller rink but not patronize the bowling alley one floor below. The cinemas in our immediate neighborhood, such as the Tivoli and the Savoy on Fourteenth Street and the Ontario on Columbia Road, refused to admit us. In Washington's official downtown, most every movie house barred blacks, except for the Little Theatre, where l laughed my head off at Marx Brothers films. Fortunately for me, Griffith Stadium took all comers in the stands, if not on the big-league roster.

In the early 1950s, Mom became active in the League of Women Voters, heading its Speakers Bureau and participating in rallies to secure voting rights for Washingtonians. In those days, residents of the nation's capital could not vote for president, much less elect our own mayor. She also joined the avowedly liberal Americans for Democratic Action (ADA), which pushed aggressively for integration. Mom rose to vice president of the Washington chapter and hobnobbed with fellow ADAers including noted attorneys Joe Rauh and Arthur Goldberg, the future secretary of labor and justice of the Supreme Court.

The nation's capital of my youth mirrored America's schizophrenia about race. In contrast to the ostensibly integrated schools north of the Mason-Dixon line, the city's public schools were rigidly segregated until the celebrated *Brown v. Board of Education* decision by the Supreme Court in 1954, which declared school segregation unconstitutional.

Bruce School was all-black during the segregation era. We had our high schools—Cardozo, Armstrong, Dunbar, and Spingarn. Whites had theirs—Coolidge, Bell, Wilson, McKinley, Roosevelt, and Western.

Ardent integrationists who could afford it sent their kids to Georgetown Day School. Kline went there first. I followed him after graduating from Bruce and for the first time studied alongside white kids, many of them the children of my mother's All Souls and ADA crowd. Georgetown Day occupied a site at 4001 Nebraska Avenue NW, home now to NBC's offices and studios where shows such as *Meet the Press* are produced. My stay was brief because the Supreme Court's ruling in *Brown*—and the companion decision in *Bolling v. Sharpe*, which applied to D.C.—outlawed public-school segregation in the nation's capital and across the country in May 1954.

Under the hard-charging leadership of our neighbor Charles Hamilton Houston, Howard's law school was the intellectual and strategic epicenter of civil rights litigation action. As his biographer, Genna Rae McNeil, noted in *Groundwork*, Houston trained his students to become superb lawyers and "social engineers" who used the Constitution and laws to help African-Americans achieve our rightful place in the nation and to make sure the system guaranteed justice and freedom for everyone. I learned while reading *Groundwork* that my parents provided financial support for Houston's school desegregation lawsuits.

The school desegregation suit in D.C. truly bubbled up from the ground, a history lesson that resonates with contemporary social movements. As recounted in the May 2004 issue of *Washingtonian* magazine commemorating the fiftieth anniversary of *Brown*, a barber named Gardner Bishop appeared at a school board meeting in 1947 to announce that he was launching a boycott of Browne Junior High, a black school attended by his daughters. Browne had eighteen hundred pupils and was so overcrowded that students attended in shifts.

The boycott persisted for months. At one point, Bishop approached Houston for help. Bishop and his lawyers filed lawsuits aimed at forcing Washington to equalize black and white schools. Their realpolitik theory was that doing so would cost the government so much money that it would eventually prefer to operate the schools under a unitary, integrated system, instead of paying for two comparably financed systems side by side.

According to Richard Kluger, author of a history of the *Brown* case entitled *Simple Justice*, the boycotting parents rallied behind Bishop's leadership and formed the Consolidated Parents group, whose ranks included my mother and her close friends Marie Smith (Alonzo's mother) and Burma Whitted. The group raised money for the lawsuits and organized additional protests. Reflecting on his pivotal role in precipitating the boycott, Bishop recalled in 1992, "I had more mouth than anyone else, and I worked for myself, so there wasn't much chance of being punished by whites. Ignorant as I was, people believed in me, and I had to do it. We didn't have no president, we didn't have no vice president, we didn't have no nothing. And we were mad at everyone— the whites, the highfalutin' blacks, the board of education—everyone."

On May 17, 1954, the Supreme Court altered the course of American history by proclaiming in the unanimous *Brown* decision that "in the field of public education the doctrine of 'separate but equal' has no place," and furthermore that "separate educational facilities are inherently unequal." The *Bolling* ruling applied the logic and conclusion of *Brown* to the D.C. schools with equal force. The high court declared, "In view of our decision that the Constitution prohibits the states from maintaining racially segregated public schools, it would be unthinkable that the same Constitution would impose a lesser duty on the federal government," which as a legal and practical matter controlled the affairs of the nation's capital.

As racial attitudes gradually softened and housing barriers crumbled, my parents figured in 1953 that it was time to venture beyond the neighborhood we had known since 1941. We stepped up in lifestyle from the brick row house on New Hampshire Avenue to a lovely three-bedroom single-family detached home at 4031 Nineteenth Street in northeast Washington, just off South Dakota Avenue. My father was proud as could be of our spacious new home. Only three years into his solo practice, he had now set a new high-water mark for the Price family in terms of home ownership. Our cousins from Charles

County gushed over the house when they came for Christmas dinner. Although Dad was the polar opposite of the garrulous father figure in the TV sitcom *The Jeffersons*, its theme song, "Movin' on Up," could have been ours as well.

Yet we quickly learned another bitter lesson about racial intolerance. The Nineteenth Street neighborhood was overwhelmingly white. Since Dad was a distinguished physician, I naively assumed we would be viewed as an asset to the community, whose economic status probably ranked a notch above solidly middle class. In fact, our family likely pushed it up a tad. I cannot imagine the neighborhood's average household income declined because of us.

Our white neighbors didn't see it this way. Within a couple of years, virtually all of them fled. An armada of moving vans descended on the neighborhood month after month. The student body at Taft Junior High just down the street did not flip quite as fast. The main reason was that it drew youngsters from the heavily Jewish neighborhood along South Dakota Avenue to the north. "Little Tel Aviv," as everyone called it, stayed ethnically stable several more years before those white families began dispersing as well.

Georgetown Day was far across town and basically had been a temporary school for me after Bruce anyway. In early September 1954, my eighth-grade year, I was among the first contingent of black students to enter the newly integrated Taft Junior High, a couple of blocks from our new home.

There were two enrollment waves of black students into Taft. The initial registrants who entered on the first day of school were pupils like me, who had just graduated from grade school or were switching from nonpublic schools. The second and much larger contingent of entrants, who arrived the following month, were students who lived in Taft's district and were transferring in from a previously segregated junior high elsewhere in the city.

Since there were only a few of us at first, the early days of desegregation stirred up little fuss. The second wave was another story. Although Taft experienced none of the virulent confrontations of Little Rock's Central High School, we did endure some mild turbulence. One day in October, a bunch of white students decided to stage a walkout to protest the arrival of more black pupils. I do not know what possessed these knuckleheads, but they actually asked black students like me who were already at the school to join them on the picket line. Of course, we told them to get lost. The only thing I can figure is that they cared more about skipping school than making a statement.

Several weeks later, my well-meaning homeroom teacher had a brainstorm that a good way to promote harmony between the races was for several of us black students to serve as hall monitors during the breaks between classes when kids moved from room to room. In other words, we were posted between opposite lanes of student traffic. Far from racial healers, we became convenient punching bags and kicking posts.

This lasted about a month before we decided to return fire. One morning when a couple of perpetrators passed by just before the bell, we collared them, hauled them into the stairwell, and roughed them up enough to let them know they should cut it out.

This encounter ended the physical confrontations but didn't cure the tension. A handful of white classmates befriended black students, but they were rarities. And no matter how much adolescent hormones were raging, forget about socializing with white girls. That was strictly verboten. Black and white kids almost never visited each other's homes back then. Thus, from the outset, classrooms and sports teams were integrated, but social life after school remained rigidly segregated.

Academics came easily for me at Taft. Several white teachers, bless their souls, betrayed nary a trace of racism and took it upon themselves to encourage me scholastically. Math was a breeze. Barbara Dekelbaum and Mr. Fisher, my math teachers, brought the subject alive. In English, Mrs. Mills stretched our reading tastes and made us write papers. She even tried to turn us on to *Beowulf*, the epic poem written sometime between the eighth and eleventh centuries. In those days, I still expected to become a big-league ballplayer. My game plan certainly didn't include maturing into a poet or an English teacher. As Mrs. Mills droned on, trying nobly to hold our attention, I doodled endlessly—cartoons, cars, anything to distract me.

Actually, I do have something useful to show today for all the doodling. During one of those dreary ninth-grade English classes, I designed the signature I planned to use when doling out autographs as a big-league ballplayer. I utilized a stylish script patterned after the way the names *Dodgers* and *Indians* were inscribed on the fronts of the home-team uniforms of Brooklyn and Cleveland, respectively.

Nearly a half-century later, when I attained a modicum of celebrity as head of the National Urban League and author of *Achievement*

Matters, I relished signing autographs using the very signature I created in that English class. Admittedly, this happened at speaking engagements and book-tour events, not outside pro baseball clubhouses or at autograph shows. That was celebrity enough for me.

In high school, I continued the giddy ride academically but banged against an even harder wall socially. These proved to be the unhappiest three years of my life. My parents and my brother always encouraged me to reach for the stars scholastically. The original plan after Taft was for me to attend one of those exclusive New England prep schools. This was the proven pathway to Ivy League colleges, which the children of my parents' closest friends had followed for decades. Andover, Mount Hermon, Exeter, Taft, and Kent—those were the fancy schools most familiar to black Washingtonians who harbored lofty dreams for their youngsters.

In the spring of my ninth-grade year, I was accepted by Mount Hermon. I geared up psychologically to go. But over the summer, my heart called a timeout. Why attend an all-male, socially isolated school in frigid New England during the prime of my adolescence, I wondered, when I could stay home and socialize with my friends? I put my foot down and declared I wasn't going away to prep school, period.

My parents accepted my decision with a proviso. If I stayed home, they insisted that I had to attend one of Washington's academically strongest high schools, even if it meant a lengthy trek by bus to a school outside my assigned district. Taft served as a feeder for McKinley Tech High School, a perfectly fine school. But it didn't rank up there with Wilson or Coolidge, considered the cream of the crop among public high schools. Both were overwhelmingly white. Wilson was located way past Rock Creek Park in northwest Washington—not far, in fact, from Georgetown Day School. However, now that we had moved to northeast D.C., I probably could hitchhike to Baltimore faster than busing to Wilson.

Therefore, we trained our sights on Coolidge, which was closer and almost on par with Wilson academically. School choice existed even back then, provided you knew how to game the system. The trick was to find a course offered by the school you wanted to attend but not by the one where you were supposed to go. Since science and math were my strongest suits, we told the school district it was essential I take German, and that Coolidge was the closest school to home that offered this course of study. I entered Coolidge in the fall of 1956.

The decision to go there worked out fine academically. But it was an unmitigated disaster socially, utterly defeating my rationale for staying in D.C. To begin with, my neighborhood buddies took umbrage that I did not move on to McKinley with them. They excommunicated me from their social set. I was seldom invited to the very parties I had remained in D.C. to enjoy. McKinley had a bevy of black girls who were gorgeous and smart. Yet since I neither took classes nor partied with them, they scarcely knew I existed. The social isolation lasted throughout high school. Was I miserable!

Coolidge offered no consolation. Barely two years into integration, black students were scarce at the school. The social atmosphere mirrored Taft's. White and black students at Coolidge were slightly more cordial toward each other, but the contact seldom extended beyond school. Again, we rarely visited each other's homes and never, ever dated or danced across color lines.

The isolation and ostracism I suffered in high school exacerbated my innate shyness. I'm outgoing by design, not by instinct, and surely no natural-born schmoozer. Heading the National Urban League many years later forced me even farther out of my shell. When it came time to work a crowd, I would take a deep breath and plunge in, admittedly with an eye always on the clock and the exits.

Now, don't get the idea I was a total hermit in high school. During junior year, I crossed paths with an elementary-school classmate who was pretty and smart as could be. We had been linked romantically at Bruce, if you can call puppy love "romance." I discovered that her family had moved to Sandy Spring, Maryland, a forty-five-minute drive from our house. We started dating and became quite attached to one another. Beyond the feelings I had for her, she rescued me from the deep well into which I had plunged.

The rekindled relationship lasted through high school. It petered out—mostly at my instigation—when we both went off to college. This wasn't one of my finest moments as a human being. High school had been such a traumatic time socially that I was determined to start afresh when I escaped Washington—brand-new identity, new locale, no shadow of my movie-star-handsome big brother hovering over my social life.

My scholastic success at Coolidge enabled me to write my own ticket to college, especially since Dad had squirreled away enough money to pay the whole freight. I recall getting only about three Bs the entire three years of high school, and those were for individual marking periods, I think, not for entire courses. The rest were As, all of them in honors classes. The bottom line was that I really kicked butt academically at Coolidge.

To be honest, my homeroom teacher, Ms. Anderson, who was white, believed so ardently in my potential that she occasionally challenged other teachers who had given me less-than-stellar grades. Millions of minority children struggle when saddled with teachers who lack faith in them and don't push them to excel, and with counselors who steer them down the wrong path, and with test results that misconstrue their ability and potential. If all minority children had talented and devoted teachers like Ms. Anderson who believed in them, then that stubborn racial achievement gap would shrivel up, sure enough.

I ranked tenth in Coolidge's senior class. Five of my classmates finished tied for first, with straight As all the way through high school. I set my sights on the best colleges east of the Mississippi River.

In the fall of senior year, I paid the obligatory visit to my guidance counselor to solicit her advice about where I should apply, based on my grades and SAT score. She was one of those curmudgeonly hold-overs from segregation known for giving black students a hard time. In a bone-chilling conversation I will never forget, the "misguidance" counselor recommended I apply to some colleges I knew were several notches below where I should be aiming. She obviously did not have my best interest at heart. Fortunately, I had the presence of mind to respond that I didn't need advice like hers, and that my parents would help me with the application process from that point forward.

In the fall of 2000, I visited the Urban League affiliate in central Long Island to talk with black parents and their youngsters who belonged to our National Achievers Society. Theresa Sanders, the talent-ed head of the affiliate, recounted an equally outrageous conversation with a guidance counselor. It seems her daughter was doing well in school and scoring way above grade level in reading and math. Sanders paid a visit to school to find out how to enroll her youngster in Advanced Placement courses. The guidance counselor said he wasn't equipped to arrange that placement, since he did not have the requisite paperwork on hand. Nor did he lift a finger to get it from the office, or even volunteer to intercede on the child's behalf. However, the counselor did ask if Sanders wanted to place her daughter in special education. He assured her that he did have those referral forms handy.

Such were—and remain—the obstacles facing many minority students who are sailing through school. Just imagine the impediments confronting youngsters who are perfectly bright, or even middle of the pack, yet whose parents are not knowledgeable or confident enough to navigate the school system on their behalf. These millions more minds are a terrible thing for society to waste.

For whites who do not understand what African-Americans mean when we rail against institutional racism, I offer these examples as evidence. This is the subtle and malicious way we often are held back behind the scenes.

In the end, I survived the scuttled dream of becoming a major leaguer, the social isolation, and the malice and discrimination to graduate from Coolidge and head for a top-flight college. High school toughened me up for the real world that lay ahead, although I could have done without rushing the maturation process by missing out on so many joys of adolescence.

CHAPTER 6

LABORATORY IN DEMOCRACY

The academic record I compiled at Coolidge positioned me to apply to some of America's preeminent colleges and universities. My parents and I targeted five—Amherst, Harvard, Oberlin, Tufts, and Penn State. Admittedly, I wavered before applying to Harvard because its aura was intimidating. But my forever optimistic brother urged me to go for it, so I did.

On admissions day—April 15, 1959—I learned that all five had accepted me. "Up yours," I muttered to ORO and that misguidance counselor who had tried to derail me. *Thanks, Mom and Dad, for believing I can do anything*, I thought. *Thanks, Kline, for your confidence in me. And thanks, Ms. Anderson, for being my tireless champion at Coolidge.*

The allure of Harvard as the most storied institution of higher learning in the United States tugged hard at me. How could I not leap at the chance to attend? Since Harvard had anointed me one of its chosen, how dare I not accept?

Yet Amherst held plenty of appeal, starting with its stellar reputation in the village that raised me. I revered my father and was profoundly influenced by his unrealized wish that he could have attended one of the "Little Three" colleges—Amherst, Williams, and Wesleyan. Dr. Montague Cobb, the husband of my fifth-grade teacher and, it would turn out, the uncle-in-law of my future wife, was a distinguished alumnus who loved the school and lobbied me to attend.

These powerful competing magnets of Harvard's aura and Amherst's family ties pulled in opposite directions, virtually neutralizing one another in my mind. I had to see the campuses for myself. When I visited Amherst, the quaint, quintessentially New England campus felt inviting and accessible. The prospect of spending the next four years in a sylvan setting appealed to me, since I doubted I would ever live anywhere like it as an adult.

Hesitant as I am to admit it, one decisive factor that sealed the choice of Amherst was nothing as high minded as superb academics or its Thoreau-like setting. At a small school, I figured, I might actually make the varsity baseball squad and—be still, my heart—the basketball team, for good measure. After all the frustration at Coolidge, I yearned for another shot at organized sports.

Shortly after Labor Day 1959, a quartet of freshmen from the Washington area set off for Amherst in an aging Cadillac owned by one of our new classmates, Steve Langford. Vintage car collectors would kill for it today. With a haughty snout up front and weighed down with luggage in the rear, Steve's Caddy, seemingly made out of cast iron, ploughed up the turnpike, daring any vehicle to cross its path. It even was outfitted with a small refrigerator beneath the dashboard, where we stashed sandwiches and sodas for the trek north.

When I dragged my duffel bag up to the fourth floor of James dorm, I instantly learned my first lesson in college life—tolerance. Emanating from one of the rooms was the deepest Southern accent I

First row, far left: A benchwarmer on the Amherst freshman baseball team
Amherst College Library Archives and Special Collections

had ever heard. It belonged to a classmate from Alabama. A Confederate flag hung on the wall in his room. Less than an hour on campus and already my freshman year was shaping up as an ominous experience. Happily, my Southern classmates and I survived this initial wariness and got on reasonably well, given the times. No confrontations, slurs, or mean-spirited pranks.

Four other black students joined me in the freshman class, all of us from the East Coast, making it 5 brothers out of 250 freshmen. There were fewer still in the upper classes. This was about the norm in those days, but hardly a great leap forward from the halcyon era of the 1920s when future African-American luminaries such as Charles Drew, Montague Cobb, William Hastie, and Mercer Cook were on campus together. In the late 1950s, historically white colleges and universities up north, which prided themselves on their open-mindedness, in truth practiced tokenism when it came to ethnic diversity. At least it was a decided improvement over many white institutions down south, which maintained an iron curtain of segregation. When the admissions barriers began crumbling in the mid- to late 1960s, black applicants didn't suddenly get smarter. Rather, they unquestionably benefited from institutional enlightenment—and affirmative action.

Some elite women's colleges in those days actually had more shameful admissions records. During my freshman year at Amherst, my future wife, Marilyn Elisabeth Lloyd, a sophomore at nearby Mount Holyoke College, was the sole African-American student on campus. Smith had only a couple of black freshmen my first year. Such was student diversity circa 1959 at America's selective colleges. Social life was a challenge, to say the least. Even in college, I wasn't into interracial dating, nor were any white girls to speak of.

A dancer, Francophile, and strikingly beautiful young woman, Marilyn immediately attracted my attention. We dated several times in the fall, but that was as far as our relationship progressed. Besides, she had suitors aplenty. Amherst men always had to contend with rivals from distant colleges including Harvard, Yale, and especially Dartmouth. Basically, we cooled our heels all fall, waiting for winter, when the roads would become so treacherous that the invaders were confined to their immediate environs until the spring thaw. By then, we hopefully would have stolen the hearts of all the Smith and Mount Holyoke co-eds who caught our eyes. This was the theory, at least. Occasionally, it actually worked.

In the spring of my freshman year, however, the social scene remained quieter than I liked. Rumor had it Wellesley College overflowed with lovely black coeds. Since I was the only brother in my class willing to hitchhike to suburban Boston, where Wellesley is located, I eagerly accepted the assignment. It seems like light-years ago, but hitchhiking was a commonplace mode of travel. In those innocent times, no one feared being robbed, assaulted, or kidnapped. Sometimes, even college girls hitchhiked.

Off I went on the eighty-mile trek along Route 9 toward Boston. The journey proved well worth the investment of a weekend. A friend of a friend who was a junior at Wellesley welcomed me and shepherded me around to meet the sisters on campus. Years later, my tour guide, Isabel Johnson, and her husband, Don Stewart, became two of our dearest friends. She headed Girls, Inc., and Don served as president of Spelman College and then the College Board.

Although I didn't end up dating anyone I met, the sheer sight of all those attractive black coeds was Murine for the eyes, as the ads used to say. The visit inspired hope that other "Seven Sisters" colleges— among them Mount Holyoke, Smith, and Radcliffe—would emulate Wellesley someday soon.

While college social life in the Pioneer Valley could not measure up to Howard University, with its sororities stocked with vivacious black coeds, the truth of the matter was that I had no right to complain. The summer before my sophomore year, Marilyn sailed off to Paris for her junior year abroad. As soon as I returned to school, I started scouting the nearby campuses to see what other coeds had arrived on the scene. My eye was drawn to another Mount Holyoke student, a lovely, exotic-looking freshman. We began dating and pretty soon were going steady. Thus, even though the pickings around Amherst remained slimmer than my classmates and I would have liked, I was a happy camper by sophomore year.

Amherst College offered an incomparable education, then as now. The professors were brilliant, many bordering on intimidating, and they pushed us hard intellectually. Every freshman had to run a grueling gauntlet by taking six courses each semester. Mind you, we all took the same courses, the choice of a foreign language being our only elective. It mattered not whether you had attended a run-of-the-mill public high school or an elite prep school. It didn't matter whether the farthest you had gotten in high school was geometry or biology.

Every freshman took calculus, physics, European history, humanities, English composition, and a foreign language. Some overwhelmed freshmen bailed out before flunking out. Amherst also had a quaint procedure of quietly labeling a student who was lagging as an "underachiever" and sending him home for a semester or a year to shape up before trying again.

English composition was my personal hell. It was taught by Professor William Baird, who alternated between being hilarious and irascible. Every week, he required us to write two or three essays of three to four pages in length. As if this weren't taxing enough, the topics he doled out were doozies. In one assignment that absolutely stymied me, Professor Baird told us to write an essay about an occasion in our lives when we were terrified. We were not to write about what had made us terrified, he instructed us. We were to write several pages about what it meant to be terrified.

I scraped by with a C- in Professor Baird's course. As I was strolling disconsolately out of the room on the final day of class, he said, "Mr. Price, you seem not to have gotten the point of this course." I replied that was about the only thing we had agreed upon the entire year.

Sophomore year, I lived for a while in a fraternity I had joined. I quickly took a shine to the social life. Over the summer, I had purchased a brand-new VW Beetle with money I earned during vacation working as a clerk-typist for the Veterans Administration. The car cost a mere eighteen hundred dollars! Keep in mind that annual tuition and room and board, which my parents covered, came to only about twenty-five hundred.

While my social stock soared, my grades cratered like the Dow Jones Industrial Average at the start of the Great Recession. In those days before undergraduates were deemed "emancipated," colleges sent your grades as well as the tuition bills home to your parents. My father, ever a man of few words and a master of subtlety, sent me a brief letter. The gist of it was that he had just received my latest set of grades. "I see you're having a good time," he wrote. In the next sentence, he noted ominously that our house had a two-car garage and one of the slots was unoccupied. He left unsaid the punch line that if my grades did not improve by next marking period, my Beetle was returning home.

Message received. Since Dad always had my best interest at heart, I never bucked him when he put his foot down. In short order, I moved out of the fraternity, got serious again, jacked up my grades—and kept the car. Chalk up another victory for no-nonsense parental involve-ment in a child's education.

Even though Amherst was—and remains—a world-class college, I developed a deep grudge against it that I harbored for many years thereafter. The college's fraternity system was the culprit. The pro-motional literature touted Amherst as a laboratory in democracy. The college publicized its fraternities and promised applicants that there was universal rushing. This meant that every freshman who wanted to join a fraternity would assuredly get into one—not necessarily the frat of his choice, but one of the thirteen on campus, for certain.

Yet the college brochures contained no caveats on the delicate sub-ject of black students and fraternities. For us, the reality of the frater-nity system fell far short of the hype. Belonging to a fraternity was a big deal in those days. Most upperclassmen lived in frats. Most parties worth attending, especially those following football games, took place at fraternities. Girls were drawn to guys who belonged to the most prestigious frats. Upperclassmen who did not join fraternities were classified somewhat derisively as "independents," which was tanta-mount to being branded as left-wingers, nerds, eccentrics, or weirdos. The main places where independents threw their own parties were the dreary social rooms in the basements of dorms. The college stacked the social deck decidedly in favor of frat members.

Those promotional brochures were also silent on another salient fact. Only five of the thirteen fraternities admitted black students. I first learned this during bull sessions in the dorms. Naive me, I still did not quite believe it until the time came for the round-robin frat visits during rushing season in the spring of freshman year. That week, I learned the hard way about racism on our idyllic campus, which left me with deep psychic scars and resentment toward the college that took a couple of decades to heal.

During the rushing period, we were entitled to visit any fraternities that interested us, whether or not they reciprocated. Anyone who has seen *Animal House* probably will never forget the scene when black and foreign students visiting a racist frat are taken on a tour of the kitchen or some such, instead of the attractive party rooms and living quar-ters in the fraternity. This actually happened to me. I was treated to perfunctory tours of porches and furnace rooms as an unsubtle way of sending me a message: "Fuggetaboutit." The unstated insult smarted. To make matters worse, several of my closest friends and I had sworn we would pledge the same fraternity as a team. When the offers were not forthcoming for all of us, we went our separate ways. I signed on with a frat where I knew a few guys but did not have any close friends.

Alpha Theta Xi, the one I joined, boasted of being a liberal fraternity that welcomed blacks, Jews, and foreign students. Plus, it probably claimed more members of the dean's list than any other frat. So it wasn't like I was consigned to purgatory. I had just learned that liberal arts colleges as laboratories of democracy weren't always as advertised. I never forgot this eye-opening lesson, which I have often invoked over the years in attempting to parse the true meaning of labels such as *liberal* and *conservative, progressive* and *reactionary*. It is necessary to dig deeper because labels often mask the real deal underneath.

Although segregation persisted in many realms of American life in those days, ostensibly enlightened colleges such as Amherst should have been ashamed of themselves for allowing blatantly racist student organizations to operate on campus with their blessing. These colleges should have served as examples of how democracy ought to work, instead of reflections of how it actually functioned.

To the college's enduring credit, other aspects of Amherst far exceeded expectations. One reason I chose it over larger schools was the hope that I would get to play intercollegiate sports. Forget about making the pros. I just wanted to wear an official uniform and compete on a team against other clubs.

Although I had never made the high-school basketball team, much less been chosen for pickup games with the hotshots on premier D.C. playgrounds such as Turkey Thicket, I tried out and actually made the freshman squad. As a center at six-two. Even though I could barely touch the rim, let alone dunk. I started some games at center despite my height. That was small-college basketball back in the day.

The truth was I couldn't much jump or shoot. However, I got a charge out of traveling to colleges to compete before enthusiastic crowds, suiting up and prancing through those pregame layup drills like a pro.

That winter, we played archrival Williams College in its bandbox gym. During warmups, rock music blared over the loudspeakers. Our side got all pumped up as we soared toward the rim with our layups. Then Williams took the floor. We stared, mouths agape, at these giants—six-eight, six-seven, six-five, and so on. They dunked the ball with such abandon it made me nauseous.

One of our chief adversaries and agitators on the Williams squad was Gordon Davis, who became a lifelong friend. Among other banner professional accomplishments, he spearheaded the creation of Jazz at Lincoln Center in New York City. His father, Allison Davis, was a Dunbar graduate like Dad and a noted cultural anthropologist who in 1942 became the first African-American to hold a full-time faculty position at a major white university, namely the University of Chicago. A world-class wisecracker, Gordon "dissed" us all through the game while Williams whipped us badly. He gleefully resumed talking trash when he barely beat me one-on-one in the Berkshires forty years later. Yet the gap in our abilities is closing. I figure I'll nail him by the time we're ninety.

I tried out for varsity basketball during sophomore year and barely made the team. But it was crystal-clear my hoop skills were skimpy. I quit the team in favor of pursuing the more active social life that eventually attracted my father's attention.

When I entered college in 1959, students focused their energies mostly on campus life—courses, sports, dating, and bullshitting the hours away. By the time I graduated four years later, however, America's college generation was rousing from its slumber and confronting injustice around the country and especially in the South. The class of 1963 bridged the eras between student apathy and activism.

Second row, third from right: Also a benchwarmer on the freshman basketball team
Amherst College Library Archives and Special Collections

Courageous students began staging sit-ins to break the back of segregation at lunch counters down south. They followed the Reverend Martin Luther King Jr. in the marches he led. Impatient with the pace of change, young activists formed two vigorous new organizations— the Student Nonviolent Coordinating Committee (SNCC) and the Students for a Democratic Society. These groups boisterously challenged the status quo. College students weren't just skipping classes to demonstrate; some were dying or being beaten by Sheriff Bull Connor of Birmingham, Alabama, and his racist ilk.

This surge in student activism gradually stirred my social conscience. I attribute the awakening to an authentic commitment to justice but also, frankly, to my growing shame that I was not as engaged as my braver contemporaries in righting society's wrongs. Probably, my mother's activist genes were slowly awakening.

In the spring of 1963, I joined busloads of students from New England colleges and universities who descended on Washington to picket in front of the White House. President John F. Kennedy, who talked a good game about civil rights but had delivered little, loomed as our target. The demonstration went off without a hitch, although there was little sign it changed his mind.

During the summer following graduation, national civil rights leaders delivered a vastly louder wake-up call to JFK and the nation when they organized the March on Washington for Jobs and Freedom. A. Philip Randolph, the visionary international president of the Brotherhood of Sleeping Car Porters, rallied other prominent black leaders to the idea and enlisted Bayard Rustin to orchestrate the march's logistics. Randolph had threatened to stage a march in 1941 to pressure President Franklin D. Roosevelt to guarantee jobs for blacks in wartime industries. When FDR capitulated by issuing an executive order, Randolph called off the march. This time, there would be no turning back.

The March on Washington ranks as one of the epiphanies of my life. Most of the people who attended undoubtedly felt the same. Crowd estimates ranged from 250,000 to 500,000; most "official" accounts put the total closer to the former. I'm always amused by how organizers of marches routinely inflate the numbers, while whoever is targeted by the marches typically low-balls the estimate. Whatever the actual count, the crowd was huge.

I volunteered to serve as a marshal for the march. We received training in how to contain any disturbances by circling the antagonists and ushering them away from the crowd. We marshals reported for duty around six on the morning of the march. As this "army without guns"—black and white, male and female, young and old—assembled on that historic morning of August 28, 1963, the empty downtown streets lined with majestic federal buildings were strikingly serene.

The action picked up when roughly two thousand chartered buses began arriving from out of town and disgorged their passengers. Thousands more marchers who had chartered trains came over from Union Station. Members of the Congress of Racial Equality arrived on foot, having walked 230 miles from Brooklyn.

My adrenaline kicked in at the sight of tens of thousands of marchers streaming down Constitution Avenue and Independence Avenue toward the Washington Monument, where the march officially began, and ultimately to the Lincoln Memorial, where the day's performances and speeches would be staged. Fortunately, I never had to put my abbreviated marshal's training to use that day. Unfortunately, I stood too far from the Lincoln Memorial to catch the songs by the likes of Joan Baez, Odetta, and Mahalia Jackson. Nor could I hear any of the soul-stirring speeches, most notably Martin Luther King's historic "I Have a Dream" address.

The march garnered mixed reviews. The ever-acerbic Malcolm X derided it as "the Farce on Washington." Stokely Carmichael, the fiery black nationalist from SNCC, dismissed it as "only a sanitized, middle-class version of the real black power movement." Russell Baker of the *New York Times* offered a brighter assessment. "No one could remember," he wrote, "an invading army quite as gentle as the two hundred thousand civil rights marchers who occupied Washington today. . . . The sweetness and patience of the crowd may have set some sort of national high-water mark in mass decency." And James Baldwin captured the emotions and cautious optimism of many hopeful attendees, including me, with an eloquence we could never emulate: "That day, for a moment, it almost seemed that we stood on a height, and could see our inheritance; perhaps we could make the kingdom real, perhaps the beloved community would not forever remain the dream one dreamed in agony."

A visceral experience of bearing witness to history, the March on Washington made an indelible impression on me. The contours of my life's calling began taking shape that sweltering summer day.

Scarcely two weeks later, reality violently intruded, demonstrating that, when it came to defeating racism, progress was seldom linear. On September 15, a bomb was tossed from a speeding car into Birmingham's Sixteenth Street Baptist Church, which was packed with children celebrating Youth Day. The explosion killed four young girls and injured twenty-one children.

CHAPTER 7

THE CENTER OF MY UNIVERSE

E asily the greatest gift Amherst gave me is Marilyn Elisabeth Lloyd, my wife of more than fifty years. Even though we both grew up in Washington, it is highly likely that, but for Amherst, I might never have courted her, fallen eternally in love with her, married her, and had three daughters who like her are truly beautiful in every sense of the word. Who knows the odds that we would have met at some other time and place? Happily, I needn't ever worry about that.

Metaphors are not my forte, maybe because I never got the point of my freshman English course. So it's utterly without embarrassment that I say she's the center of my universe and my Rock of Gibraltar. Has been since the day we started going steady. Will be until the day I depart these shores.

Since graduating from law school, I have had a dozen careers. A restless professional adventurer like me needs to be tethered to a life partner who indulges her mate's perpetual quest for discovery and fulfillment, while preventing him from floating into orbit on some utterly foolhardy journey. That's my beloved bride.

Our intertwined roots go back to the village that raised both of us. In fact, my father and her mother's older sisters, Hilda and Otwiner Smith, grew up across T Street from each other in D.C.'s LeDroit Park neighborhood, within the shadow of Howard University. They all attended fabled Dunbar High School around the same time. My father operated on Marilyn's maternal grandfather. Her aunt Hilda taught me at Bruce School, and Hilda's husband, Monty Cobb, was my principal booster for Amherst. Years later, Marilyn's mother and her uncle Monty, anatomy professors both, taught my brother at Howard Medical School.

Marilyn comes by her centeredness naturally. In 1941, her mother, Ruth Smith Lloyd, who pursued her graduate studies at Case Western Reserve University, became the first black woman in the United States to earn a PhD in anatomy and only the sixth black woman to obtain a doctoral degree in one of the STEM disciplines. She received a prestigious Julius Rosenwald Fellowship, awarded to promising African-American scholars and artists. Ruth then joined the faculty of Howard Medical School, where the renowned biologist Ernest Everett Just served as her mentor. Over the course of thirty-five years, she taught most, if not all, of the future doctors and dentists trained at Howard. Ruth specialized in "the cadaver walk," the gruesome stroll through the lab in which she led med students in discussing corpses that were being dissected like frogs in junior-high biology class. The prospect of taking the walk was enough to dissuade me from pursuing a career in medicine.

Marilyn's mother ministered to the emotional and family needs of so many students that she earned the nickname "Mama." Whenever I spoke before large black crowds and mentioned her name, many a Howard Medical School grad came up to me afterward with fond recollections of Mama Lloyd.

Ruth Lloyd was a real card. After a wonderful but wearying day of commencement ceremonies when Marilyn graduated from Mount Holyoke, her mother's feet grew tired from all the standing. So while wearing her hat and white gloves, she shed her high-heel shoes and commandeered her teenage son's black high-top sneakers.

She was a nonstop raconteur with an earthy, PG-13 sense of humor. Her grandchildren learned early on that if they wanted to get a word in edgewise once she got rolling, they had better leap in when she was catching her breath. Ruth specialized in original sayings that made people dissolve in gales of laughter. Once, she told of someone who "looked like sent for and couldn't come." Regrettably, no one thought to take notes during her riffs in order to preserve her witticisms for posterity.

Throughout her life, Ruth placed family first and foremost. Her devotion clearly showed in the fact that she and Marilyn's father reared three extremely smart, curious, compassionate, and utterly decent children. Happily, Marilyn possesses those most precious character traits in abundance and has passed them on to our daughters. Other attributes—ambition, wealth, celebrity—matter far less when the final reckoning comes.

Marilyn's father, Dr. Sterling Lloyd, was quieter but no less accomplished. Born in Phoebus, Virginia, adjacent to what was then Hampton Institute, he was the baby of four brothers. Their father, Dr. Rupert Lloyd Sr., a physician and surgeon, also served as campus physician for Hampton early in his career. Their mother, Daisy Blanche Lloyd, was a Bible-toting housewife who had her hands full with these bright and mischievous boys. When the family gathered for dinner, she required her sons to recite a saying from the Bible. One of the brothers, Rupert Jr., delighted in quoting risqué passages and, in response to his mother's withering glare, would add, "It's in the Bible, Mother."

When the time came, the Lloyd brothers journeyed north to attend Dunbar High in Washington. Though it was a public school, it functioned like a prep school without dorms for the out-of-town teenagers, who boarded with local families. After Dunbar, Sterling followed his older brother Rupert to Williams College. Rupert, by the way, was one of the earliest blacks to enter the U.S. Foreign Service. Next stop for Sterling after Williams was Howard Medical School, where he finished first in his class.

While our parents knew each other, Marilyn and I seldom crossed paths as youngsters. Like a lot of brainy young black girls, she skipped a grade in school, putting her a year ahead of me, even though we're the same age. Plus, she was artsy. Marilyn fell in love with dance and for years took ballet classes after school at the Jones-Haywood School of Dance, whose illustrious alumni include Broadway legend Chita Rivera.

One of my favorite photos of Marilyn

It was good fortune that we ended up at colleges barely ten miles apart. Marilyn entered Mount Holyoke in South Hadley, Massachusetts, a year before I arrived at Amherst. As I reflect on it, college dating and mating rituals in those days seem downright quaint by today's standards. To judge by the relative success rates in producing long-term marriages, it's also arguable that these antiquated methods worked better.

One time-honored method of socializing that fascinated me was the college mixer. Busloads of freshman boys from Amherst would descend on Saturday night on the campus of nearby Mount Holyoke or Smith. We would head straight for a huge hall filled with freshman girls. It was heaven—for white guys. Hardly any college students crossed the color line in those days, and black women were a rarity.

The other practice we had the temerity to try was showing up unannounced at a women's dorm to meet black coeds. First, we scoped them out in the freshman guides. Since our white classmates weren't shy about meeting women this way, we tried it, too. I felt sorry for the coeds we pulled this stunt on. After all, we knew up front what they looked like. Imagine their anxiety as they descended the stairs to set eyes on us for the first time. Think of the polite exit strategies they must have been plotting in case they thought we looked like gargoyles.

I sampled these meet-and-greet methods but decided to go solo as well. It took awhile, but I finally mustered the courage to call Marilyn for a date. I approached the encounter with trepidation. After all, self-confidence never ranked as my strong suit when it came to courting women. My brother looked like a movie star, but no one ever mistook me for one. Plus, I was shy and studious, never blessed with an innate gift of gab.

To make matters worse, I had already placed Marilyn on a pedestal. She was striking, yet artsy, sophisticated, cerebral, and quiet. Marilyn was a ballet dancer, which dazzled me, and spoke French fluently, which lost me. With her thick, long hair braided in the back, she looked every bit the intellectual she was. Plus, she already had a boyfriend, and black college guys all over New England were chasing her. As if those weren't obstacles enough, she was an "older" woman, in college age if not chronologically. But since one big reason I left D.C. for college was to become more assertive socially, I resolved to join in the pursuit of the African-American belle of the Pioneer Valley.

We dated occasionally that year, although romantic sparks never ignited between us. The following September, Marilyn sailed to France for junior year in Paris. Despairing that she would fall prey to the charms of some suave Frenchman while I stayed home alone, I returned to Amherst for sophomore year and immediately began scouting the incoming freshman classes at Mount Holyoke and Smith.

To my delight and relief, I discovered that a lovely black coed from Brooklyn had entered Mount Holyoke in the fall. I approached her for a date, and eventually we became an item. The relationship continued throughout the academic year and into the summer. Some weekends, I drove from Washington to New York City to see her. After the drive, I usually spent Friday night at the home of my aunt Louise Latimer, the daughter of my great-great-uncle Lewis Latimer. She lived in her father's home, now a museum in Queens known as Latimer House. First thing Saturday morning, it was off to Brooklyn to pick up my girlfriend and head out to Sag Harbor, the chic Long Island vacation mecca frequented by black families, where her parents had a summer house.

Since it was too taxing financially and physically to drive up to Brooklyn and Sag Harbor most weekends, I moped around a lot at home during the summer of 1961. Noting my ennui one day, Mom said rather innocently, "Isn't that Lloyd girl you used to date back home from France? Why don't you call her sometime and see what she's doing?"

I did, and the rest is history, although it took several months to crystallize. I asked Marilyn out for a date, mainly to catch up and hear how her junior year in Paris had gone. I was dazzled anew when I dropped by her house to pick her up. Gone were the braids, replaced by a chic French "do." She was more outgoing, sophisticated, and worldly than before. The Parisian aura made her even more stunning.

We went out several times that summer, the most memorable occasion being our canoe excursion on the Potomac River. One bright day, we rented a metal canoe from a boathouse in Georgetown and took off downriver. On our way back, the sky turned steel gray, a surefire sign of a hellacious storm headed our way. As a camper many years earlier, I had witnessed how a lightning strike set the surface of a lake to sizzling. I wanted no part of that. Suddenly, I understood what Professor Baird had meant when he asked us to write about what it was to be terrified.

In my best Romeo impersonation, I had been paddling and romancing Marilyn as she absorbed the scenery. Now, we had to hightail it off the river. While I'm no electrician, I knew the canoe would get a big charge if lightning struck the water. I asked Marilyn if she knew how to paddle. When she shook her head, I told her to grab a paddle for some urgent on-the-job training. We stroked frantically and made it to shore without incident. The threatened calamity drew us closer.

We returned to college that fall, she as a senior and I as a junior. In November, I took her to the Harvard-Yale football classic in New Haven. She stayed with her cousins, the Reverend and Mrs. Julian Taylor. The Reverend Taylor was a nationally prominent Baptist preacher and the uncle of jazz great Billy Taylor. In 1994, one of the couple's daughters, Shirlee Taylor Haizlip, wrote the widely acclaimed book *The Sweeter the Juice*. It's the deeply affecting story of her successful quest to reunite her mother with an older sister who had crossed over to live as white generations earlier and severed all contact with her black roots. The story resonated with my own.

When I arrived at the Taylor home to pick up Marilyn, the ever-protective Reverend Taylor summoned me into the den. His stern demeanor masked a wry sense of humor. He stared at me and gravely asked, "Price, who are your people?" I was offended by the question,

Marilyn with President Clinton
Official White House Photo

given my parents' prominence in D.C. But I dutifully laid out my pedigree because the Reverend Taylor had rattled me. Besides, I knew I couldn't get Marilyn out the front door without his permission.

The football game was enjoyable and the after-parties even more fun. The protracted time we spent together that weekend—driving down and back from college, attending the game and the parties, being around her extended family—really ignited our romantic spark. Though I did not realize it at the time, there was now no turning back in our relationship.

After graduating from Mount Holyoke in 1962, Marilyn enrolled in the master's program in linguistics at Columbia University in New York City. Many a weekend, I drove to see her. Since we had scant spending change, we entertained ourselves on the cheap. She exposed me to new culinary vistas and big-city treats. Scrumptious turkey and roast beef sandwiches with Russian dressing at the West End Café on Broadway near Columbia. Clam spaghetti dinners for four bucks at Kettle of Fish in Greenwich Village. Sunset rides on the Staten Island Ferry. Midnight double features at the Thalia Theater just a couple of blocks down Broadway from campus.

She lived in a graduate women's dorm called Johnson Hall, next to the law school. In those prehistoric times, males were not allowed past the living room. I usually stayed in dirt-cheap SROs (single-room-occupancy buildings) on the Upper West Side near the campus. Those rooms were so narrow that, in order to wash my face and shave at the sink without banging my head against the mirror, I had to stand flush against the wall opposite the basin, slide my butt down a foot or so, and then bend over.

A year later, in June 1963, I graduated from Amherst. In between commencement activities one evening, we sat by the War Memorial overlooking the Holyoke Range, where I proposed to her. I realize it sounds corny. But at fifty-plus years of marriage and counting, it's obvious the storybook venue worked wonders that night.

Marilyn returned to Columbia in the fall, while I entered Yale Law School. She rented a room in the apartment of an elderly Hungarian woman, Mrs. Lucas. Even more old-school than the matrons at Johnson Hall, Mrs. Lucas would not let me cross the doorstep when I came to visit. I had to wait in the hallway until Marilyn was ready. It mattered not to her landlady that we were engaged, barely four months shy of tying the knot.

We got married over the Christmas holiday in 1963, midway through my first year in law school. Marilyn shuttled back and forth between New Haven and New York. In a major concession to the fact we were now married, Mrs. Lucas let me into the kitchen when I came to the city to visit my wife.

Our first daughter, Traer, was born a year later. She wasted no time making her entrance. One weekend in late November, I returned from playing touch football to find Marilyn crouched by the kitchen sink, in pain from cramps. I promptly called the obstetrician to find out what was happening, since her water had not broken. The doctor informed us that the cramps probably were contractions and instructed us to measure the intervals between them. When we conveyed that information to him, he told us to hightail it to the hospital. Marilyn's first cousin Brian Lloyd, who was visiting, took us because I was too anxious and excited to drive safely. I was still registering Marilyn when, barely a half-hour after we arrived, the nurses wheeled her into the delivery room. It was as if Traer suddenly downshifted into first gear and came roaring out, ready or not.

Marilyn and I seal our vows with wedding cake.
The Scurlock Studio

This was years before hospitals allowed fathers to witness deliveries. No matter. I would have declined anyway, out of concern that I'd faint at the first sign of bodily fluids, which surely would have been no help to Marilyn. So I paced nervously in the corridor outside, just the way expectant fathers used to do in the movies.

A short while later, the medics brought Marilyn and our infant daughter into the recovery room. They plopped our newborn into my arms, closed the door behind them, and promptly forgot about us for what seemed like a couple of hours. It truly was a revelation. Marilyn had been around young children, having two younger brothers. The wee hours of

November 28, 1964, marked the first time in my life I had held an infant. I had little inkling how tiny and light, yet squirmy and strong, they are. We cooed and cuddled while Marilyn lay in bed, thrilled and exhausted.

We entered parenthood the old-fashioned way—unplanned pregnancy, no inkling of our child's gender, no clue what day she would come into the world, and little idea, on my part, at least, of what we had gotten ourselves into. Some relative gave us a copy of Dr. Spock's classic book about child rearing, but neither of us glanced at it. Truth be told, we have managed to raise three gentle and compassionate children without ever cracking a page, thanks to a fortuitous combination of intuition, mother wit, and abundant grandmotherly advice from both sides of the aisle. Our route may not be right for everyone, but the end results, personified by our lovely daughters, speak for themselves.

Marilyn withdrew from Columbia after our first daughter's birth. She explored transferring to the graduate linguistics program at Yale but found that it, like Columbia's program, was focused on PhD students and was no longer admitting candidates for master's degrees. Plus, she had cooled on linguistics as a prospective career.

The fall after our eldest was born, Marilyn landed a job teaching fifth grade at Winchester School in New Haven. A grandmotherly woman named Miss Mary McDuffie took care of Traer during the day. This continued until our second daughter, Janeen, was born in 1969. Lauren, our youngest, arrived two years later. By then, Marilyn had left teaching to focus full-time on raising our children. She remained out of the labor market for a decade. It was a decision she has never regretted because raising children is an intimate, intense, and gratifying experience that cannot be rivaled.

Marilyn is a gentle and loving soul who to this day is the center of my universe. She proved grounded and rock-steady while I swirled about fighting professional ennui and perpetually exploring new career terrain. She is the calm one we all snuggle up to after the day's tension and turmoil. Thanks to our enduring love and distinctive chemistry, we have survived and thrived.

CHAPTER 8

TRAINING FOR THE LAW AND FOR LIFE

S ince attorneys played a pivotal role in the struggle for civil rights, the notion of attending law school after Amherst College strongly appealed to me. Once this was settled in my head, there was only one choice: Yale. Why so? Yale Law School was—and remains—the pinnacle of higher education, in my estimation. It has been the nation's top-ranked law school for decades. It welcomed only 150 students per class when I applied. The student body, selected from the very top of a nationwide applicant pool, sizzled with intellect, energy, and ambition.

Admittedly, those are attributes of any exalted institution of higher learning. What made Yale unique was the ethos of public service that pervaded the law school. The list of fabled alumni ran the gamut from presidents, senators, congressmen, governors, and Supreme Court justices to renowned attorneys, corporate executives, and nonprofit leaders.

I decided to roll the dice and apply solely to Yale. No other law school would do. In fact, I didn't even apply to graduate school, although the Columbia School of International Affairs intrigued me if Yale did not pan out. In the fall of 1962, I took the LSAT. Since I had done well on the SAT four years earlier, I figured I should fare all right on the LSAT. The night before the exam, I went to see *West Side Story*, just to get my mind off the exam. Evidently, it was still switched off the next day because I butchered the test. No two ways about it. I'd provide my score here except I've repressed the memory. It was that awful.

Once I learned my score, I assumed getting into Yale was a lost cause. But I decided to visit anyway, just to see up close what I would

79

be missing. I scheduled an appointment with the assistant dean of admissions, Charles Runyon. Despite the power he wielded over thousands of applicants, Dean Runyon turned out to be an easygoing man with an enigmatic smile. The interview felt like it went well, and he seemed to take a genuine interest in me.

When the meeting ended, Dean Runyon invited me to accompany him, Eugene Rostow, the dean of the law school, and Frederick Beinecke, the S&H Green Stamps mogul, to the dedication of the new Beinecke Rare Book Library next door. Following the ceremony, the four of us were whisked off in Beinicke's spacious Mercedes-Benz to a reception at Dean Rostow's house. This was a heady experience for a lowly applicant who had butchered the law boards.

As I drove back to Amherst, I could not for the life of me figure out what I had done to deserve such rarified treatment. The mystery was compounded several months later when Yale admitted me, miserable test score notwithstanding. Evidently, Dean Runyon placed a bet that he had spotted some potential in me that I couldn't see in myself.

The next three years whizzed by. Happily distracted by marriage, and coping with the financial demands of helping support our young family, I mostly went through the motions in class. Since we lived off campus, I never participated fully in the academic, extracurricular, and social life of the school. The mandatory courses and handful of electives during the first two years confirmed that I was not cut out for traditional legal practice with a private law firm.

While I was at Yale, one way I earned extra money to support our young family helped to shape my subsequent career. The antipoverty agency in New Haven, Community Progress, Inc., hired me to serve as a social group worker with a half-dozen junior-high boys who were in and out of juvenile court. These fellows qualified as bad actors by the standards of the day. They robbed parking meters, tossed lighted matches into the gas tanks of automobiles, and committed other mischief like that. They were a huge headache to the courts and were on course to become thugs and criminals. The idea behind hiring me was to link them with a caring adult who might be able to get them back on the right track before they became lost causes.

I worked three afternoons a week at Prince Street School in the Hill neighborhood of New Haven. It took awhile to break the ice with these fellows and win their trust. After all, they were street toughs and

I, a Yalie, was anything but. They greeted me with skepticism, and I initially felt insecure dealing with them.

Nevertheless, we bonded eventually. We hung out together and talked about everything and nothing. We shot hoops and even formed a team, which I coached, that competed in the parks-and-recreation basketball league. This was important because it introduced structure and teamwork into their aimless lives. I took them to New York City to see the sights and ride the Staten Island Ferry. They visited our apartment, where we baked cakes. I dropped by their homes to get to know their families—in most cases, a mother or grandmother and some siblings, but seldom a father in sight.

During the two years we were together, these guys had nary another hostile encounter with the cops. They stayed completely out of trouble and soldiered on through school, though it was a struggle. In other words, we really connected. Some of the guidance and support I hoped to provide actually penetrated.

I did not realize how much our relationship had come to mean to them until I showed up late one day because a law school class had run over. Speaking on behalf of his buddies, one of the youngsters told me something that has stuck with me ever since. "Mr. Price," he began, "being together with you and the guys at three o'clock has become the most important thing in our lives. If we're going to keep this going, we need to know that being here with us at three o'clock is also the most important thing in your life. If you're ever late again, we'll know it isn't, and that'll be it for us."

Interestingly enough, this blunt message accorded with real-world experience and subsequent research. Years later, I served on a commission established by the Carnegie Corporation that focused on the efficacy and importance of after-school programs. I recall reading a poignant book, *The Kindness of Strangers* by Marc Freedman, that made precisely the same point. The basic lesson is that, for many youngsters, occasional mentoring by volunteers is valuable, even though working adults cannot always control their schedules and honor their commitments to their kids. But for youngsters saddled with significant social-emotional needs and unstructured lives, there simply is no substitute for regularly scheduled youth development programs after school, during weekends, and over the summer that are staffed by people who believe in them, know what they are doing, and show up when they are supposed to. This investment and trust enable these youngsters to confirm that the adults who say they want to help them are truly serious.

My mentoring experience awakened me to the fact that many youngsters who land in trouble and are written off by society aren't lost causes after all. They respond favorably to second chances and the authentic support of caring adults. In fact, the positive impact on my mentees so inspired me that, during my final year, I wrote my senior paper on legal strategies for curbing juvenile delinquency. This proved the beginning of a lifelong professional focus on the field of youth development. After drifting through law school, I had at last begun to figure out how I wanted to use the education I had received.

The summer before my final year at Yale, I landed a job interning in the Hill neighborhood office of the New Haven Legal Assistance Association. LAA provided free representation for low-income people with legal trouble. Its lawyers handled civil and criminal cases. They also brought class-action suits and represented community-based organizations in the inner-city neighborhoods they served.

As an intern, I handled intake on new clients, helped draft legal documents, and conducted light research for the attorneys. LAA opened my eyes even wider to inner-city life. One afternoon, a new client showed up in the office. As I filled out the intake form, I noticed he had a ten-year gap between jobs. When I asked the middle-aged man why this was, he explained that he had spent those years in prison for killing his son. I made a mental note never to get him riled up.

LAA was the first legal environment that genuinely appealed to me. I could imagine becoming a legal services lawyer because it blended my professional training with an emerging desire to help poor people improve their circumstances. Out of curiosity, I interviewed with one traditional law firm during recruiting season. I quickly realized the work law firms typically did was not for me. After a year of drafting wills and contracts, I would be swinging from the chandeliers. The interviewer probably detected those qualms on my part. So we shook hands and amicably parted company.

I joined LAA straight out of law school in 1966, earning the princely entry-level salary of seven thousand dollars per annum. Since the going rate for new lawyers at private firms in town was only a few thousand dollars more, this represented some financial sacrifice, but hardly a staggering one.

The work captured my interest in the beginning. I handled a wide range of cases, from felonious assaults and armed robberies to divorces and landlord-tenant disputes. Many of our clients were real characters who spun amazing yarns and sometimes told bald-faced lies. As young attorneys, some of my LAA colleagues and I believed there were both honorable and disreputable drug addicts. The former were hooked on drugs and did dumb stuff, we reassuringly told ourselves, but never aided the police by informing on other junkies. The dishonorable ones compounded their personal problems by ratting out their friends. Or so I thought until I started reading the presentencing reports on my presumably honorable clients who had pleaded guilty or been found guilty. Invariably, I would find an obscure notation in the file about how cooperative my client had been and how the sentencing judge should take this into account. This was yet another lesson I never learned in my criminal law course.

A truly insidious part of Connecticut's criminal code in those days was an "offense" called "lascivious carriage." Translated, this meant that unmarried people who were caught cohabiting could be charged with a crime. I'm serious! That sure would crimp people's dating and mating habits in this day and age. Probably half the adult population in America would be behind bars if the law remained on the books.

When teaching at Princeton in recent years, I have enjoyed asking my students if they have any idea what the crime of lascivious carriage entails. Not surprisingly, they never guess the answer, probably because the term fails the transparency test and, no doubt, because the "crime" itself is utterly incomprehensible to their generation.

Anyway, grownups being grownups, people used to shack up. If they were addicts or drug traffickers who had not snitched on anyone recently, or were users whom the police wanted to turn into informants, the cops would get word on where they were holed up with a girlfriend or boyfriend, barge in, and arrest them for lascivious carriage. If the defendants agreed to cooperate, the charges would then be dropped.

Since I spent loads of time in the criminal courts, it dawned on me that precious few unhitched lovers from the high-class neighborhoods or suburbs were prosecuted for lascivious carriage. Perhaps they were all celibate. This was another eye-opening revelation early in my professional career about the double standards embedded in the criminal justice system that all too often screwed minorities and poor people. The abuse of authority was plain as day. Fortunately, the Byzantine crime of lascivious carriage did not survive the sexual revolution, although it may remain hidden in the criminal statutes of some states.

American cities percolated with tension in the sixties. There were confrontations galore over police brutality, dilapidated housing, slum clearance, urban renewal/Negro removal, and "maximum feasible" community participation in government-funded antipoverty programs, to name just a few flashpoints. Cities erupted in violence year after year. Among the bloodiest were Los Angeles, Newark, Detroit, and Washington, the latter following the assassination of Martin Luther King Jr. in 1968.

Although smaller in size, New Haven suffered alongside the nation's other cities. Inner-city residents became increasingly agitated about intrusive police practices (including arrests for lascivious carriage), disturbing instances of police brutality, and high-profile shootings of civilians who were unarmed, even though they may have been up to no good. Newly formed community groups such as the Hill Parents Association protested against these practices. Temperatures in New Haven soared.

In an effort to address these police-community tensions, several neighborhood groups formed the Hill-Dwight Citizens' Commission on Police-Community Relations. The commission enlisted me as its lawyer, pro bono staff director, scribe, and all-purpose factotum. Since the group received no grants and its members were mostly community people, the commission easily qualified as an indigent client.

The role thrust me into the cauldron of community change for the first time in my fledgling career. I relished the dynamics, the tension, the media coverage, the chance to help mold public opinion, the challenge of marshaling evidence and trying to move stubborn municipal bureaucracies, and, in the final analysis, the opportunity to improve public policy and practice.

Staffing the commission taught me volumes at a tender age about realpolitik and real people. Sometimes, I resort to a football metaphor when thinking about collaborative endeavors. Which teammates, I always want to know, are determined to head resolutely downfield toward the end zone and across the goal line? Which ones prefer to stay in the huddle and never lay it on the line? Which ones go for the sidelines or crumble instead of taking a hit? Which ones drop passes that should have been caught or even take off running the wrong way?

I learned early on how to spot colleagues who wanted to march downfield and how to steer clear of all the others. Indeed, I discovered years later that some of the most vocal community activists I dealt with were drug addicts who may have been deployed by the police to undermine our efforts. While I am not paranoid by nature, this politically fraught community work taught me to keep my personal radar tuned for infiltration and disinformation.

Our citizens' commission held public hearings, which I transcribed by hand. In the end, it issued a report, written by me, which presented findings and recommended reforms in police policy and practice. The commission's report gained enough credibility that it was cited in the so-called Kerner Report, issued by the eleven-member National Advisory Commission on Civil Disorders, which President Lyndon Johnson appointed in July 1967 and which Otto Kerner, the governor of Illinois, chaired.

The Kerner Commission reached a prescient conclusion that, sadly enough, resonates to this day, despite the considerable progress that's been made. Warning that America faced a system of apartheid in major cities, the commission declared the nation was "moving toward two societies, one black, one white—separate and unequal." These days, impoverished blacks have company—namely, low-income and working-class whites, Latinos, and other immigrants. They all remain trapped in poverty by lousy schools, lousy health care, lousy jobs, lousy local economies, and lousy housing. Indeed, the more things change, the more they stay the same.

The fact that our citizens' commission gained a modicum of national recognition was a big deal in New Haven and a source of pride for the folk who served on it. The New Haven Police Department probably did not share our sense of accomplishment.

Regrettably, the yeoman's work of the citizens' commission could not forestall a riot in New Haven. Rumor mills churned during the summer of 1967 about whether or not the "model city" could avoid an uprising. In early August, I departed with my family for a vacation in Ocean City, New Jersey. We planned to stay in a house rented by Marilyn's parents. On the way out the office door, I jokingly told my secretary, Janice Gore, not to phone me with any tales about how New Haven had erupted in flames.

Scarcely forty-eight hours later—on August 19, to be exact—Janice called me in Ocean City with precisely that message. New Haven had indeed blown. The riot encompassed the Hill district, where our law offices were located. It also covered the Dixwell-Newhallville neighborhood, where we lived. A number of local people I knew, many of them current and former clients, were behind bars on charges of looting. I told Marilyn I had to return but thought it advisable for her to stay put until I could assess the situation.

In the wee hours of the following morning, I hit the road for New Haven, arriving around eight. I went immediately to "the Hill" to look around. It was like driving into a real-life battle zone or onto the set of a *Mad Max* movie. National Guard troops armed with rifles and machine guns patrolled the streets. Military vehicles blocked the intersections. A haze from fires hung over the neighborhood. Hardly anyone walked the streets. It was an eerie and harrowing sight.

Headlines in the *New Haven Register* conveyed the unsettled and scary atmosphere: "Arrests Mount in City Disorder." "Fire Bombs Mark 3rd Night of Strife." "Blazes Erupt Throughout City." "300 Frightened Hill Residents Fled to Shelters in Suburbs." And finally, "Police, Curfew Break Back of Strife."

Amazingly, our LAA office in the Hill survived the hostilities comparatively unscathed. I obtained a list of my clients who had been arrested during the riot and headed to the jail to talk with them. To a person, they vehemently denied engaging in any looting. They said they had been cowering at home or visiting relatives out of state.

Still clinging to the conviction that I had honorable defendants, I dashed to see the prosecutor in order to proclaim my clients' innocence and demand the charges be dropped or, at a minimum, that my clients be released without bail on their own recognizance. The prosecutor flashed a bemused smile and beckoned me over to peek inside the case files. Almost without fail, the police accounts, corroborated by eyewitnesses, placed my clients at the scene with stolen items in hand or arms inside the plate-glass windows of looted stores. Since the jails were overflowing with riot suspects, I managed to negotiate reduced bails so my clients could return home, even though I could not get the charges dropped.

My clients maintained their innocence until trial day, when it was time to fish or cut bait. The way the criminal courts worked, if the prosecutors deemed the charges unfounded or weak, they usually dropped the cases so they could concentrate on the sure bets and bad actors. But if a defendant forced them to go to the trouble of trying the case and was found guilty, then the punishment would be much harsher than if he had pled guilty in exchange for a lighter sentence, sometimes even probation.

On trial day, my clients faced a moment of truth. Those who truly were innocent could press for dismissal or insist on a trial. Usually, they would prevail. Those who were guilty of something but were holding out would sidle up to me and say something like, "You know, Attorney Price, I actually wasn't in South Carolina that night after all. Point of fact, I was near the store. Please see if I can take a plea to a lesser charge in exchange for probation or a light sentence." The seasoned defendants were shrewder plea bargainers than I.

In a surge of optimism bordering on hyperbole, Robert Weaver, my father's friend from Dunbar who as secretary of the Department of Housing and Urban Development became the first black member of a president's cabinet, had once proclaimed, "New Haven is coming closest to our dream of a slumless city." The riots punctured that image of an enlightened city and tarnished Mayor Richard C. Lee's reputation as an innovative architect of urban revitalization. "If we are a model city, God save the rest of the cities," Lee moaned after the riots. Even Lee, as committed, creative, and energetic as mayors came in that era, could not counteract the economic erosion caused by the industrial decay and suburbanization that engulfed rust-belt cities such as New Haven.

Representing community groups and staffing the commission were energizing and intellectually stimulating. But lawyering per se left me cold. I soon discovered that I thought like the youth worker I once was, not like a defense lawyer hell-bent on winning acquittals for my clients. For instance, I once represented a teenage client who, to be frank, was a knucklehead. Not a bad kid, just a happy-go-lucky jerk who got into one jam after another. One time, he stole a car to take on a joyride. He was arrested and asked me to represent him. This fellow readily confessed to me that he had taken the car.

At the court hearing, it was the prosecutor's job to establish probable cause that my client had stolen the car, in order to charge him with a felony. The prosecutor showed beyond a doubt that the car had been swiped and that my client was apprehended driving it, yet he missed an obscure link in the chain of evidence—so obscure, in fact, that I no longer remember what it was. Anyway, I did not notice the evidentiary gap in the state's case because I knew the young man had stolen the car. I was focused instead on getting him into a halfway house for delinquent teens, in the hope that he would shape up. In other words, I might have been able to get him off on the charge, but the youth worker in me was obsessed with helping him get on with his life. The prosecutor met the burden of proof and ultimately convicted my client. It began to dawn on me that it might be in my clients' best interests, as well as mine, if I ceased practicing law.

This case helped close the curtain on my legal career barely eighteen months after it began. I next accepted a position with the city of New Haven as deputy director of its federally funded Model Cities program, which sought to rejuvenate the neighborhoods torn asunder by the riots. The job lasted merely three months because the community groups I once represented staged a political coup. In those days, one of the hottest political issues was community participation in the planning and implementation of government programs. Emboldened by federal laws calling for "maximum feasible participation," community leaders mobilized against city hall, in New Haven and elsewhere, after watching bulldozers level their neighborhoods in the name of urban renewal. Occasionally, affordable housing rose in its place. But oftentimes, shopping malls, sports arenas, and highways were built instead. The poor people who once lived on these bulldozed blocks typically vanished to who knew where.

In New Haven, the mayor and the board of aldermen were at loggerheads politically. Community leaders in the Hill neighborhood, which was the target area for Model Cities, shrewdly took advantage of the schism and persuaded the aldermen to give all the Model Cities planning money to the Hill Neighborhood Corporation, a community group I had incorporated and represented while with LAA. Behind the scenes, I was supportive of the effort. Ironically, I fell victim to the law of unintended consequences when my job evaporated because the community snared all the planning money.

The city suggested a new position, but I was already being courted by the founders of the Black Coalition, an umbrella organization of black groups in New Haven. It had been created the previous fall in the aftermath of the riots to try to restore faith in the city, exert influence for blacks, and orchestrate the physical and spiritual rebuilding of communities damaged by the disturbances.

Hank Parker, a charismatic schoolteacher with his eye on bigger things, chaired the Black Coalition. Other key founders included Al

Tindall, the folksy but shrewd head of the Dixwell Community House, and Fred Harris, the firebrand leader of the Hill Parents Association. They asked me to become the first executive director of the Black Coalition. As is my wont when an opportunity stokes my competitive juices, I accepted the offer without hesitation.

Just as she has throughout my career, Marilyn went along. This move illustrated what came to be my philosophy in choosing careers. Basically, I have tried to have as much fun as I could professionally, so long as we could get away with it financially. Since we hadn't encountered any problems paying the household bills, so far, so good.

When I informed my parents of this third professional move in barely two years, however, they were puzzled, concerned—and clueless about what the Black Coalition was. My description of its origins, purpose, and wobbly funding hardly allayed their anxiety about our financial security and whether I was squandering my privileged Amherst and Yale Law School education. Yet like other young people during the intensely activist 1960s, I was drawn like metal filings to the magnet of the civil rights movement and its Northern counterpart, the antipoverty crusade.

The Black Coalition thrust me smack into the center of the action at the tender age of twenty-six. Operating behind the scenes and often in front of TV cameras, I relished the work and, to be truthful, enjoyed the growing public exposure. A year earlier, I had been a fledgling legal services lawyer. Now, I was negotiating face to face with the president of Yale University, the head of the New Haven Foundation, and the CEOs of local corporations. Our press conferences demanding this from the city and protesting that municipal policy generated widespread local media and aroused reactions from city hall. I used to dash home from press events to watch the coverage on the evening television news. This was heady stuff for an impressionable young attorney whose classmates probably were holed up in law libraries drafting writs and researching briefs for their firms' senior partners.

Rest assured, the Black Coalition was about much more than self-actualization and ego gratification. We forged an agenda that we followed pretty faithfully. To lift the spirits of our battered community in the summer of 1968, we staged a concert fittingly called "Soul in the Bowl," held in the Yale Bowl almost a year to the day after the riots. Instead of fretting whether or not there would be another uprising, the coalition decided to wade into the anxiety by staging a celebratory event aimed at unifying the city and chilling everyone out. Yale could have turned us down, citing perfectly justifiable security concerns for its facility and for the tranquil upper-middle-class neighborhood surrounding the bowl. Yet to its everlasting credit, it granted us permission and thus helped bolster the spirits of the entire city.

The night of the concert, we courted disaster when we discovered, five minutes before showtime, that Hugh Masekela, the South African trumpeter of "Grazing in the Grass" fame who was the featured attraction, was nowhere to be found. Waiting nervously backstage, I imagined how quickly the crowd would turn hostile if Masekela stiffed us. I told the police sergeant on duty—an old adversary from my LAA days who specialized in narcotics and lascivious carriage busts—that I'd make book on which of us would exit the bowl faster if Masekela failed to show. Fortunately, after a brief bit of stalling by the emcee, the star drove up in a limo, and the show went on.

I matured in a hurry with the coalition. Its board consisted of leaders from virtually every walk of black life in New Haven. Militant community leaders and heads of upstart community groups served on the board. It also included directors of groups that young Turks like me considered old-line—namely, the Urban League, the NAACP, and the local black ministerial alliance. I met a leader from the Nation of Islam, Minister Abdul Karriem, for the first time when he joined our board. Like many black folk in those days, I was spooked by the Black Muslims' aura of secrecy, the rumors of violence, the strident rhetoric, and their insistence on frisking visitors to their mosques. Minister Karriem utterly defied that image and proved a wise and steady member of the board.

When the Black Coalition received a hundred-thousand-dollar grant, many of my old friends from the Hill, including some leaders who served on our board, suddenly turned against both the organization and me. I believe they envied the grant and viewed us now as an extension of the New Haven establishment. While we continued to work together, the mistrust and tension persisted throughout my tenure. It taught me again never to take organizational behavior or human nature for granted.

Or to assume that those ostensibly on our side actually were. One evening at the Black Coalition's headquarters, we convened a meeting of its founders and other community leaders to discuss what to do about persistent tensions with the local police. In keeping with our constructive posture, we crafted a seven-point plan for improving police-community relations. The plan was carefully considered and entirely constructive in tone.

The meeting adjourned around midnight, after we agreed to hold a press conference the following afternoon in time to make the evening television news. I awoke as usual around six-thirty the next morning, raring to go with our media event. When I opened the morning newspaper, I discovered to my utter disbelief that the chief of police had experienced a revelation after we adjourned and called a newspaper reporter in the wee hours to outline his own seven-point plan. It was all our ideas, almost to the comma. Not surprisingly, there was no mention whatsoever of the Black Coalition's recommendations, since we had not released them yet. The police chief's announcement took the wind completely out of our sails, precipitating the cancellation of our press event.

Clearly, someone on our side had called the chief right after the meeting and spilled the beans. I learned from that day forward that I could never really know who was on my team. The revelation did not make me paranoid. It just made me even more watchful of my colleagues' behavior and about what I said outside of immediate family.

In the late 1960s, the New Haven police fixated on wiretapping local leaders. In fact, the list of targets was so exhaustive—community activists and even prosecutors, probate court judges, and defense lawyers—that if you fancied yourself important, you became insulted if you were not wiretapped. I had the dubious distinction of making the list. Often when Marilyn or I used our home phone, we heard odd clicks and pauses, as though a real person, not just a machine, was listening in. We guarded against saying anything we did not want overheard, not that we had any secrets worth exploiting. Years later, a prominent attorney filed a class-action lawsuit on behalf of the wiretap victims. We signed on and eventually collected a couple of thousand dollars as compensation for the unlawful intrusion.

The Black Panthers came to town while I was running the coalition. They were drawn there by a Black Panther Party activist whose husband, a New Haven native and member of the party, had been killed in a shootout in a lunchroom at the University of Southern California. The Panthers launched a New Haven chapter and recruited members on a y'all-come basis. This mystified me, since the FBI and the local police clearly were intent on infiltrating and undermining the organization.

While we let the Black Panthers use our mimeograph machines and office supplies, we never invited them to join the coalition. Personally, I had little use for the group. I never knew who was for real and who was an informant. They recruited new members openly, seemingly oblivious to the probability and perils of infiltration. I never forgot—or forgave—the fact that a mysterious Black Panthers organizer would swoop into New Haven, mobilize some impressionable high-school kids to toss Molotov cocktails around town, and then vanish while the students were arrested and hauled off to jail.

A local acquaintance of mine named Warren Kimbro joined the Panthers and let them operate out of his home. Early one morning in 1969, Marilyn and I awoke to the startling news on the radio that the police had arrested Warren and several other Black Panthers, including some high-school students, for allegedly murdering a party member named Alex Rackley and dumping his body into a marsh out of town. Prior to the shooting, Rackley reportedly had been held and tortured in Kimbro's home on suspicion of informing on the Panthers for the FBI. Although I lacked details, I nodded knowingly when I heard the police had made the arrests so quickly after the shooting. Without help from an infiltrator, it probably would have taken days to find a body in the remote swamp.

An immediately remorseful Kimbro cooperated with the police investigation, pled guilty to second-degree murder, and served only four years in prison before earning parole. The sequel to this bizarre case illustrates why conservatives have a field day with liberal elites. When Kimbro got out of prison, he was admitted to the Harvard University Graduate School of Education and subsequently served as an associate dean at Eastern Connecticut State University. I greatly admire that he got his life back on track. But parents whose children were rejected by the Ivy League graduate school understandably went ballistic when they learned that a confessed murderer had gained one of the prized slots.

Rackley's murder set the stage for the celebrated trial of national Black Panthers leader Bobby Seale, who was charged with presiding over the tribunal at Kimbro's place, during which the victim supposedly was "convicted" by the Panthers. Protesters from around the country gathered on May Day 1970 on the New Haven Green to support Seale and to register their anger that he was being tried. Another motive for coming was to upstage Yale's Kingman Brewster, who had become the highest-profile university president in the United States and was viewed in those antiestablishment times as the symbol of everything the protestors abhorred. Local groups including the Black Coalition, which had spent two arduous years repairing the fabric of the traumatized black community following the riots, told the protest organizers to confine their demonstration to the green and to stay out of the neighborhoods. They heard and heeded our message.

The protestors had little inkling of what they were up against in President Brewster. In my dealings with him, I always marveled at his intellect, shrewdness, and tactical dexterity. He was impossible to corner. For instance, the Black Coalition would present him with an ambitious set of demands for what Yale should do to help revitalize the black community after the riots. He would mull them and then respond by offering a set of counterproposals that went beyond our imaginations and our ability to implement. This invariably bought him time as we scrambled to catch up. It also enabled him to test our bona fides and delivery capacity.

At the May Day rally, Kingman Brewster surprised the protesters—and enraged Yale alumni—by declaring that he was "skeptical of the ability of black revolutionaries to achieve a fair trial anywhere in the United States." This confounded his critics, who now thought he might be on their side after all. What's more, he told the demonstrators that Yale's dorms were available to those who had nowhere else to stay, and that breakfast hours would be extended to accommodate those who arose late. This took all of the steam out of the protesters who had come to trash both Yale and Brewster's reputation. The extent to which he dodged a bullet was underscored just three days later, when National Guardsmen fired into a crowd of protesters at Kent State University, killing four students. Brewster's virtuoso performance was a highly principled, yet cunningly pragmatic, masterpiece of broken-field maneuvering that spared Yale incalculable damage.

Reflecting on my admittedly brief tenure at the helm of the Black Coalition, I believe we helped stitch the fractured city back together following the riots. With the "Soul in the Bowl" concert and our Black Cultural Festival, we lifted the spirits and contributed to restoring black pride. As omnipresent advocates, we gave insistent voice to our community's grievances about police mistrust and abuse, rampant housing dislocation, poor housing conditions, and inadequate schools. We set community revitalization projects in motion and aided neighborhood groups with plans of their own. We restored frayed relationships across racial lines and established a respected black presence in the corridors of power. We conducted community-organizing and voter mobilization efforts that contributed to a sharp increase in black representation on the board of aldermen. Henry Parker, the original chair of the coalition, capitalized on the stature of his position by mounting successive, if unsuccessful, campaigns for mayor before winning election as state treasurer.

Happily, activism never led me into temptation or stupidity. I resigned from the Black Coalition after two exciting and gratifying years, during which I grew professionally and matured personally. Years later, I learned from an article in the *Hartford Courant* that the New Haven police considered me dangerous but had never managed to catch me doing anything illegal. I could have told them my momma didn't raise a son who was dangerous or dumb enough to flout the law.

Reflecting on those tempestuous times, the 1960s riots in America's cities spawned a new generation of black elected officials and grassroots leaders and galvanized the conscience of colleges and employers to be more inclusive in their admissions and hiring practices. Black capitalism emerged from this era as well. Cities such as Cleveland and Gary elected the first generation of black mayors of major American cities. Municipal work forces became more integrated. Inner-city residents who were motivated and reasonably skilled took advantage of these openings to gain access to safer housing, higher education, and better jobs. These certainly constituted huge leaps forward for black people.

Thomas Sugrue, author of *Sweet Land of Liberty*, a definitive study of the antipoverty and welfare rights movements in the North, argued that they reshaped the struggle for racial equality. How so? By shifting the locus of action for dealing with racial justice and community improvement from the federal government to the local level. Spurred by the demands for black power and community control, these movements triggered the widespread creation of community development corporations and other neighborhood groups that to this day remain focused on housing and economic and human-capital development.

In the aftermath of the riots, the agenda for black activists in cities segued from revolution to revitalization, from protest to empowerment. Some riot-torn communities have recovered, fueled by reinvestment and, yes, robust gentrification. Yet the cruel irony is that by the time D.C.'s new Fourteenth Street was born, gentrification in nearby neighborhoods was so rampant that one wonders how many residents from 1968 even benefited, much less still live there.

The turbulence cost countless riot-torn communities and their residents dearly and, in many cases, irretrievably. As with any destructive and disruptive force, there were near-term and long-term downsides from the urban uprisings. Despite the gains by many, the riots failed miserably at lifting all boats. In fact, some physically devastated neighborhoods sank into a deeper economic funk of isolation, despair, poverty, and dysfunction. Merchants whose shops were torched and looted refused to come back. Long-established commercial corridors such as Fourteenth Street in D.C. took decades to recover.

To this day, when I tour cities, it is easy to spot the physical, economic, and psychic scars that linger from the riots and the general demise of inner-city neighborhoods due to disinvestment, redlining, out-migration of factories, and evaporation of decent-paying jobs. The riots helped some people flee the suffocating confines of urban poverty, but they consigned those who could not move to a generation of hopelessness. The opportunity-cost calculation never tilted in favor of the riots, in my estimation.

The Hippocratic oath—"First, do no harm"—seemingly never applies to riots or rioters.

CHAPTER 9

MOVING TOWARD THE MAINSTREAM

Approaching my late twenties, I gravitated toward more mainstream occupations. Having a wife and three children plus buying a first home will do that to you. In 1968, we purchased a house for the now-incomprehensible sum of $13,500. The $450 down payment probably wouldn't cover a courtside ticket to see the New York Knicks in this day and age. The monthly bill for principal, interest, and taxes barely topped $150. We owned a small three-bedroom house on Ford Street in the Newhallville neighborhood of New Haven. The modest backyard, with its fragrant lilac bushes, was just the right size for our kids to romp around in.

Our second daughter was born the following year. With two children and a growing menagerie of pets, we were squeezed because all the rooms were small except for the kitchen. In addition to every domesticated rodent imaginable, we had a mouthy beagle named Pup-Pup, who barked at the slightest provocation. Pup-Pup devoured Toll House chocolate chip cookies. I assumed man's best friend would provide some security. Yet crooks burglarized our house with carefree abandon. Six times in four years, to be exact. I came to suspect that the thieves would bake a batch of cookies, slip some to Pup-Pup on their way in, and then calmly go about their business.

One Sunday afternoon during pro football season, we went to visit my aunt Vi. To pretend someone was home, I left the lights on and parked one of our cars in front of the house. When we returned later in the afternoon, still in full daylight, the front door had been kicked in. After so many robberies, I followed a standard routine of leaving my family in the car, scouting the house, and, if the coast was clear, signaling for them to come in.

Following the birth of our youngest daughter, space on Ford Street got really tight. Plus, I became fed up with the anxiety and inconvenience of all those break-ins. The neighborhood started to deteriorate noticeably; some houses nearby were abandoned or torched by arsonists. I didn't like what I was seeing, for either the sake of my family or our investment. Reluctant as I am to admit it, staying there required more social conscience than I could muster.

We sold our little house and bought a larger one in a lovely neighborhood called Westville, located within walking distance of the Yale Bowl. We netted four thousand dollars on the Ford Street house after only four years. For a brief spell, I strutted around like a real-estate mogul. Then I ran the numbers on our new house, which cost considerably more. Without letting on to Marilyn, I worried we were movin' on up to the poorhouse.

The erosion of a modest working-class community such as Newhallville was heart-wrenching. For years, these neighborhoods were a reliable source of affordable first homes, decent schools, and safe playgrounds for working families, young couples, and their kids. Most cities had communities like these. But many never recovered from the riots, while others declined due to race-based redlining, exacerbated by the disappearance of nearby factories and the solid livelihoods they provided. The collapse of these neighborhoods coupled with escalation in housing prices made home ownership a more elusive dream than ever for young adults of modest means in many parts of the country. The Great Recession a generation later compounded the decline by cutting a tornado of abandonment and foreclosure through many struggling neighborhoods.

When I decided that my brief, if energizing, career with the Black Coalition had run its course, I talked with a friend from my short stint in city government. Joel Cogen, who once served as co-director of the New Haven Redevelopment Agency, had left city government to start a consulting firm. He recruited me by arguing that if I ever wanted to move beyond advocating for progress and start doing something tangible about it, I should join the firm.

The proposition intrigued me because Joel's partners and associates were smart and decent people who were doers. The firm's scope of services and client list fascinated me as well. Cogen Holt and Associates served as the staff of the Connecticut Conference of Mayors. This would afford me a window on a wide range of urban policy issues. The firm was building a portfolio of strategic planning, program design, and program evaluation assignments. And it served as the development consultant for nonprofit groups building affordable housing and for city agencies bent on reviving their downtowns. In 1970, I signed on as a senior associate.

The work broadened my professional horizons right away. Mike Sviridoff, former head of CPI, the antipoverty agency in New Haven, had recently left the administration of New York City mayor John Lindsay to become vice president of the Ford Foundation. He presided over Ford's vast domestic program division. Providing support for community development corporations, voter registration projects, and civil rights agencies—all of which I cared about—fell under his purview.

It turned out Mike had spotted me as an up-and-coming attorney and advocate when I represented those community groups in their efforts to wrest control of antipoverty programs from the city and CPI. He became a professional rabbi and godfather to me, as well as a treasured lifelong friend. I was one of a dozen or so young professionals whose careers he shepherded and promoted and who were proud to be known as "Mike's Boys."

Mike contracted with Cogen Holt for me to conduct evaluations of some of Ford's favored grantees. The assignments exposed me to the national scene and put me in direct contact with leaders and role models whom I had admired from afar. Thus, in the early 1970s, still in the formative stages of my career, I met Whitney Young, Vernon Jordan, and John Jacob, my illustrious predecessors as president of the National Urban League, when I evaluated the League's New Thrust program. Other assignments introduced me to Franklin Thomas, head of the Bedford-Stuyvesant Restoration Corporation and later president of the Ford Foundation; Charles Bannerman of the Delta Foundation in Mississippi; and John Lewis, the revered congressman who had cofounded the Student Nonviolent Coordinating Committee and run the Voter Education Project. I also met the Reverend Leon Sullivan of Philadelphia, a towering figure intellectually and physically, who gave stemwinding speeches about community development that made true believers of all who heard him.

These evaluation assignments took me to the Deep South for the first time. The South I had assiduously avoided. Growing up, I had an aunt and uncle, Corrine and Louie Schuster, who lived in Petersburg, Virginia, about a hundred miles south of Washington. Louie, who was Mom's brother, taught business administration at Virginia State University there. Petersburg was as far south as I had ventured.

My maiden trip for the Ford Foundation took me to Tuskegee, Alabama, in 1973. The journey made me nervous because Alabama and its cantankerous governor, George Wallace, both had notorious reputations when it came to race relations. As a Northerner, I feared I did not comprehend the rules of the game when it came to how to comport oneself, how to interact with white strangers, even what it would be like to stay in a hotel down there. Saddled with a vivid imagination that sometimes was hard to contain, I fretted about Alabama's notorious history of lynching blacks who had inadvertently or knowingly crossed some forbidden line.

Upon arrival, I checked into the Holiday Inn there in Tuskegee. The fact that black clerks worked behind the desk did not strike me as unusual. After all, at least some nooks and crannies of the labor market must have become integrated by then.

Unsure what it would be like to eat in the hotel restaurant, I ordered dinner from room service and tuned the TV to the local evening news. I watched in amazement as the anchor described how, earlier in the day, Governor Wallace had appeared at the annual meeting of the Southern Conference of Black Mayors. The conference had been held right there at that Holiday Inn, which was owned by African-Americans. The TV coverage featured Wallace actually planting a congratulatory kiss on the cheek of Miss Southern Conference of Black Mayors. Talk about not believing my eyes! The old codger had either experienced an epiphany or learned how to count votes in the aftermath of the Voting Rights Act of 1965. Whatever the explanation, I thought, *Welcome, Hugh Price, to the New South.* While it took many a trip before I became reasonably comfortable, at least I ceased being afraid of my shadow whenever I ventured south.

Of all the groups I evaluated for Ford, the burgeoning community development corporation (CDC) sector especially intrigued me because of the role these unique organizations played in rebuilding urban neighborhoods and rural communities that had fallen on hard economic times due to general poverty, riots, or factory closures. At

their best, CDCs built and renovated housing, developed neighborhood shopping centers, and provided essential social services including
job training and child care. They were the darlings of politicians seeking to empathize with poor folk. Senator Bobby Kennedy launched the
mother of all CDCs, the Bedford-Stuyvesant Restoration Corporation,
after a high-profile walking tour of Bed-Stuy in Brooklyn in 1967.

CDCs represented a unique blend of compassion for the down-
trodden and hard-nosed business discipline about how to uplift them.
The more I came to understand and appreciate them through my
evaluations of Bedford-Stuyvesant, the Southeast Alabama Self-Help
Association, and the Delta Foundation in Mississippi, the more convinced I became that this was the preferred way of revitalizing poor
communities, and that someday I would like to run one of them.

CDCs set the stage for the recovery of inner cities, even the gentrification phenomenon, of the 1990s. After the urban riots in the 1960s,
fewer and fewer private corporations and entrepreneurs wanted anything to do with inner-city neighborhoods. They refused to return to
the burned-out blocks. The jobs, livelihoods, and commercial services
that made neighborhoods viable vanished with them.

Fortunately, a few foundations such as Ford and the Rockefeller
Brothers Fund bucked the trend and backed these fledgling CDCs.
Foundation grants got the ball rolling, years before private businesses
regained sufficient confidence to return. Next came the federal government in the form of the Office of Economic Opportunity, which
provided substantial operating support for CDCs. This was what
might be called the premarket phase of the revitalization cycle. More
and more nonprofit groups stepped into the void, building affordable
housing with government subsidies. Federally designated enterprise
zones offered tax relief for businesses willing to venture into these
neighborhoods.

Consulting, especially in a small firm, can be a precarious way to
make a living. Invariably, we experienced ebbs and flows in the vol-
ume of business. The mid-1970s were not kind to our type of consulting. When business slowed, we still had a payroll to meet. Since our
firm was like family and consisted of people who had worked together
for many years, we were loath to slash expenses by laying off loyal
colleagues.

The firm's partners—who included me by then—paid the piper
by cutting our own salaries. In fact, in 1975, we were almost halfway

through the fiscal year when it became clear that business would not rebound in the foreseeable future. My income from the firm dipped by roughly a quarter, even as I accumulated financial obligations based on the anticipated higher income. This was in an era, mind you, of oil price shocks and stiff inflation.

The pay cut wreaked havoc on our household budget and for a spell cost me some credit cards and a solid credit rating. On one business trip, when I tried to check out of a hotel, the clerk requested my American Express card, looked into it, and then announced she was keeping it, on instructions from Amex. She then asked how I intended to pay the hotel bill. Fortunately, I could produce a second card, which cleared. The experience embarrassed me to no end. With a wife who was not working, three young children, and a mortgage, I started to the see the appeal of other careers with steady paychecks.

I enjoyed the consulting world and working with my colleagues at Cogen Holt. The experience provided remarkable opportunities for growth in my program evaluation, project management, and overall business skills. The work for the foundations expanded my professional horizons and network of contacts outside New Haven. Yet after six years with the firm, I continued to be anxious about our family finances, given the mercurial economics of consulting. As proved to be the pattern throughout my career, I tended to zig and zag between contemplative positions, such as writing and consulting, and active ones in which I actually ran something. I again wanted back in the action.

In the fall of 1975, Frank Logue, the newly elected mayor of New Haven, asked me to become the human resources administrator in his administration. Not the chief personnel officer, mind you, but the cabinet-level administrator responsible for overseeing the city's human services programs for senior citizens, preschoolers, and students in after-school programs.

I brought to this assignment an invaluable lesson from President Ronald Reagan, with whom I seldom agreed. He once uttered a phrase I will never forget: "Trust but verify." I instructed our agency to hire a squad of graduate students to make announced and then unannounced visits to the programs we funded. The simple point was to make certain that the government and taxpayers were getting their money's worth.

The program operators grumbled at first, especially when our monitors occasionally discovered that the promised programs did not yet exist or were patronized way below reported levels. However, they calmed down when they discovered our objective wasn't to expose and embarrass them, but to make certain every project we funded really existed and worked reasonably well. Bona fide but weak programs requiring improvement were one thing. But I had no tolerance for bogus programs run by shysters who cheated taxpayers and besmirched the reputation of government and nonprofit agencies trying to do the right thing.

I enjoyed most everything about municipal service in New Haven, except for the two-year election cycle for mayor. A mayoral administration barely got rolling with its initiatives, much less reaped the benefits of having them gain traction, before it was time to resume campaigning. The short tenure also meant that senior officials who served at the mayor's pleasure placed their family's security at risk every twenty-four months. This caused indigestion for a man who had children and mortgage payments but precious little savings.

Frank Logue had defeated a deeply entrenched political machine. Instead of accepting the changing of the guard, his foes dug in, expecting to recapture city hall two years hence. The heads of many community-based programs funded by my agency, including some of my erstwhile friends from Black Coalition days, were aligned with the previous political regime and were reluctant to jump ship. So they fought the Logue administration—and me—tooth and nail.

Things got nasty at times. One evening at a public hearing on the municipal budget allocations I oversaw, a speaker whom I knew called me a "miscegenated" something or other. The allusion to my skin tone and the fact that my family tree was integrated infuriated me. I had never been attacked so viciously in public.

After the hearing, the speaker and several of his compatriots who had once been friends of mine suggested we all go out for drinks. I probably should have accepted, but I never have been much of a schmoozer. I told them to forget it; I was going home to my family. They correctly read my reply as a brush-off. The ringleader said this was a game of political hardball, and that I should not take it personally. I did not see it that way, since he had gotten so personal in the hearing—and also because I would be out of a job if they had their way.

The games continued with plenty of political thrust and parry. Our opponents attempted to maintain control of the antipoverty agency in town by preventing Mayor Logue from appointing his designees to the board of directors, as required by law. I finally ran out of patience and wrote the federal department that funded the antipoverty agency, noting that our opponents were blatantly violating the law by refusing to seat the mayor's appointees.

The feds agreed with our position and stripped the agency of its certification and funding, much of which was flowing to the very community groups that staunchly opposed the mayor. With this funding lifeline cut off, the heads of these groups came hat in hand to see me with an appeal for emergency support. I declined their request, explaining that, in hardball, there were winners and losers. This time, they had lost. While it had long ago ceased being my sport of choice, I never shied away from playing hardball if the cause was just.

The mayor won reelection in a squeaker. Although I did not reveal it prior to the election, I had already decided after two politically tumultuous years that I would not be at the depot the next time the train rolled in. I had the confidence to make that fateful decision because, shortly before the November election, an unexpected and unimaginable opportunity had popped up utterly out of the blue.

CHAPTER 10

THE *NEW YORK TIMES* KNOCKS

One day in the fall of 1977 as I sat in my city hall office in New Haven, my secretary buzzed to say Max Frankel of the *New York Times* was on the phone. I instantly recognized the name of this Pulitzer Prize–winning journalist, since I read the *Times* faithfully. For the life of me, though, I could not figure out why he was calling. The Logue administration had not done anything recently that warranted coverage in the newspaper of record.

Max introduced himself, and we exchanged pleasantries. Then he moved quickly to the punch line. He was calling, he said, to let me know I was under serious consideration for appointment to the editorial board of the *Times*. After a moment's pause, I revealed my ignorance of the newspaper business by asking if this was a group of external advisers who met occasionally with the editors and reporters to opine on how the *Times* was doing from our outside perspective.

He may have been taken aback by the question and wondered if the call was a wise idea after all. Still, he pressed on, explaining that serving on the editorial board was a full-time position that entailed writing the unsigned editorials that appeared daily in the newspaper. The board consisted of a dozen or so editorialists who were experts in various fields and who generated the steady stream of editorials speaking for the newspaper on a wide array of issues. To avoid being totally anonymous, Max added, they also got to write signed "editorial notebooks" from time to time.

Though I now understood the position, I remained puzzled why I was being wooed. I had once penned a regular column for the Black Coalition's modest community newspaper, *The Crow*. This didn't even qualify as the low minor leagues of journalism. I had written many evaluation reports for the Ford Foundation, but they certainly were no match for editorials in the nation's, and arguably the world's, preeminent newspaper.

As flattering as it was to be approached, I could not fathom how I had popped up on the paper's radar screen. Patient and persuasive man that he was, Max invited me to visit the *Times* to meet with him and Jack Rosenthal, the deputy editor. I leapt at the suggestion because, to be frank, when an internationally renowned institution knocked, what was the harm in opening the door to see what it was selling?

The visit went well. I was intrigued by what I heard. By then, I had checked out the situation with a few mentors, most notably Mike Sviridoff. It turned out he and Jack were longtime friends, and that he had put my name in play.

I found Max and Jack to be brilliant, and personable to boot. That's a combination I have always prized in bosses and colleagues because it helps ensure that the environment is stimulating and harmonious. Everywhere I work, I want to grow professionally. But first and foremost, I insist on being respected personally. I have no tolerance for employers who might treat me as a peon or who might think the way to reach me is to raise their voices. I respond best to criticism spoken at normal decibel levels.

At the conclusion of our meeting, Max asked me to write a couple of sample editorials on topics of my choosing. I quickly threw myself into the audition because it has always been my philosophy that, once I've gotten the attention of someone important, I want to keep it until we either close the deal or call it off. I actually submitted a couple more samples than Max requested, just to signal that he had really piqued my interest. I tend not to play hard to get when I am genuinely interested in a position. This directness may weaken my bargaining leverage, but it's who I am. Basically, I am pretty visceral and intuitive when it comes to making career choices. When my head, my heart, my gut, and, yes, my wallet are all in sync, I forge ahead. If any of the four, especially my gut, balks, then no amount of reflection or conversation can convince me, and I back away. Over the years, I may have intuited my way out of opportunities I should have pursued. But I seldom second-guess my instincts.

While this process was percolating, I discovered that Max was courting another black candidate—namely, Bob Curvin, a PhD in political science and onetime Newark activist who had also conducted program evaluations for Ford. Mike was behind this referral as well. I learned about Bob's candidacy through a friend in New Haven named Phil White. He knew both of us well and agonized along with us as the recruitment process unfolded. We all assumed that since Roger Wilkins, the sole African-American on the editorial board, was stepping down, the *Times* would select only one of us to replace him. To my surprise and the newspaper's credit, Max hired both of us.

The final step in the recruitment process, and the one I thought would be the scariest, turned out to be the most fun of all. This was meeting with the publisher, Arthur Ochs Sulzberger Jr. The combination of his forbidding title and equally forbidding aura caused some anxiety as the date approached. Quite fortuitously, a week before the appointment, *Time* magazine ran a feature story about Sulzberger, or "Punch," as he was affectionately called. The article portrayed him as an easygoing sort who enjoyed fiddling with gadgets.

I indeed found him to be approachable and affable. He immediately put me at ease. The conversation seemed to go well. When we were done, I headed down the corridor toward the elevator. Over my shoulder, I heard Punch come out of his office, extolling the virtues of a new burglar alarm that he, an inveterate do-it-yourselfer, intended to install on his country home over the weekend. I struggled to visualize the publisher of the world's most important newspaper up on his roof, affixing this gizmo. But as the French say, "*Chacun à son goût.*"

As the years passed in New Haven, I had begun to wonder if a sufficiently enticing job would come along that would lure us away. Moreover, I assumed that if such a job materialized, our destination probably would be Washington, still the hometown for both sets of parents and our siblings. When Jimmy Carter won the presidential election in 1976, I felt this was my best shot to work at a federal agency or even on the White House staff. But no offers of consequence came my way. From time to time, I mulled a couple of opportunities with nonprofit groups in D.C., but nothing quite caught my fancy.

The opportunity with the *Times* intrigued me from the outset. To begin with, serving on the editorial board would be akin to joining the faculty of a great graduate school filled with renowned experts on a wide array of subjects in the news. Seeing if I could cut it fueled my curiosity and competitive instinct.

While some of my colleagues on the editorial board who already were accomplished writers groused about being closely edited, I relished the chance to mature as a writer under the daily tutelage of Max Frankel. Most alluring of all, I held strong views about the issues I planned to cover, among them urban policy and race relations. What better platform than the *Times* for propagating my viewpoint internationally? Personal and family reasons played major roles in the decision as well. New York was the most exciting city on earth, hands down. Marilyn and I relished the all-too-rare occasions when we journeyed from New Haven for a cultural or entertainment excursion in the city.

I started at the *Times* right after New Year's Day 1978. Bob Curvin began around the same time. For six months, I commuted by train from New Haven. It was horrible because Conrail, as Metro North was called back then, broke down constantly, especially in frigid, snowy weather. Some trips took four hours one way. Mind you, I'm talking only seventy-five miles. I came to view the commute as a prison sentence that would end by midsummer, when we took up residence in the New York City area.

On July 18, 1978, we moved to New Rochelle, just north of the city. That summer, *Saturday Night Fever* was the hottest film in the country. We relished driving into the city from our suburban Westchester County home with songs from the movie's soundtrack pulsating on the radio, listening to "Stayin' Alive" as we crossed the Triborough Bridge with the stunning skyline beckoning us.

Tony Manero, the John Travolta character in the film, dreamt of making the move from Brooklyn to Manhattan. I was finally getting my shot on the big stage professionally. Joel Cogen, my former partner at the consulting firm in New Haven, had given me some reassuring advice. "New Yorkers are no different than anyone else," he said. "They put their pants on one leg at a time. You can compete. All you gotta do is add a few zeroes to all the numbers because everything there is bigger."

Three weeks after we moved to New Rochelle—on August 10, to be exact—the world caved in on us financially. The Printing Pressmen's Union declared a strike and shut down the *Times*, along with the other daily newspapers in town. The Newspaper Guild, to which I belonged, had no choice but to go along. Suddenly, I was out of work and off a payroll for the first time in my married life.

At first, everyone assumed the strike would not last long. Conventional wisdom was that it would be over by back-to-school time in late August because the newspapers were loath to forgo all the advertising revenue. But when Labor Day passed without an accord, our family settled in for the long haul. We lived off the savings we had squirreled away to paint the house and furnish the living room.

As the strike wore on, I started to worry about running out of savings. My strike benefits barely covered half a week's groceries. When pragmatism finally overtook pride, I called Mike Sviridoff to scrounge up some consulting work. I hoped he was feeling a tad guilty, since he had turned me on to the *Times* and it on to me.

Mike responded as a supportive friend by hiring me to flesh out a preliminary idea that Franklin Thomas, Ford's president, had proposed. He envisioned creating a national organization to lift the community development movement to the next plateau of scale and impact. The assignment kept me busy and captured my interest, given my longstanding belief in the importance and potential of CDCs. Working from home in this pre-laptop, pre-spell-check era, I painstakingly pecked away at my electric typewriter. A couple of months later, I submitted my report to the foundation. This proved an immensely gratifying assignment because the entity that grew out of Frank and Mike's idea and my preliminary amplification of it lives on to this day as the highly regarded Local Initiatives Support Corporation, which became in effect the mother ship of the community development movement.

Sporadic consulting aside, the strike meant I had ample time on my hands. If there was an upside, idleness enabled me to get more involved in our children's schooling than I had managed to before. When we registered our eldest daughter, then a ninth-grader, at Albert Leonard Junior High in New Rochelle, school officials placed her in the academic track just beneath honors, even though she clearly belonged in the most challenging track. We were annoyed because she had always excelled academically and was fresh from attending one of New Haven's finest private schools.

Marilyn contacted our daughter's guidance counselor to try to get her reassigned. But she got the typical bureaucratic brush-off. So I decided to get involved by paying a visit to the school. As I often remark in speeches, it's a big deal when black fathers come to school—so much so, I add half-jokingly, that school officials don't know whether to call the press or the police.

When I asked our daughter's homeroom teacher why she had not been assigned to honors, I received two explanations that almost floored me. First, I was told that our daughter would be well served where the school had placed her. Translation: do not second-guess the judgment of professional educators. I assured the teacher I didn't mean to do that. But I then told her in a measured tone but in no uncertain terms that my child belonged in honors and explained why I felt this way.

Next, the teacher indicated there was a lengthy waiting list of youngsters who had come up through the New Rochelle schools and who were lined up to get into honors. It was inappropriate, she gently scolded me, to try to leapfrog the queue, given the fact we had just moved to town. Again, I apologized for being so pushy and inconsiderate. Then I reiterated that our daughter deserved to be in honors based on her academic credentials, and that I did not care how long the waiting list was. It was wrong to keep her out of courses in which she unquestionably belonged. If I couldn't get satisfaction on the spot, I told the teacher, I intended to call the superintendent of schools first thing in the morning to seek redress. Before I could place the call the next day, a school official phoned to tell us our daughter had been reassigned according to our wishes.

What struck me as outrageous, then as now, was this: If there were many students who could handle the most demanding work the school could throw at them, why husband the best education for just a handful? Rationing opportunities for excellence is wrong-headed when our society needs to educate young people to their fullest potential. The U.S. economy and all of society win when they are. Conversely, we lose when they aren't.

After three months of enforced idleness, the newspaper strike ended on November 5 when the publishers and the pressmen's union finally cut a deal. My union, the Newspaper Guild, immediately announced that its issues remained unresolved. The union summoned its members to picket the headquarters of the *Times*. I was so exasperated by then that I ignored the call. The guild capitulated quickly when the Printing Pressmen's Union declared the strike was over. Under the settlement, the *Times* awarded editorial writers a lower raise than reporters—around 3 percent, if I recall correctly—evidently on the theory that we were paid more than they were to begin with. This made sense in principle. But the whole situation frustrated me because I had lost one-quarter of our family's income and gained a measly 3 percent per annum under the settlement, at a time when inflation approached 9 percent. I would never make up the lost income.

The economics simply did not add up, as I vowed to remember when the union contract came up for negotiation again three years later. By then, our eldest daughter would be a year away from college. This kind of paltry raise, especially when coupled with the risk of another labor strike, would not do when those hefty tuition bills started impacting our budget.

With the strike finally over, my editorial career resumed—or, more appropriately, commenced—in earnest. I faced a dilemma, though. I had come to the *Times* to write about urban policy, among other topics. Before we went out on strike, President Jimmy Carter had announced an ambitious new national urban policy that promised to provide plenty of fodder for editorials. By the time we resumed editorializing, however, Carter's urban policy was dead in the water. Since nobody inside the D.C. Beltway bought it, it made no sense to drone on editorially about why our readers should take it seriously either.

I scrambled for replacement topics in order to meet the productivity expectations set by Max. It dawned on me that one shrewd way to expand my portfolio would be to stake a claim to a major subject area as soon as it was up for grabs if an incumbent editorial writer retired or moved on. Thus, when Fred Hechinger, the esteemed expert on education, transitioned from the editorial board to become head of the *New York Times* Foundation, I wasted nary a day in telling Max and Jack how eager I was to cover this vacated beat. After all, education was and remains a critically important issue for minorities and cities, the topics closest to my heart and my professional experience. This was also how I later added the telecommunications beat, although I knew far less about it when I staked the claim. I was eager by then to break free of writing entirely about cities, poverty, minorities, and civil rights. I needed to reboot my brain and write about fresh topics.

Writing editorials for the *Times* was a rarified experience. I enjoyed direct access to cabinet secretaries and other luminaries. I got to quiz presidential candidates and heads of state at publisher's lunches. The editing process sharpened my analytic and writing skills. It also affirmed the value of my law school education. When you think about it, an editorial resembles a miniature legal brief. The fundamental components of an editorial are pretty straightforward. It usually starts with a terse description of the issue and why it matters. Following that comes an articulation and analysis of the pros and cons. It closes with an explication of where the newspaper comes out on the issue, and why. This structure stood me in good stead for years to come when writing decision memos and position papers for clients, supervisors, boards of trustees, policymakers, the media, and general audiences.

Policy debates in our editorial meetings were spirited but never raucous and always respectful. Two aspects of the job especially astounded and delighted me. The first was the freedom I enjoyed to pick the topics I wrote about. The other was how my perspective invariably became the editorial viewpoint of the newspaper. I picked upwards of 90 percent of my topics over the course of five years, and my viewpoint became the newspaper's almost every time.

Serving on the editorial board provided the added dividend of working closely with colleagues who sometimes saw the world very differently than I. Bob Curvin and I got along famously and were simpatico philosophically. Another colleague I really liked was Roger Starr, who was equal parts curmudgeon, conservative, and humorist. Prior to joining the newspaper, when New York City was reeling under budget deficits in the mid-1970s, Roger, who was city housing commissioner at the time, conjured up the notorious phrase "planned shrinkage," which ignited a political uproar. His idea was to withdraw public services from decaying parts of the city and let them shrivel up as the population shrank. The notion struck me as inhumane and naive. Roger was not cowed by criticism, and I respected him for it. I learned much from him about the thinking behind world views that contrasted sharply with mine.

Editorial writing reinforced what I had learned in law school about the importance of examining issues from opposing perspectives. Not only did it strengthen my ability to rebut opponents, but I often discovered that my adversaries had a valid point or useful insight. I was deeply troubled by reports from the *Concord Review* some years ago that high school teachers were assigning fewer and fewer papers requiring students to do research and analysis. Instead, they were allowing students to write brief essays that enabled them simply to spout their opinions. This may have polished their prose, but it wouldn't sharpen their minds.

Years later, a college student named Travis Bristol interned with the National Urban League one summer while I was president. He dropped into my office unannounced one day. I admired his moxie and invited him to sit down. Travis told me he had just finished his freshman year at Amherst, my alma mater. When I inquired how it had gone, he shook his head and said the heavy-duty writing assignments had almost defeated him. I then asked how much writing he had done at the public high school he attended in New York City. His reply flabbergasted me. Although he had taken three Advanced Placement courses, including English and political science, Travis said he had written only one three-and-a-half-page paper his entire high-school career. The rest of the writing assignments were five-hundred-word essays, to help prepare students to "get over" on the AP exams.

In my view, this borders on child neglect by educators. College professors and employers complain these days that young people cannot write. The fault rests primarily with the adults who fail to teach them to write, not the students who are never taught. If students are not expected, required, and taught how to write as they progress through school, how on earth are they supposed to perform at crunch time in college or on the job?

About four years into writing editorials for the *Times*, I began to get antsy about the looming specter of college tuition bills and miniscule salary increases. In the back of my mind, I also began to worry that if I stayed at the newspaper too long, people in the outside world would view me in perpetuity as a writer and start to doubt that I could ever run anything.

Not only did I enjoy recommending public policy, I relished the action itself. I liked running programs and organizations dedicated to good works that helped people get ahead and brought joy, illumination, and understanding into their lives. This meant tackling operational challenges such as devising and executing mission statements. Implementing, assessing, refining, and overseeing programs that improved the well-being of real people. Marshaling institutional resources and, yes, even raising money. I especially enjoyed creating new entities out of whole cloth and turning around struggling organizations by infusing them with fresh talent, energy, ideas, and resources. I also got a profound sense of personal and professional gratification from improving the way teams of people functioned and from having my hand on the throttle of programs and organizations devoted to causes I cared deeply about.

I looked into how editorial writers like me who weren't career journalists managed to get ahead at the newspaper. When I inquired what I had to do to become a columnist on the Op-Ed page, I learned that it would be a lengthy wait because many veteran editors and reporters were way ahead of me in the queue, and that very few would ever ascend to the top. Next, I asked about becoming, say, metropolitan editor. To do that, I probably would first have to cover a beat and work my way up through the reportorial ranks. Since I had been akin to a deputy mayor before joining the *Times*, I viewed this as a sideways move at best, with an uncertain payoff down the road. Lastly, I inquired about possibilities on the business side of the paper. This wasn't likely, however, because editorial writers and reporters were not viewed as business people.

I reluctantly concluded that I was living professionally on a lovely tree-lined cul-de-sac. Writing editorials for the newspaper of record truly was a privilege, and the department itself was a stimulating and collegial place to work. But I had given it my all. I was anxious now to get mind and body back into running, making, or "doing" something, as opposed to writing about it. Having zigged into a reflective role, it was time again to zag into an operational one. I needed the everyday psychological, visceral, and intellectual stimulation generated by the motion and commotion, the debates and decisions, the risks and rewards that accompanied running things.

Although I was grateful for the incomparable opportunity and experience, it was time to bid a reluctant adieu to the *Times*.

CHAPTER 11

LET'S GO TO THE VIDEOTAPE

O nce the urge to run something rather than write took hold, I swung into search mode by alerting several strategically situated friends that I was amenable to moving on. Since there was no rush, I gave myself six months to a year to see what might crop up in the natural course of events before forcing the issue by shopping aggressively and openly.

Several months into this low-key prospecting, Jay Iselin, the president of WNET/Thirteen, the public television station in New York City, called to invite me to lunch. He had heard I was on the prowl for a new position. The notion of venturing into public TV intrigued me. WNET ranked as the largest public television station in the nation and created many acclaimed series for PBS. I knew nothing whatsoever about the industry and did not watch much PBS programming because the signal in that pre-cable era was weak in Westchester County.

The position Jay wanted to discuss was senior vice president in charge of the Metropolitan Division. This entailed oversight of the local program schedule, of acquisitions for local broadcast and programming, of on-air pledges, and of direct-mail solicitation. I knew nada about any of this, which made the idea of accepting the position all the more tantalizing. Jay was drawn to me because I brought administrative experience coupled with knowledge of the kinds of urban issues the station's local shows ought to cover. Just as Max had bet I could learn to write editorials, Jay was willing to chance that I would acquire a working knowledge of public television.

As I weighed the offer, I realized that not only was I eager to run something again, I also wanted a respite from agonizing over the fate of minorities, cities, and the poor. I badly needed a break, intellectually and emotionally, from pushing those medicine balls uphill.

I accepted the offer and started work in November 1982. Punch Sulzberger, Max, and my colleagues on the editorial board held a going-away reception in my honor. I wasn't sure what I had done to merit such a warm gesture, but I basked in the recognition and appreciate it to this day.

Entering public television was an even more unorthodox career step than becoming an editorial writer because I would be totally removed from my natural professional habitat. This made the challenge all the more daunting and energizing. Whenever I take on such a task, I begin by getting a fix on the nature of the position and what is required in order to succeed on its terms. As I become acclimated, I start thinking out of the box. My aim is to map a strategy for nudging the enterprise beyond its accustomed boundaries and inducing it to perform on a higher level than it had been before I took the helm.

In addition to my administrative duties inside the station, I was also determined to become a player in the public television industry by writing for trade publications and speaking at conferences. In other words, I wanted to be viewed as adding value to the enterprise and the industry above and beyond the call of duty. This meant extra work, to be sure. But that's how I have approached every job I've ever held.

Public television proved the ideal transition professionally. For a year and a half, I ran the Metropolitan Division, which in effect was the station that viewers in the greater New York area watched. We produced some purely local programming, but this was difficult to sustain because the station was too strapped financially to keep it going out of its own coffers. Thus, one of my primary reasons for joining the station in the first place barely materialized. Nevertheless, I got a kick out of learning a new industry, technology, and lingo.

My challenge and enjoyment increased exponentially when I was asked in 1984 to take over the National Division, which produced and distributed such award-winning PBS series as *Great Performances* and *Nature*. It also coproduced the *MacNeil/Lehrer NewsHour*. When I took the reins, the unit was fresh from creating two renowned documentary series—*The Brain* and *Civilization and the Jews*. Yet the National Division was dispirited. It frequently incurred sizable budget overruns on its productions, which made the station wary of bankrolling future series. Plus, the cupboard was bare when it came to major new television series slated for production.

To complicate matters, the award-winning producers in the unit were puzzled and agitated over why I—an utter novice who had never produced anything other than snapshots, and a black guy to boot—was now their boss. I could almost see the questions etched on their brows the first time we met. What did I know about their work? How could I possibly make their lives and the station better? Was this just another of those unconventional ideas for which Jay was known?

I approached this professional challenge essentially the same way I had tackled others. I first set out to learn how the division operated and how each genre of programming bearing WNET's logo was created and financed. Next, I diagnosed what was amiss and started crafting a plan for remedying it. Given my skimpy background in public broadcasting, I undertook this strategic assessment in close conjunction with the cabinet I established, comprised of the senior-most producers and colleagues in the division.

During the reconnaissance, I privately compiled a preliminary checklist of success indicators. In other words, what did I need to accomplish in order to be deemed a success in a position many people at the station and in the industry probably believed I did not deserve? Had I been in their shoes, I probably would have felt the same way on traditional qualifications alone. Just knowing the undercurrent of doubt was out there made me all the more determined to confound the skeptics and prevail. I would be less than honest if I didn't admit that being African-American under those circumstances really got my competitive juices flowing.

To turn this into a win-win-win for my new colleagues, for the station, and for me, I resolved to do several things. For openers, I had to reignite creativity in the National Division and get new programming ideas into the pipeline. I discovered quickly that creative people such as public television producers are very driven. If their energy isn't outer-directed and focused on the act of creation, then it turns inward and drives everyone crazy. So I challenged the team to start generating ideas and secured some planning funds from the station to seed their thought processes.

Next, I knew that if I did not rein in the propensity of some producers to exceed their production budgets, the station would not take chances on our ideas, for fear of continued overruns. Nonprofits can be fragile institutions financially. Rude fiscal surprises such as large unexpected deficits can plunge them into a hole that takes forever to climb out of. Overruns in one unit can cause havoc in others, which are then forced to cut back, even though they aren't the culprits.

I told our producers in no uncertain terms that budget overruns were an indulgence of the past and unacceptable going forward. I instituted tight oversight measures to keep spending from careening out of control. This wasn't easy because our production teams often operated half a world away. To their credit, they got the point that I was dead serious about budgetary accountability.

As our unit began to demonstrate fiscal discipline, the station regained confidence in our ability to create quality programs on budget. We beefed up fundraising and became more adept at raising production underwriting, generating tie-in book deals, and finding coproduction partners overseas to help finance our programs. Once these initiatives gained traction, the station grew more willing to authorize us to launch a production even if we had not raised every last dollar because it knew we would finish the job on budget and not rest until we had raised enough money to cover the station's up-front bet and then some. With the station's comfort level restored and new program ideas moving from concept to reality, our producers gradually became happier campers. By enabling them to be more successful, I succeeded as well, convincing the skeptics that this outsider actually could generate the wherewithal needed to produce noteworthy programs and thus add value to the enterprise.

We continued to produce *Great Performances* and *Nature*, two award-winning staples of the PBS schedule. On my watch, our terrific producers created or coproduced many new series including *The Mind, American Masters, Television, Art of the Western World, The Struggles for Poland, Childhood, Global Rivals, Dancing,* and *Travels.* This was a remarkably fertile period for our talented production team.

I wasn't done, however. Remember, I wanted to establish myself outside the confines of the station in the broader public television industry. The opportunity presented itself sooner than expected. Several months after becoming head of the National Division, I traveled to Seattle for the annual summer convention of the public television system. The previous fall, the former *MacNeil/Lehrer Report* had expanded from a half-hour to an hour and was now known as the *MacNeil/Lehrer*

NewsHour. As was often the case with new ventures, the shakedown cruise for the updated format did not go smoothly. Some local station managers complained bitterly about the longer format and resented the loss of a half-hour of local programming squeezed out of their schedules by the lengthened *NewsHour*.

These annual conferences served as a marketplace that helped determine the fate of many PBS shows. In plenary sessions comprised of local station presidents and schedulers, the producers made presentations and showed preview trailers of upcoming series they aspired to offer PBS. In those days, the local station managers actually voted on whether or not they wanted to invest their money in the production of many of the staples on public television. Poor showings in these early tallies could kill off programs because there would be no money to make them.

As we gathered in Seattle, the scuttlebutt in the corridors was that the *NewsHour* was going down for the count. It certainly did not help that coanchor Jim Lehrer had sustained a heart attack and was out of commission. After hearing the pitch to renew the *NewsHour*, the station managers then took a straw pool. The show of hands suggested that only about 40 percent of them supported continued funding for this distinctive program. If that feeble show of support held fast, the hour-long program would die only one season after its launch.

Those of us who ardently believed in the *NewsHour* were shocked and initially unsure just what to do next. Since our station was deeply invested in the show as its coproducer, and since I knew Jay Iselin considered this one of his legacy contributions to the industry, I unilaterally decided that inaction wasn't an option. The worst thing would be to stand by and let the initial nonsupport harden into a firm negative vote.

I decided to roll the dice. Even though I was new to the industry and unknown to most of the local station representatives, I requested permission to address the crowd. This was nervy of me, no doubt about it. But someone on our side had to do something to try to stop this runaway train from crushing the program. I figured that since I ran the division that produced much of the programming the audience members broadcast, they probably would pay attention to what I had to say, even if they then hooted me off the stage.

I began by introducing myself and indicating that I had not wanted us to meet this way. Next, I touted the virtues of the *NewsHour* and observed that any new enterprise typically went through a period when it tested things, garnered reaction, and then tweaked matters or else dropped them entirely. The program was still in the early phase of its development, I added. I urged the stations to be patient and constructive.

Then I really ran the risk of offending this audience of public television pros by arguing that commercial television was known—and notorious—for precipitously pulling the plug on programs before giving them a fair chance to get their bearings. Public television was supposed to—and was indeed chartered to—behave differently, I commented. We shouldn't be so ratings-driven and so oriented toward glossy production values that we didn't give a new venture such as the *NewsHour*, which was central to our mission, a reasonable opportunity to blossom.

I closed by imploring the station managers to rethink their opposition and by pledging to visit many of them in the weeks immediately ahead to try to understand why the *NewsHour* was not working from their perspective. Then I exited the stage as the room buzzed in amazement. No doubt, some folks who had wondered who I was when I mounted the stage were now asking aloud just who the hell I thought I was to lecture them about how their industry should behave. Some colleagues probably thought I had lost my mind by going up there and calling out the station managers.

Yet a fascinating thing happened at the plenary session the following morning. A whole series of local station managers who had been silent the day before took the stage to say they now believed there had been a rush to judgment on the *NewsHour*. Without mentioning my remarks or me by name, they urged their colleagues to cool down and give the program a further chance to improve by financing it for another year. Since the next round of votes on funding would not occur until the fall, their comments managed to stop the train while buying time for us to listen to the local station leaders and tweak the program.

True to my promise, I visited many stations in the ensuing weeks and learned firsthand why they were upset with the program. One station manager explained that the hour-long program had crowded out his thirty-minute local newscast, which ran at half-past the hour and utilized footage free of charge from the commercial newscasts at the top of the hour. What's more, his imperiled program focused, among other things, on the state legislature, which provided much of his station's funding. I assured him I now understood why he was unhappy.

Not surprisingly, neither the *NewsHour* producers nor our station and WETA in Washington, which coproduced it, were willing to accede to this concern and scale back the program's length. However, the producers made some modifications based on feedback from the stations. Some actually improved the program; other modest changes at least showed the station managers they had been heard. Thus, my listening tour proved helpful.

Still, the sale would not be closed until the final vote by the stations on whether or not to renew funding. When the next round of tallies came in, my colleagues and I scanned them to assess where the opposition remained and, frankly, what powers of persuasion we could employ to sway them. Some naysayers produced programs themselves that were broadcast on our station, which, after all, was and remains the largest public television market in the country. Whether and where in our schedule we broadcast their programs mattered immensely to those producing stations and especially to the companies that underwrote their shows.

I called those station managers who were equivocating about the *NewsHour* to tell them we were reviewing our schedule and mulling whether or not their shows, which we had traditionally run in prime time, might perform better in the wee hours of the early morning. First came an audible gasp, followed by protracted silence on the other end of the line. Also, some of the skeptics were seeking PBS funding for their programs and needed our vote, which carried proportionally more weight than the votes of other stations because our market was the biggest.

When the next vote of the stations was taken, the *NewsHour* secured just enough support to survive. In the ensuing years, the program, known in recent times as the *PBS NewsHour*, gained respect and popularity among local station managers as an indispensable staple of public television.

The public television job proved a bonanza, given my newfound love of international travel. Each year in late April, several colleagues and I journeyed to Cannes, France, for an international television festival. There, we met TV executives from all over the world and screened programs produced abroad that we might want to buy for broadcast on our station. The Palais in Cannes, the equivalent of a small convention center, was laid out like a trade show. Broadcast companies and independent producers maintained booths with screening rooms there.

People dressed as cartoon characters and models in skimpy bikinis prowled the floor hawking the shows they had been hired to promote. We spent the bulk of our time trolling for coproduction partners, negotiating deals, and rounding up the resources needed to produce our programs.

I would be lying if I claimed this was arduous or boring duty. Since WNET was a purchaser and producer of TV programming, the festival covered my registration and hotel expenses. It put me up at the luxurious Carlton Hotel, scene of the wonderful caper film *To Catch a Thief*, starring Grace Kelly and Cary Grant. In those early days of faxing, I played a game of inflating my importance in the eyes of haughty French hotel personnel by sending a fax to myself at the Carlton prior to leaving the office. Upon checking in, I would head for the concierge desk and smugly inquire, "*Avez vous un fax pour moi?*"

The weather in Cannes usually cooperated by turning sunny and warm. The daily drill went something like this: Tennis, followed by light breakfast on the terrace of one of the grand hotels along the Croisette, the majestic boulevard lined with palm trees that fronted the Mediterranean Sea, often followed by a morning tour of the Palais, where we screened program offerings and arranged appointments with prospective partners. Then came lunch at the Carlton Hotel's restaurant right on the beach, where we negotiated coproduction deals with one eye on the sea and the other, I confess, on the topless French women cavorting in the sand just a few feet away. Afternoons brought more exploratory appointments, usually on the verandas of other luxurious hotels overlooking the Mediterranean. Next were lavish receptions on grand yachts moored in the Cannes harbor. Then it was off to a sumptuous dinner, which usually was paid for by a European broadcaster with a seemingly limitless expense account. Paying jobs like this one seldom came along, so I reveled in every minute of it.

Believe it or not, this hazardous duty often produced handsome dividends. One evening, our team dined out with the head of an independent British television company. He brought his wife, which prompted some grousing, since the rest of us wanted to confine the conversation to business. We did not see where she fit into the picture, especially since our spouses were not with us. However, since he was paying, his wife came. So much for our bellyaching.

Over dinner, we swapped descriptions of the favorite projects for which we were seeking partners. Nothing clicked as we worked through our respective wish lists. Near the end of what was shaping up as a fruitless conversation, Marian Swaybill, our enterprising head of coproductions, mentioned that we intended to produce a series called *Art of the Western World*. She basically tossed it out there, not expecting it to catch the CEO's attention, since his programming tastes were decidedly commercial and this series might be a bit highbrow for him.

The TV executive's wife sat bolt upright and exclaimed to her husband, "Art, art! You must do it." He acquiesced then and there. Her intervention triggered an investment of several million dollars, if memory serves. This put us over the top financially and enabled us to produce the series. I never groused again about who was coming to dinner in Cannes.

Work-related travel gradually transformed me from a neophyte into a hungry student of the world outside the United States. Trips to London and Paris, Salzburg and Hamburg, Monte Carlo and Madrid became second nature. I took in Rio, Tokyo, and Bangkok, the latter for the Rockefeller Brothers Fund, whose board I had joined.

In early 1986, I journeyed to West Berlin for an international workshop on public broadcasting. I paired this with a business trip to Vienna once the conference ended. East-West tensions were still dangerously high. Merely a week or so before I arrived, Soviet dissident Anatoly Sharansky had crossed over to West Berlin with hordes of media covering the East-West prisoner exchange. East German soldiers were routinely shooting would-be defectors who tried scaling the Berlin Wall. This trip was no cakewalk like Cannes; it definitely had an edge to it.

As soon as I arrived in West Berlin, I hopped a tour bus and headed to East Berlin for my first ever trip behind the Iron Curtain. The sights there appalled and depressed me. The apartment buildings, made of bricks gathered from the rubble of bombed-out structures, were as ugly as any I had ever seen. The tour guide's words were guarded and decidedly politically correct. Vast monuments to Soviet domination dotted the skyline. At a snack bar, we were served stale sandwiches that were barely digestible.

After the conference, I planned to fly straight from communist East Berlin to Vienna, instead of returning from West Berlin to another West German city before traveling on to Vienna, as the treaties required. This wasn't about saving time. Rather, I wanted another glimpse of life on the other side of the Berlin Wall. I hopped a municipal bus that regularly crossed from West to East Berlin. When it reached the border, heavily armed East German guards boarded the bus and searched everything. I wondered if I had made a wise choice when I saw they had no sense of humor whatsoever.

The bus cleared the search and headed for East Berlin's Schönefeld Airport. Once deposited there, I dutifully followed the signs to the waiting area set aside for travelers from the West. There, we were segregated from travelers from communist-bloc countries. In the waiting room, I spotted a newsstand and ventured over. The only English-language newspaper available was the *Daily Worker*, the communist paper. In an ironic sign of how times have changed since the fall of the Berlin Wall, Schönefeld is touted these days as Berlin's Holiday Airport.

I trudged back to my seat in the segregated waiting room and pulled some reading matter out of my briefcase. At the time, we were collaborating with a British TV company and an independent filmmaker on a documentary series called *The Struggles for Poland*. The idea behind it was to chronicle the heroic efforts of the Polish people to remain free of Soviet domination, psychologically if not militarily. The manuscript I extracted from my briefcase was the lengthy script for the series. I began to edit the document. A few moments later, it dawned on me how indescribably dumb it was to have this document in my possession, much less in full view on my lap. Had an East German guard sashayed over and insisted on examining it, the government surely would have thrown the book at me. I slid it unceremoniously back into the briefcase and meekly twiddled my thumbs until the flight was called. All the while, I thought, *Maybe my mother raised a dummy after all.*

Flying a Soviet-built jet on Air Interflug, the East German airline, was worth experiencing—once. The pilot flew like a cowboy, making abrupt dips and turns. The furnishings were Spartan, as was the food. As we exited in Vienna, I made my contribution to hastening *perestroika* by surreptitiously leaving the copy of the *International Herald Tribune* I had bought in West Berlin on the airplane seat. I just couldn't contain my rebellious streak any longer.

Public television was a growth experience, no question about it. I learned how to sit perfectly still, seemingly unperturbed, as a cockroach crawled up my leg in a swanky Fifth Avenue apartment during a fundraising pitch to the wealthy matron who lived there. While serving on the Rockefeller Brothers Fund board, I toured Bangkok with fellow trustees David Rockefeller and Henry Kissinger, watching them being treated like visiting potentates in scenes reminiscent of those 1940s Movietone News clips. I witnessed the early days of globalization in the unlikeliest of places, such as a flyspeck island far off Thailand's Phuket Island, toward the idyllic Pee Pee Islands, where barefoot men listened to Madonna on a boom box as they climbed bamboo ladders in a cave, searching for sparrows' nests with a view toward extracting the birds' saliva for use as an aphrodisiac. In Rio de Janeiro on a co-production prospecting trip, I strolled along the glorious Ipanema and Copacabana Beaches and ogled so many stunning women of striking ethnic blends that I concluded the town fathers must have installed an invisible electronic fence to keep unattractive bathers away. In a Viennese disco, I gawked as a world-renowned opera star stripped down to her skivvies and danced the night away following a stirring performance earlier that evening in a production at the Staatsoper state opera. Back home, I discovered trendy New York City discos including the Palladium and the Tunnel, which WNET used as venues for glittery receptions to launch new series. At the station's swank fundraising events, I met and danced with "social x-rays"—the aging, rail-thin women of great wealth who insisted on wearing miniskirts designed for runway models and who Tom Wolfe profiled so hilariously in *Bonfire of the Vanities*.

Yes, I became a worldlier person thanks to public television. Outfitted in a tux one evening in Vienna's Staatsoper, I pondered the light-years separating this professional life from the one I had pursued as a legal services lawyer and head of the Black Coalition. I considered how far riot-scarred New Haven was from Vienna and the other world capitals I routinely visited on business. I reviewed how these European and Asian production executives had to deal with an African-American counterpart if they hoped to do business with the biggest public television station in the largest viewing market in America. The world had come a surprising distance in recent years. So had I.

Just as cable television was coming of age, Jay Iselin stepped down as president in 1987 after fifteen remarkably creative and productive years at the helm. He had accomplished a great deal for the station and the industry but was running out of gas, as high-octane leaders of dynamic organizations invariably do.

Heeding my brother's encouragement to go for it, I decided to make a run for the presidency, figuring I had an excellent shot. Between the local broadcast side and the national production operation, I had overseen about two-thirds of the organization—in fact, almost every facet except engineering and human resources. I felt I had done a good job. After all, a passel of notable new PBS series had been conceived, coproduced, and launched on my watch. I had played a consequential role in saving the *NewsHour* from an early demise. Since I had attended first-rate schools, the elitist in me figured my academic credentials were in my favor. What more could the selection committee want? At a minimum, I assumed it would take a serious look at me.

Was I ever wrong! The search committee granted me a perfunctory twenty-minute interview. As I left the room, I shook my head in disbelief. My ego was crushed, smashed to smithereens on the proverbial glass ceiling. This was the first time I had smacked into it, and the blow smarted. I took scant consolation in the fact that the committee treated the other inside candidates, who were also senior executives, just as cavalierly. Nor was race apparently a factor, since my fellow insiders were a white male, a white female, and another African-American, who, as chief operating officer, ranked higher than the rest of us on the organizational totem pole. Evidently, the search committee was intent on enlisting a veteran commercial TV executive as the new leader. Even so, what baffled and infuriated me about the search process was how little respect we insiders were accorded after working our asses off to rescue the station from near-bankruptcy and getting it solidly back on track.

I badly wanted the presidency for many reasons. I had grown to love public television, with its lofty mission and international scope. The industry was intellectually stimulating and chock-full of challenges and fascinating people. The appointment would have made history because I stood to become the first African-American to head a public TV station in the United States. With prominent blacks such as Clifton Wharton, Frank Thomas, and Vernon Jordan shattering assorted glass ceilings, the egotist in me wanted to join their ranks in yet another previously unpenetrated realm of American life. I felt I had earned it by my performance, and that I had the right stuff to win the position.

The rejection put me in a funk that lasted for months. Not getting the job frustrated me. Not even being taken seriously by the search committee insulted and infuriated me. I went through the motions at work. Heart and body were no longer in it because the dismissive way I had been treated snapped my psychic bond of loyalty to the institution.

From then on, it was just a job. The other insiders who were rejected told me they felt much the same way.

With cable television making our lives in national production increasingly miserable, I concluded that if I wasn't in the driver's seat guiding change, why be stuck in the caboose getting whipsawed by enormous challenges? Had our family been wealthy, I would have quit in a huff. Thankfully, Marilyn persuaded me not to do anything rash that would hurt our family or my professional reputation. I decided to hang on and see if a new professional opportunity presented itself. Never one to leave this entirely to chance, I once again sent word through my professional network that I was available if the right situation came along.

Our daughter Traer snapped me out of the doldrums several months later. She attended church regularly back then and was quite spiritual. I was standing in the kitchen with my by-then accustomed hangdog look. She suddenly said, "Don't worry about not getting that job. You're being saved for something more important." I cannot explain why, but suddenly my mood brightened. I finally put the rejection behind me and regained peace of mind.

Since I faced a decision about whether to remain in television or return to the knitting—namely, resume dealing with issues related to cities, minorities, and the poor—I decided to talk with a couple of acquaintances in commercial television to explore if I had any future there. One was a network news executive; the other ran a big-city cable television system. The former advised me to steer clear because the news business was under siege, due to mounting pressure to curb costs and generate profits. The cable exec indicated that his industry did not view public-TV types as business people. I chuckled and thought to myself that we probably were tougher-minded business people than they'd ever be because we operated on tighter financial margins. After all, our world-class producers created programs on location all over the world, instead of in hermetically sealed studios. We had to produce on budget, with little potential to make money and no tolerance for losing any. I departed these meetings resigned to the fact that my career as a television executive had run its course.

As good fortune would have it, a friend named Peter Goldmark was appointed president of the Rockefeller Foundation around this time. I sent him a congratulatory letter that also included some thoughts about the state of urban America. In other words, it was an oblique signal that I was available if he wanted to chat about bringing me onto his team at Rockefeller.

Peter got the unsubtle hint and called soon after receiving the letter. He asked me to become vice president of the foundation. I quickly accepted and resigned from the station with genuine regrets about leaving my compatriots, who were a treat to work with and who had demystified television for me, starting with how to operate a VCR. Yet I was completely at peace with putting my detour into public television behind me. It was high time I got back to my life's work of empowering poor and minority people to enter the American mainstream.

CHAPTER 12

OTHER PEOPLE'S MONEY

The Rockefeller Foundation felt just right after my sojourn in public television. The name alone was legendary in the world of philanthropy. Its combination of money and power made important things happen. While I cannot speak for how Rockefeller operates now, in those days, it functioned as a proactive foundation that did not wait to receive proposals, place bets on what it considered winners, and then dispense grants. For the most part, program officers at Rockefeller took initiative, devised strategies, and forged alliances to advance its mission. The foundation's money served as the rocket fuel to propel its work. This style of philanthropy suited me perfectly.

I came to Rockefeller to oversee its grant making in the area of promoting equal opportunity for minorities and to craft a portfolio of new initiatives to help improve urban education. Since the former was ably overseen by a veteran urban affairs expert named James Gibson, the latter consumed most of my creative energy and required all the ingenuity and leverage I could muster, since our school reform unit did not have much money to spend. I recruited two bright colleagues—Marla Ucelli, a former chief education adviser to Governor Tom Kean of New Jersey, and Jamie Beck Jensen, a PhD candidate in education—to assist me.

True to my practice of going beyond the call of duty, I was determined to become a player in the field of school reform, not merely a funder. This I accomplished by publishing articles and giving speeches around the country. I often likened our school reform efforts to a black barbershop. How so? When a customer sits in the barber chair gazing at the mirrors on opposite walls, the shop looks vastly bigger than it actually is.

A perfect example of how we leveraged our modest resources was the National Commission on Teaching and America's Future. My colleagues and I actually conceived of the commission during a strategic discussion around my desk. This was a case of blending something borrowed with something new. For many years, the Carnegie Corporation had utilized the commission model—basically, a high-profile collection of experts and public-spirited corporate and civic leaders—to examine critical issues and promulgate reports chock-full of findings and policy recommendations.

We decided to employ this approach to examine the professional development of teachers in America's public schools, especially those not serving children as well as they should. Then as now, inner-city schools suffered from a chronic shortage of qualified and experienced teachers. My colleagues and I felt a high-powered commission could help galvanize the attention of the public, the media, and ultimately the politicians who had to appropriate the money to enable schools systems to train and upgrade good teachers. A key ingredient we added to the commission format was follow-up grants to help interested states implement the commission's recommendations. We wanted this report to impact policy and practice, not gather dust propping up bookends on a shelf.

To spearhead the commission, I recruited Linda Darling-Hammond, a distinguished professor at Columbia Teachers College who was and remains one of America's foremost experts on teacher quality and training. I delighted in the fact that Linda, an African-American, was a student of mine at Yale when I taught there part-time, as well as a neighbor in Westchester County. Leading the commission instantly catapulted her into position as the country's preeminent and highest-profile expert on this critical subject. The move also advanced another agenda of mine—namely, integrating the virtually all-male, all-white fraternity of renowned school reform experts by using Rockefeller's cachet, cash, and convening power to thrust more female and minority experts onto center stage in the field.

Although the commission was conceived in my office, we did not wish to go it alone. We invited the Carnegie Corporation to join in co-sponsoring the enterprise. It readily accepted. Carnegie's involvement gave the effort added clout and resources, especially given its impressive track record in making these kinds of vehicles work.

While Linda would serve as executive director of the commission, she came up with the astute idea of recruiting North Carolina governor Jim Hunt to chair it. Devoted to improving public education, he brought expertise and political savvy to the project. Linda also insisted on expanding the scope of the commission to encompass recruitment and preservice training of new classroom teachers. This way, the commission would address recruitment and in-service training as part of a continuum, not as disjointed episodes in the lives of educators.

I count the National Commission on Teaching and America's Future, launched in 1994, among my proudest contributions to the cause of improving public schools. Thanks to the power of the underlying idea and the enormous credibility of its leadership and membership, it evolved into one of the most influential commissions of its type. In the fall of 1996, a mere two years after it was founded, the commission released its first report, entitled *What Matters Most: Teaching for America's Future*. The widely covered report called for sweeping changes in how teachers were recruited, prepared, and trained. In fact, *Education Week*, the leading national newspaper covering K-12 education, credited *What Matters Most* with pushing teaching to the forefront of the education policy landscape. As recently as August 2016, the commission released an influential report titled *What Matters Now: A New Compact for Teaching and Learning*. In early 2017, the commission merged with a like-minded organization known as Learning Forward and will operate going forward under that name. Thus, it continues to impact education policy and practice more than two decades after my Rockefeller Foundation colleagues and I hatched it in my office.

I joined the foundation determined to use its resources to help ratchet up the scale and profile of Dr. James Comer's School Development Program (SDP). Marilyn and I had experienced firsthand the power of his approach when we lived in the Newhallville neighborhood of New Haven. Our eldest daughter had attended Martin Luther King School, one of the earliest schools to implement the SDP. We saw up close how parents could play a constructive role in inner-city schools and how educators and parents, working in tandem, could help develop youngsters' social skills and turn them on to learning. Dr. Comer preached that education was a critically important facet of children's overall development, not a hermitically sealed experience unrelated to their surrounding environment. He backed his philosophy with

statistics that showed encouraging academic gains in schools that embraced his approach.

To my mind, more urban schools needed to try the SDP, and more
educators and policymakers needed to hear Dr. Comer's message. I persuaded the foundation to invest in building the capacity of Dr. Comer's
team to work with many more school districts. We also financed the
creation of videos that captured his method as a way of disseminating
it beyond the schools districts he and his colleagues helped personally.

Like many other school reform efforts, the SDP went smoothly
in many districts but sputtered in others. The foundation's backing of
Dr. Comer paid gratifying dividends. Although the videos we funded did not attract the hoped-for attention from school officials, our
grants expanded the reach of his work and boosted his national profile.
With our money and imprimatur, we helped consolidate his ranking
as one of the nation's premier school reform experts. For roughly a
half-century, Dr. Comer has led the way in helping educators, policymakers, academicians, advocates, and the media see the light when it
comes to the importance of fostering youngsters' academic, social, and
emotional development. U.S. presidents, first ladies, and secretaries of
education eagerly court him and seek his opinion. Schools of education at universities have introduced courses based on his insights and
approach.

Another example of using the Rockefeller Foundation's leverage to
augment our modest budget and mobilize the resources of other organizations to advance a cause grew out of a keynote address I delivered
at the annual meeting of community foundations in Seattle in 1990.
This speaking engagement also furthered my game plan to become
not just a grant maker but a player who proposed innovative ideas, exhorted leaders to act, and spawned coalitions where possible. I devoted
this speech to imploring community foundations, which at the time
were the fastest-growing sector of American philanthropy, to join forces to help improve the well-being of America's children, particularly
youngsters in poor urban and rural areas. Community foundations had
received criticism for being overly cautious, reactive, and short term—
instead of proactive, innovative, and strategic—in addressing the needs
of America's children.

Unbeknownst to me at the time, the speech resonated deeply with
the audience of community foundation presidents and program officers.
Several months later, Jan Kreamer, the charming and hard-charging

head of the Greater Kansas City Community Foundation, approached me after a meeting in New York to say that the speech had ignited a spark among community foundation leaders. She suggested we get together to explore where this tentative interest might lead. I proposed lunch the next day.

Jan and I got along famously. Together, we decided to invite some of the most influential CEOs of community foundations to a meeting in Kansas City to explore whether or not there was genuine interest in forging some kind of joint effort. In surprisingly short order, they reached consensus that a collaborative initiative made sense. They agreed to craft a preliminary charter for the group and settled on a name—the Coalition of Community Foundations for Youth. At subsequent planning meetings, additional foundations signed on and devised an initial plan of action for CCFY.

In April 1991, some thirty heads of the largest community foundations officially launched CCFY at an inaugural meeting in Dallas. The founders defined its purpose as a clearinghouse and sounding board for innovative projects to promote the intellectual, social, physical, and moral development of poor children and their families. In addition to organizing symposia, CCFY published such reports as *Best Practices in Youth Philanthropy* in 2002.

I stayed close to CCFY throughout its formative stages. Rockefeller gave the organization seed money to underwrite its initial meetings and provided the first operating grant to get its program off the ground. My goal was to leverage our convening power and modest resources to train the attention—and, of course, the bountiful collective resources—of community foundations on such vital issues as expanding after-school programs and improving public schools for low-income children. CCFY mushroomed into a network of more than two hundred community foundations, staying true to its fundamental mission of strengthening the leadership capacity of community foundations to improve the lives of children, youth, and families.

Much like the National Commission on Teaching and America's Future, CCFY still lives roughly a quarter-century after its founding. It subsequently rebranded itself as CFLeads (Community Foundations Leading Change) and broadened its scope beyond a sole focus on children to building thriving communities. It functions as a national learning cooperative for community foundations seeking to tackle challenging issues, to pursue cross-sectional solutions, and to marshal resources to improve communities and provide opportunities for all. CFLeads offers webinars, operates leadership networks for members, distributes community foundation case studies, and issues reports such as *Community Foundations Take the Lead: Promising Approaches to Building Inclusive and Equitable Communities.*

While CCFY and CFLeads haven't brightened the lives of every needy child, they continue to this day to strengthen the commitment and fortify the capacity of the community foundation sector to proactively address the needs of their communities and constituents. In my book, that's a compelling long-term social dividend from leveraging other people's money.

CHAPTER 13

THE MILITARY AND ME

The most innovative idea I championed at the Rockefeller Foundation easily ranked as the most gratifying as well. It derived from my improbable alliance with the military. Mind you, I never served in the armed forces. Didn't get drafted or even take the physical exam. I'm neither a warmonger nor a peacenik.

Friends who served in the Vietnam War say that, given the setting and constraints, coupled with the difficulty of telling friend from foe, fighting there was truly scary. Some buddies of mine who served, especially in the infantry, will not talk about their experience to this day. I have unbounded admiration for the soldiers of my generation who carried the U.S. flag in that frightening and ultimately futile conflict. I never criticized those who served. I just wasn't eager for the army to call my number. As fate, not design, would have it, I had enrolled in law school, gotten married, and become a father by the time the war escalated. This fortuitous sequence of deferments kept me out of the military.

The odyssey of my improbable idea began in the mid-1970s, when I was a partner at Cogen Holt. The Taconic Foundation, a small family foundation headed by a Yale Law School professor, gave our firm a modest grant to examine the nagging issue of why so many black teenagers, particularly males, languished outside the labor market—and more importantly, whether something creative and, above all, effective could be done about it. This was the heyday of liberalism, when caring people conjured up programs they believed would help solve—or at least ameliorate—stubborn social problems.

The issue of chronically high teenage unemployment leapt out from all the research and statistics. The theories behind why this was the case ran the gamut from lousy education and stunted social skills to outright discrimination by employers, evaporation of decent-paying blue-collar jobs, and structural flaws in the labor market. Translated, the latter meant there simply weren't enough jobs near where black teens lived, and that these young people persistently drew the short straws because of their other deficits. In my experience, each of these theories rang true to some extent.

Abstract theories are fine. Reliable statistics that substantiate the scope of a problem are indispensable. Yet for me, the pivotal question always is whether or not there are program interventions that can attract the support of policymakers and justify a sizable-enough public investment to make a dent in the problem.

As my colleagues Doris Zelinsky and Harry Wexler and I cast about for ideas about what to propose, I recalled growing up in Washington. When I was a teenager in the 1950s, many of my male classmates couldn't have cared less about school. Try as the teachers might, they just could not turn these fellows on to learning. Some were cutups or truants. A few boys were what we quaintly called "roughnecks," "knuckleheads," or "thugs," who barely avoided reform school. Perhaps they possessed some of those nonacademic "intelligences" that Howard Gardner of the Harvard Graduate School of Education identified and that made school an unbearable bore.

As soon as they could, these aimless teenage boys dropped out of school and out of sight. I remembered encountering several of them a few years later. They had enlisted in the army or else been drafted. Either way, they strutted about ramrod straight in their crisp uniforms, full of pride and purpose. Since I never served in the military, I was clueless about what had happened to them and how they had been transformed. The radical change in these young people's mindsets and deportment mystified and intrigued me.

The military eventually terminated the draft and mostly stopped accepting high school dropouts. As war and weaponry became more sophisticated, the Pentagon needed soldiers who were better educated. This completely understandable escalation of admission standards nonetheless blocked an important escape route and road to salvation for desperate inner-city and rural youngsters lacking high school diplomas who had nowhere else to turn. This has cost society—and successive generations of these young people—dearly. Ironically, during the booming labor market in the late 1990s, the military encountered such problems recruiting volunteers that Secretary of the Army Louis Caldera advocated allowing his branch to accept more dropouts.

I served as project leader for the study by our consulting firm. When my colleagues and I examined the presumed benefits of military service for rudderless boys, we started imagining a civilian equivalent of the army experience and came up with the concept of a quasi-military domestic youth corps for dropouts. Essentially, our idea was that youngsters would enroll voluntarily and be assigned to military bases, where they would receive intensive academic training, perform community service, and develop self-discipline.

We were excited by what we thought was a breakthrough idea. I sent a draft description of it to my mentor at the Ford Foundation, Mike Sviridoff, to see if it piqued his interest. He replied affirmatively and offered to convene a group of eminent labor economists to hear our case and critique the concept. We trekked to Ford's imposing headquarters in New York City, confident we could persuade these renowned experts that we had discovered the antipoverty equivalent of nuclear fusion.

The economists assembled by Sviridoff listened politely, perhaps even indulgently, as we laid out our concept. Then they opened fire from every direction. I do not recall a favorable comment the entire time, although I may have been so shell-shocked that I've repressed all memory of this meeting. None of our responses to their pointed questions satisfied the naysayers.

How to explain the debacle? No doubt, there were flaws in our idea and operational challenges we had not thought through. But the experts displayed so little curiosity that I remain persuaded to this day that a big reason for the chilly reception was dreadful timing. With the nation emerging in the mid-1970s from the politically fractious Vietnam War, policymakers, government officials, and foundation executives simply were in no mood to embrace a military-like or military-lite solution to a domestic problem, especially one involving young people. Many liberals, presumably like some of the economists in the room, recoiled at the idea of anything that smacked of the military. When the meeting ended, we sheepishly zipped up our briefcases, tucked tail, and headed home to New Haven.

By nature, I am patient and persistent—some might even say pig-headed—when convinced my cause is right. So when I joined the New Haven city government several years later as human resources administrator, I saw a chance to rekindle the quasi-military corps idea. My office ran or funded an array of after-school, senior citizen, pre-school, and antipoverty programs. Doris Zelinsky joined me as the agency's director of strategic planning. Soon after taking office, we approached the head of the local public housing authority, which coped with idle teenagers on a daily basis. Together, we devised a variant of the corps that would operate within the New Haven Housing Authority. Participants would be assigned to various units in the agency, from the central office and property management to maintenance and landscaping. They would be supervised and mentored by full-time personnel. They would receive training and could climb the ladder of responsibility if they performed well. Those who succeeded might land permanent jobs with the agency.

We needed external funding to implement this version of the corps. I intended to use a combination of municipal funding under CETA (the federal public service employment program authorized by the Comprehensive Employment and Training Act) and other federal demonstration grants. According to the city government's organizational chart, I supervised the public jobs program, and we expected to apply to the U.S. Department of Labor for the latter.

However, my funding scheme came a cropper because the CETA funds were deployed, understandably enough, to help curb unemployment by hiring jobless workers and averting municipal layoffs. The director of CETA, who supposedly reported to me, did the mayor's bidding and ignored my plan. I never questioned the mayor's prerogative to make this call. Yet from this unhappy experience, I learned a lesson I've never forgotten about getting portfolios and reporting lines absolutely straight before accepting a job. Thus, my second attempt at launching a quasi-military youth corps proved again to be a nonstarter.

Fast-forward two careers and a decade later to the Rockefeller Foundation. In the fall of 1988, one month after joining the foundation, I attended a school reform conference at the Stanford University School of Education. Groggy from jet lag, I perked up when one of the speakers—Edmund Gordon, a mentor, distinguished Yale psychologist, and avowed pacifist—ventured the provocative opinion that the conditions in which inner-city teens were being reared were so detrimental that it might be time to consider conscripting them for their own good.

I sat bolt upright at the mention of conscription and muttered to myself, "Have I got a program idea for you!" Could we, I wondered anew, get one of the branches of the military to create a domestic youth corps for school dropouts? It would operate on military bases with all the structure and training of the military except that kids would perform community service instead of learning to wage war. One of the many privileges of serving as vice president of Rockefeller was that I could make modest grants to seed innovative ideas. I decided on the spot to pull the quasi-military corps out of hibernation and try yet again to make it happen. Perhaps the third time would indeed be a charm.

As a check against getting carried away with the idea, further due diligence was my first order of business. The idea again needed to run the gauntlet of seasoned experts who would spare no criticism. Eddie Williams, a friend who headed the think tank known as the Joint Center for Political and Economic Studies, put me in touch with a colleague there named Ed Dorn, a former assistant secretary of defense who subsequently became dean of the Lyndon Baines Johnson School of Public Administration at the University of Texas. Dorn in turn convened a cross-section of experts and advocates to vet the idea anew.

I emerged from the spirited exchange encouraged that, while some still questioned the quasi-military approach, others felt it had considerable merit. Interestingly enough, the doubters tended to be child advocates, who typically fretted the loudest about the plight of black teenagers. Most valuable of all, this session brought me into contact with key players in the defense establishment, including noted military sociologist Charles Moskos and former assistant secretary of defense Larry Korb.

By then, I was convinced that if the concept was to get anywhere this time, it had to be championed, indeed "owned," by an entity closely associated with and perhaps even embedded within the national defense establishment. I reasoned that an ostensibly liberal foundation such as Rockefeller could not carry the water on this one because military officials and defense experts would dismiss it almost reflexively.

Therefore, in my exploratory conversations, I trolled for some prominent individual or resourceful entity in the military sphere that would catch the vision and run with it. Pride of authorship took a backseat to propelling the idea forward. If some strategically situated organization capable of aggressively driving the idea wanted to assume ownership, I considered this an institutional and personal sacrifice well worth making.

More than a decade after the idea had dawned on me, I finally struck pay dirt. Aided by Dorn and Korb, I obtained two introductions that, in football parlance, finally moved the idea downfield. First was William Taylor of the Center for Strategic and International Studies (CSIS), a prominent defense policy think tank in Washington. I also obtained entrée to General Herbert Temple, commander of the National Guard. Both agreed to see me.

I approached these meetings in the spring of 1989 with a mixture of anticipation and trepidation. This was the closest I had ever gotten to the upper echelons of the military establishment. After all, I did not socialize with these folks and had never set foot inside the Pentagon, where General Temple worked. I summoned all of my brief-writing skills to prepare the most convincing case I could muster. This was my best, and possibly only, shot.

Both meetings exceeded my most optimistic expectations. After all those years of false starts and frustration, I could not believe my ears. I first met with Bill Taylor of CSIS. He proposed creating a high-profile task force of leading policymakers and military experts to study the feasibility of the concept. If all went well, they would then issue a favorable report endorsing it. Since CSIS had scant experience working with urban youth, I introduced it to friends at Public/Private Ventures, a highly regarded outfit that at the time operated and evaluated youth development programs for at-risk youngsters. I felt that the complementary expertise and credibility of these two groups would be useful during the feasibility analysis and in marketing the idea, assuming we got that far.

Invoking the discretion I enjoyed as vice president of the foundation, I authorized grants to CSIS and P/PV to collaborate in conducting the feasibility analysis. I believed that a seal of approval by a highly respected and politically wired defense think tank such as CSIS was crucial to the credibility of the idea inside Pentagon and congressional circles. Working with P/PV, CSIS then established a study group known as the National Community Service for Out-of-School Youth Project, which was cochaired by Senator John McCain and Congressman Dave McCurdy.

The other introduction, orchestrated by Larry Korb, turned out to be even more of a game changer. In our meeting, General Temple was joined by Dan Donohue, the National Guard's director of public information. To my astonishment, both of them embraced the idea with minimal persuasion on my part. General Temple surprised me even further when he commented that military people were basically youth workers at heart who happened to instruct their charges in making war, but who could train youngsters to do and be anything.

Without downplaying the CSIS-P/PV effort, General Temple and Dan Donohue said feasibility studies were fine. However, they intended to forge ahead with mobilizing the National Guard to launch the quasi-military corps for dropouts, including rounding up funds from Congress for pilot sites.

Little did I realize when I met him that Dan was one of those unheralded organizational geniuses who knew how to move complex bureaucracies forward and make things happen. In a further stroke of good fortune and fortuitous timing, he had wanted for years to develop an intervention akin to this quasi-military idea. With General Temple's enthusiastic backing, Dan focused on designing the intervention and persuading Congress to appropriate funds for pilot sites.

True to their commitment, both groups barreled along with their work. CSIS and P/PV completed the feasibility analysis and, with a second dose of funding from the foundation, moved into the design phase for the corps. Meanwhile, the National Guard charged ahead at an even faster clip, initiating conversations on Capitol Hill to line up funding for a trial run. The National Guard got to the finish line first, which was fine by me. The reports prepared by CSIS and P/PV helped smooth the way for the idea in the upper echelons of the military and political establishments.

As I wrote in my book *Strugglers Into Strivers: What the Military Can Teach Us About How Young People Learn and Grow*, this collective effort spawned what came to the known as the National Guard Youth ChalleNGe Corps (subsequently rebranded the ChalleNGe Program). In 1993, ten pilot sites opened in ten states, including Camp Ella Grasso in Connecticut. The nation's first contingent of ChalleNGe cadets graduated from Camp Grasso later that year. The U.S. Coast Guard in nearby New London hosted the ceremony. Young people who six months earlier had been written off as borderline worthless strode down the aisle, proudly decked out in caps and gowns. An audience of nearly a thousand parents, grandparents, children, and other well-wishers cheered them on. Some grizzled vets bestowed the American Legion's

"Top Student" honor on one of the graduates. A chorus made up of participants sang several tunes, and surprisingly well at that.

CNN covered the ceremony. I am not weepy by nature, but I would be lying if I didn't confess that I was teary eyed throughout much of the ceremony. I was overcome with joy for the youngsters and their loved ones. And to be honest, I wept for yours truly. My vision and tenacity had paid off. *Up yours, big-shot economists, wherever you are.*

Despite this early triumph, rocky times lay ahead. When the National Guard decided to move from a pilot test to a broader program, I tried to get the foundation to finance a full-scale evaluation. Yet I continued to encounter skepticism among my colleagues. The grant request eventually cleared this internal hurdle and headed for the board, which had to approve sizable proposals. At the board meeting, several trustees expressed qualms about exposing youngsters to the military and about whether or not female dropouts would be welcome in what on the surface seemed like a male-oriented program. One trustee argued that if the Defense Department really wanted to do this, it should provide all the funding. Other trustees praised me for thinking outside the box. In the end, however, the board declined by a narrow margin to support the project. In one of the most wrenching experiences

Visiting with Puerto Rico ChalleNGe Program cadets
Puerto Rico National Guard

of my career, I was obliged to withdraw the foundation from further involvement.

Happily, with the National Guard fully committed to its creation, ChalleNGe had ample momentum by then. The setback at the foundation never deterred me from proselytizing for the program. Dan and I appeared on the nationally syndicated *Montel Williams Show* with a bunch of participants dressed in their uniforms. As a navy veteran, Montel loved ChalleNGe. The appearance was a hoot, especially when he staged a corny reunion between a boy who had joined the corps and his father, who thought he'd never amount to "nuthin." This was reality TV with something serious on its mind.

In the summer of 1994, I managed to arrange a meeting for Dan and me with Secretary of Labor Robert Reich and Undersecretary of Defense Jan Deutsch. The agenda, plain and simple, was to engineer a major expansion of the ChalleNGe Corps to more states. Our plan fizzled, however, when the Republican Party, energized by Newt Gingrich and his Contract with America, took control of Congress in the fall. The new conservative leadership promptly declared that soldiers weren't social workers. It took all of Dan's deft political maneuvering to keep Congress from killing the program.

The original concept of ChalleNGe has held largely intact over the twenty-plus years since its inception. A robust and successful civilian intervention devoted to turning around the aspirations and life prospects of school dropouts, the program treats academic and social development as coequal objectives. The basic experience consists of a twenty-two-week residential stint on a military base. These days, ChalleNGe operates thirty-four sites in twenty-seven states, Puerto Rico, and the District of Columbia, serving roughly 5,000 sixteen- to eighteen-year-olds annually. Since the program's inception in 1993, nearly 150,000 former dropouts have graduated as of 2016.

Over the years, ChalleNGe became a favorite of politicians whose constituents needed somewhere to send youngsters they could not handle or who were adrift. I once introduced myself to President Bill Clinton and Senate majority leader Trent Lott at a gala dinner in D.C. in the mid-1990s. When I mentioned my association with the ChalleNGe Corps, broad grins crossed their faces as they told me how much they loved the program. As further indication of the program's popularity, the National Guard Youth Foundation, a nonprofit support organization, stages an annual gala in Washington that draws hundreds of patrons, plus members of Congress, Pentagon brass, governors, their spouses, and entertainment and sports celebrities.

While the program attracts dropouts from all walks of life, they share certain characteristics, among them disenchantment with school, truancy, disruptive and violent behavior, disrespect for teachers, family conflict, poverty, parental and personal substance abuse, drug dealing, gang membership, and physical abuse.

Eight core components reflect the program's commitment to academic and social development. The *Academic Excellence* component prepares participants to obtain a high-school diploma or GED certificate or, at a bare minimum, to become functionally literate and employable. Through *Leadership/Followership* training, cadets earn opportunities to lead their peers while also learning to heed the instructions of teachers and mentors. *Responsible Citizenship* covers the rights and obligations of citizens, voting, the role of government, and the legal system. Cadets devote at least forty hours to *Community Service*, such as building a walking path in a park. These activities provide opportunities for experiential learning in which participants practice their reading, math, planning, and teamwork skills. Military researchers have found that, compared with general literacy instruction, this kind of learning-to-do instruction generates rapid and robust gains in job-related reading and math literacy that endure over time. In *Life-Coping Skills*, participants develop techniques for dealing with anger, stress, and frustration, handling peer pressure, and making constructive choices. *Job Skills* focuses on exploring career options, developing résumés, filling out job applications, and preparing for interviews. *Physical Fitness* and *Health and Hygiene* cover what one would expect.

A random-assignment evaluation by MDRC, the esteemed program evaluation outfit, provided convincing evidence that ChalleNGe works. At the outset of the evaluation, MDRC randomly sorted applicants into two groups—namely, participants and nonparticipants. Roughly two years after graduating, cadets were much more likely than controls to have obtained high-school diplomas or GED certificates. They also were more likely to have received vocational training, earned college credits, or enrolled in college. Fifty-eight percent of participants held jobs, compared to 51 percent of nonparticipants, and they averaged 20 percent more in earnings annually. Although MDRC reported no significant behavioral differences, there are promising indications from some sites that ChalleNGe may help curb teenage pregnancy.

The RAND Corporation, a renowned policy research and analysis firm, conducted a cost-benefit study using MDRC's results. It concluded that ChalleNGe pays tangible dividends to society. Per cadet, RAND concluded, "total benefits of $40,985 are 2.66 times total costs, implying that the ChalleNGe program generates $2.66 in benefits for every dollar spent on the program. The estimated return on investment . . . is 166 percent." Actually, RAND believed the payoff could be greater because the benefits of higher-education attainment were not fully captured by the evaluation.

In an MDRC survey of ChalleNGe graduates, the interviewees enthusiastically recounted how the program enabled them to break habits and generated profound, positive changes in their attitudes, expectations, and self-confidence.

In April 2015, I visited the ChalleNGe program in Puerto Rico. It was going strong, so much so that National Guard officials wished to double the size. I delighted in speaking to the young women and men on a scorching day in a barren field on the parched side of the island. I told them they were my heroes, and I meant it. I lauded them for setting out to turn their lives around by enrolling in ChalleNGe, adding that I wasn't sure I could handle such a grueling experience. Over lunch, I learned about their backgrounds—troubles in school, brushes with the law, and conflicts with parents. One nerdy fellow with thick eyeglasses told me he had been a "black hat" hacker who came to realize the perils of that pathway. They all expressed relief that they had found ChalleNGe, pride that they had endured the taxing experience thus far, and confidence that it would steer them in the right direction.

Far too many American youngsters are marginalized academically, are deeply disengaged from school, and are destined for social and economic oblivion in the twenty-first century. They will be unable to uphold their obligations as citizens and providers. Their plight stems from many factors: family poverty and economic circumstances beyond their control; their own indifference to achievement and disenchantment with formal education as they have known it; and the inflexibility of public schools that fail to meet these troubled young people halfway.

Of course, parents, churches, and communities bear primary responsibility for socializing children. But if they are not up to it, what then? Consigning these youngsters to academic purgatory or, worse still, the criminal justice system serves neither society's interests nor, obviously, theirs. I remain convinced from my experience with Chal- leNGe—and from the evidence of its impact—that school districts should create schools that, like the program, are committed to, and appropriately staffed to, address the academic, social, and emotional development of youngsters who are struggling in traditional schools.

The plain fact is that the U.S. military figured out how to nurture and unleash the potential of young people like these generations ago. By examining and adapting what the Pentagon knows about educating and developing aimless young people, we can transform these troubled and troublesome young Americans into valued social and economic assets.

CHAPTER 14

THERE AT THE CREATION

I n the fall of 1989 while I was with the Rockefeller Foundation, James Joseph, a friend who headed the Council of Foundations, invited a group of philanthropists and foundation executives on a tour of southern Africa that would include South Africa. I accepted immediately because I had long been curious about the continent, if not the country, but had never had occasion to visit. South Africa was under intense international pressure to end apartheid and liberate Nelson Mandela from Robben Island prison. If and when its government would do so was anybody's guess. A high-profile visit by American philanthropists would fortify the anti-apartheid cause and presumably signal that foundation aid might be forthcoming if the country would take a historic leap forward.

We arrived in Johannesburg on January 27, 1990. How to describe the city? Its architecture was nondescript at best. Ringed by gold mines, Johannesburg back then exhibited little other raison d'être. No graceful rivers bisected it; no scenic terrain smoothed out the city's sharp edges.

In short order, my astonishment at the immorality and sheer audacity of apartheid escalated into anger. It was clear from a quick stroll along the streets that "Joburg" was a black city in a black nation. The afternoon of our arrival, we toured Alexandra Township. Thousands of families lived in miniscule shanties amid squalor and stench that literally took one's breath away. The camp was a cauldron of anger and activism as groups organized to protect their space. The Johannesburg skyline, in plain view from Alexandra, reminded its residents of the good life just beyond their grasp.

The visit to Alexandra prepared us for the shock of Soweto the next day. Approximately 2.5 million people were living in this "Levittown" of South African townships. Most Sowetans occupied tiny hovels lined side by side along dirt roads. Squatter camps and barracks housed hundreds of thousands more, while an incongruous cluster of upper-middle-class homes overlooked the acres of despair. We saw schoolchildren everywhere, rays of hope in their Sarafina outfits. Awestruck and admiring residents trailed a female foundation executive in our entourage who dressed like a fashion model. Yet there was tension, too. In fact, the route we took had to be cleared well in advance to assure that our minivans would not be stoned.

After a brief side trip to Windhoek in neighboring Namibia, our next stop in South Africa was Cape Town. At first glance, the stunning city seemed a respite from its unappealing sibling to the north. Cape Town also took one's breath away, for wonderful reasons. Majestic mountains, marvelous vistas, vast white-sand beaches, quaint Cape Dutch bungalows, municipal parks worthy of Paris, European ambiance—the city's bounteous charms easily rivaled those of Rio and San Francisco.

The civility of Cape Town almost masked the evil of apartheid as imposed even there. Just days before we arrived, the police had brutally dispersed a demonstration by shoving the marchers, mostly teenagers, into razor wire with bursts from water cannons. Blacks occupied several vast squatter camps near the airport but were otherwise out of sight and out of mind. Urbanization was so robust in South Africa that, according to government officials, nearly fifty-five hundred rural blacks arrived in the cities monthly, placing an unmanageable strain on the hopelessly overcrowded "communities." The population of the shantytowns near the airport nearly equaled that of Cape Town itself.

As good fortune, canny advance planning, or perhaps both would have it, February 2 found both South African president F. W. de Klerk and our entourage in Cape Town. In the days preceding his eagerly awaited speech to Parliament, the local media teased readers with trial balloons and misleading stories. Aside from the likelihood of Nelson Mandela's release, no other details about the speech leaked out. As I scanned the press coverage, I began to suspect that Mr. de Klerk had studied under LBJ, the master of presidential surprise. I remembered how adroitly President Johnson kept the press and public off the trail of a major announcement, only to spring the news with maximum dramatic and political effect. I suspected de Klerk was up to the same tricks, and that his speech would be a watershed event.

We stayed at the Inn on the Square, a venerable hotel in the heart of Cape Town. I awakened on the morning of February 2 to the rhythmic chants of demonstrators massing in Market Square directly beneath my window. They shouted exuberantly and did the toyi-toyi, the triumphant dance depicted so vividly in the moving documentary film *Amandla!*

Camera in tow, I dashed downstairs and melted into the throng, intent on playing amateur photojournalist. What a day, what a morning! Remember, in 1963, I had served as a marshal for the March on Washington. There were similarities, to be sure, but the differences this day were palpable. The 1963 march was a somber affair, as tens of thousands strode slowly down Constitution Avenue singing "We Shall Overcome." Few of us harbored any hope that things would get significantly better right away. Quite the contrary in Cape Town that early February day. Everyone sensed that President de Klerk's speech

Playing photojournalist at the historic Cape Town rally
on February 2, 1990
Amherst College Library Archives and Special Collections

would break historic ground, if for no other reason than the expected release of Mandela. Anticipating victory, the marchers' mood was triumphant.

I watched in awe as Archbishop Desmond Tutu arrived in the square to a rousing welcome, followed soon by Winnie Mandela. I stood within feet of them, excitedly snapping close-up photos of these globally celebrated freedom fighters. They both held the hyperventilating crowd spellbound with exhortations of victory interspersed with pledges of solidarity and pleas for orderly behavior. Local police stood casually by on street corners, under orders, for a change, to leave the marchers alone. February 2 was indeed a watershed in many ways.

Once the marchers departed for Parliament, I dashed upstairs to watch the speech on television. True to LBJ's form, it far exceeded expectations. De Klerk caught nearly everyone off guard by not only announcing the release of Mandela but proclaiming the end of apartheid. White conservatives sputtered with rage. The surprised anti-apartheid leadership bought time with alternately warm and cool responses as it sought even higher rhetorical and political ground. To judge by the press coverage, most whites breathed a sigh of relief, resigned to the fact that it finally was time for South Africa to get on with its post-apartheid future. For instance, the lead headline in the *Cape Times* proclaimed, "New Era for SA."

Durban was our final stop in South Africa. With its high-rise hotels overlooking the Indian Ocean, the coastal city reminded me of Miami Beach. This was South Africa's playground, where whites traditionally came to romp in the sand and surf. The rules of apartheid were relaxed here. I saw integrated couples in hotels, even heading upstairs together on the elevator. I watched as blacks stepped gingerly onto the once-segregated beaches.

Far from the view of the sun worshippers lay KwaMashu, a township that was the site of a violent rivalry between the African National Congress–affiliated United Democratic Front and the Inkatha, aligned with Zulu chief Gatsha Buthelezi. Two people were killed there the day before our tour, following one hundred during the preceding thirty days. The schism was illustrated by a message spray-painted on a wall: "ANC leaders ran away. Inkatha is here to stay."

From South Africa, we took a brief side trip to Mozambique, a once-beautiful country torn asunder by civil war. The organizers cautioned us when we arrived at the airport that there weren't any regularly scheduled flights into Maputo, the capital, so we chartered some airplanes. My comfort level plunged when I spotted the tiny ten-seat prop planes that supposedly flew at altitudes up to twenty-five thousand feet. To make matters worse, we learned that since the government controlled only the city, while the rebels controlled the countryside, our planes would not make a normal approach into the Maputo airport. That's because if we descended gradually, we'd likely get shot at. Thus, the plan was to come in right over the city, then descend in a tight circle, as though flying inside a cylinder. *That's just great*, I thought, popping a Dramamine pill for the first time in my life.

Maputo was a revelation. I had never visited a city in the midst of war. Most shops were shuttered tight. Our hosts cautioned us not to wander off, for if we came too close to the boundary of government control, we risked being kidnapped by the rebels. Roads inside the city were torn up, cluttered with a sea of automobile skeletons, cavernous potholes, mud, and debris. Abandoned buildings, some stalled in mid-construction, dotted the landscape. It was so terribly sad.

Our group spent the night at the Hotel Polona, a handsome relic now caught in a time warp. It was seedy and run-down. The light in my dreary room consisted of a naked bulb dangling on a cord from the ceiling. The radio beside my bed reminded me of the bulky one I had listened to as a kid in the 1940s, complete with the cloth covering the speaker. The grounds were unkept, though a solitary worker tried gamely to pluck weeds from the walkway. Aside from our group, the only foreigners resembled what I imagined Eastern European gunrunners would look like. If I closed my eyes, I could imagine myself on the set of *Casablanca*, relocated to Maputo.

The president of Mozambique, joined by "senior" members of his cabinet, consented to meet with us. The sight of the country's leaders gathered around the table was disconcerting because none looked a day over forty. As we listened to them describe conditions in their country, my heart went out to them, even though I didn't share their Marxist ideology. Mozambique was trapped by the evil of apartheid in South Africa, by colonialism, and by the protagonists of the Cold War. Eager to shed the yoke of colonialism imposed by Portugal, Mozambique looked to the West but found no support. So it succumbed to the Soviet Union's entreaties. Meanwhile, South Africa, determined to stymie any revolutionary activity emanating from neighboring Mozambique, fomented and financed an uprising there to destabilize the government and minimize any threat. The tragic result was a nation blessed with abundant natural resources, torn to shreds by a senseless civil war instigated and bankrolled by outsiders.

We stopped briefly in Zimbabwe on the way home. Like Cape Town, Harare, the capital, was a graceful city with a well-maintained infrastructure that many an American city would envy. I had been eager to visit this proud nation from the moment it attained independence in 1980, while I worked at the *New York Times*.

As a former journalist and public broadcasting executive, I watch local television when I travel to get a feel for places and their people. When I tuned into the evening news the night we stayed in Harare, I began to feel claustrophobic. The coverage focused almost exclusively on the comings and goings of government ministers. I had read before coming that dissent was percolating inside the country. Yet the government-controlled channels reported none of it on the night I watched.

Bearing witness in Cape Town on February 2, 1990,
at the birth of the new South Africa
Amherst College Library Archives and Special Collections

President Robert Mugabe received us at his official residence for what we assumed would be a brief courtesy visit. Roughly fifteen minutes into the meeting, several of us started to fidget in our seats, fearing we were overstaying our welcome. Then the side doors suddenly opened, and white-gloved waiters brought in trays of tea and cookies.

Though forewarned that Mugabe was a man of few words, we caught him in a discursive mood and with an uncluttered calendar. His remarks spanned the entire region. There was no question, he observed, that a promising new age was dawning in the aftermath of the de Klerk speech. With a post-apartheid South African no longer a disruptive force, Zimbabwe and its neighbors could redirect their sizable and financially crippling defense outlays toward dealing with acute domestic priorities. In his view, this welcome development could set the stage for a largely self-reliant southern African economic community. After roughly an hour, we departed the president's mansion in a daze, wondering what we had done to deserve such a lengthy audience.

Our other meeting in Harare, with local human rights activists, was quite another story. The session opened with the customary introductions and pleasantries. As the conversation continued, I became increasingly skeptical of the conciliatory language these human rights groups used in describing their interactions with the government. The erstwhile lawyer and editorial writer in me decided to probe more deeply by asking a pointed question.

I began by saying that I assumed many of those in the room had been educated in the West and thus understood the traditions of free speech, free press, and freedom of assembly. Yet the regime in Zimbabwe seemed determined to circumscribe the exercise of these freedoms, I suggested, as illustrated by the content and tone of the newscast I had watched the previous night. I then inquired if they acknowledged these constraints and felt comfortable with them. More importantly, I asked, what was the justification for them, from their perspective?

Well, you would have thought I had just stepped on the tender toes of every Zimbabwean in the room. Some responded angrily: how dare I ask that question? Others accused me of being planted by the CIA. I squirmed in my seat, worrying that I had spoiled the visit. My purpose in posing these questions was to encourage a frank dialogue among Americans and Zimbabweans who shared roughly the same values, or so I thought. I certainly never expected to incite a mini-riot. It took ten to fifteen minutes for tempers to cool off.

Their responses, grudgingly offered, were instructive. Some leaders said the exercise of these freedoms must be managed in order to contain unrealistic expectations that the government could not possibly meet and to cope with tribal rivalries that ignored democratic traditions, yet could be a disruptive force. Other human rights advocates at the meeting argued that modest restraints were necessary to curb externally funded destabilization efforts masquerading as internal dissent. For years, they said, the white South African government had surreptitiously financed mischief in the region to protect its racist interests.

As we listened to these justifications and tried as outsiders to weigh their legitimacy, a young black man from South Africa's African National Congress party who was traveling with us rose to speak. He directed his remarks to the Zimbabweans. "Sisters and brothers," he said, "I cannot begin to tell you how much it crushes my heart to hear you rationalize away the freedoms that we South Africans have given our lives and our blood to obtain." The room turned deathly silent as we all absorbed his words. The Zimbabwean human rights leaders could think of no rejoinder, so we adjourned.

From Harare, we flew to London before continuing to New York. As we waited in the lounge during the layover, we watched Nelson Mandela emerge from prison, a free man for the first time in twenty-seven years and the icon of his newly liberated nation. A soul-stirring sight took my breath away for the third time on this trip.

I carried away from South Africa a mixture of exhilaration and anxiety for the reborn nation. Up close, apartheid had proven even more insidious and despicable than I imagined from afar. The country maintained an illusion of marginal inclusiveness. Back then, blacks appeared on billboards and in commercials. Government-controlled television stations carried black news and entertainment programming, even black-oriented music videos. During prime time one evening, I had watched a drama, produced in South Africa, that included a vignette about a black family moving into a white neighborhood. Another segment of the same show dealt with the relationship between a white woman and a black man who, of all things, kissed on screen. From the credits at the end, I learned that the program had been filmed several years earlier, in 1987, when apartheid still ruled the land.

The anomalies extended beyond television. The downtowns and affluent neighborhoods of South Africa's major cities were more First

World—spiffy and efficient—than many in the United States. This
made all the more galling the squalid conditions in the urban townships and squatter camps. Half of all blacks in South Africa lived in
cities as of 1990. By century's end, the ratio was expected to soar to 80
percent. The country was spawning an urban underclass at an alarming
clip. Ironically and tragically, this social time bomb might explode on
the watch of a post-apartheid government dominated by blacks. Life
wasn't fair.

After assuming control, South African blacks faced the challenge of
figuring out how to navigate a problem that has bedeviled American
blacks ever since the civil rights breakthroughs of the 1950s and 1960s.
The abolition of overt segregation in the United States opened the
doors of opportunity for educated and motivated African-Americans.
Although that was a positive development, it also has widened the
chasm between black "haves" and "have-nots" in our country.

After liberation, I reflected as our trip wound down, the anti-
apartheid movement could morph into the rule of able and well-
educated blacks over their poor rural and urban brethren. As
happened in American cities, middle-class families might exit Soweto and its ilk in droves once restrictive housing laws were abolished.
Ironically, when we were visiting the country, some black leaders
who sent their children to integrated schools already fretted that
their youngsters were exhibiting "yuppie" tendencies. Could natural human aspirations to get ahead find outlets without undercutting
black solidarity and crippling the post-apartheid government? Once
the euphoria over majority rule subsided, could the new government
respond quickly and compassionately enough to avert an outbreak of
pent-up despair?

Developing countries are known to compromise on democratic principles, even years after independence. Yet constraints on free
speech and free press often provide protective cover for incompetence,
corruption, and repression. I felt cautiously optimistic that democracy
would survive and thrive in South Africa because apartheid had succumbed more to civil disobedience and democratic protest than to
armed resistance. The principles of unfettered speech, assembly, and
press, as well as universal suffrage, were deeply ingrained in the credo
of the liberation movement. Nevertheless, the crunch would inevitably
come when its poor constituents became restive and insistent about
their needs.

The two-week tour of southern Africa left me excited about the diplomatic opportunity that was opening up to America as a new political and economic pragmatism took hold on the subcontinent. South Africa finally had faced up to its future. Marxist ideology was giving way to market economics in Mozambique and elsewhere. Namibia's new constitution roughly mirrored those in the West. I prayed that the United States and its allies in the developed world would respond to this historic opportunity with gusto instead of token gestures to help make Africa finally work for all Africans.

History has taught us the hard way why it usually is prudent to temper the noun *optimism* with the adjective *cautious* when dealing with regions of the world in flux. Democracy has survived in South Africa, to be sure. Yet the appetites and needs of the people after decades of deprivation may outstrip the capacity of the government to respond. Progress in housing and education is being made with deliberate speed at best. And HIV/AIDS, hardly a blip on Africa's radar screen in 1990, subsequently ravaged the population and economies of the subcontinent, most notably in South Africa itself.

Robert Mugabe's optimistic vision for southern Africa has yielded to his desperate ambitions to cling to power in his country, regardless of the consequences for his people. Civil war, terrorism, and corruption plague other African countries. So many crippling problems! So many conflicting aspirations! Yet so much promise! Such bountiful resources!

Democracy and economic growth are taking root in sub-Saharan Africa. For far too long, the subcontinent brought up the rear among the community of nations. The exhilaration I felt upon the birth of the new South Africa persists as the continent of my ancestors steadily gains ground.

CHAPTER 15

A DREAM DEFERRED COMES TRUE

enjoyed foundation life immensely and felt no particular itch to move on. But then a job I had dreamt of my entire professional life materialized rather suddenly, if not entirely out of the blue.

In the spring of 1994, a prominent New York City attorney named Charles Hamilton called to invite me to breakfast at the Harvard Club. A longtime member of the National Urban League board, he was chairing the search committee to select a new president and CEO to replace John Jacob, who was stepping down after a dozen years in office. I wasted no time in agreeing to meet because the League is one of the most important organizations in the annals of black people and the presidency historically has been among the most coveted posts in the constellation of national African-American leadership positions.

Besides its mission and its reputation as one of America's premier black organizations, another reason I was drawn to the idea of leading the League was the stability and staying power it had exhibited over the years. Since its inception in 1910, the organization had been led by only six chief executives: George Edmund Haynes, the first African-American to receive a PhD from Columbia University, who cofounded the group with a crusading white philanthropist named Ruth Standish Baldwin; Eugene Kinckle Jones, who led the League for twenty years and who also helped found the Alpha Phi Alpha fraternity (and whose daughter roomed with my mother at Howard University); Lester Granger, who during World War II helped spearhead the integration of the military services and the defense industry; Whitney

Young, the revered former dean of the Atlanta School of Social Work who headed the League during the civil rights and black power movements in the 1960s; Vernon Jordan, the charismatic lawyer who dramatically boosted the profile of the movement; and John Jacob, a lifetime Urban Leaguer who led the organization with dignity and resolve through the difficult retrenchment years of the Reagan era.

That was really tall cotton, as old folks used to say. I yearned for the chance to join their august company.

Soon after the search got under way, I heard from Rockefeller's president, Peter Goldmark, that I was on the list of candidates. Leaving nothing to chance, I mentioned to Don Stewart, a great friend who headed the College Board at the time and who was wired into everyone, that I was eager to take a run at the position if the opportunity presented itself.

Many months then passed without further word. I put the possibility out of my mind. After all, I had learned from my painful experience at WNET not to get my hopes up. Then the call came. Although I had tried to maintain my cool about the situation, I jumped at the chance to be considered for the job.

The initial breakfast at the Harvard Club reinforced my interest. Hamilton was joined by John Gibbs, the League's consultant from the global executive search firm of Spencer Stuart. They briefed me on the position, as well as the organizational and financial challenges facing the next CEO. I listened intently, although I didn't really need much by way of background.

Then it was my turn to describe what I would bring to the enterprise and how I would approach what lay ahead. I indicated without equivocation that I was enthusiastic about the prospect of taking the helm. The more formidable the challenges, I told them, the more I relished the opportunity to tackle them—and, I told myself, the greater the chance of making a national name for myself.

At one point during breakfast, I inquired where they were in the search process. Hamilton said I was on the short list of finalists. When I asked how many others were still in the hunt, he replied tantalizingly, if opaquely, "Fewer than there are fingers on one hand." His response almost set me to hyperventilating. *Finally*, I thought, *a chance to fulfill the dream that used to rattle around in my brain driving into Manhattan and listening to* Saturday Night Fever. This was my best shot—maybe, at fifty-two, even my last shot—to dance on the big stage in a leading role.

I decided not to play coy with Charles and John about how keenly I wanted the job. When they asked whether or not I would accept if it was offered, it took me less than a moment to answer affirmatively. I trusted them to give me the straight scoop about what I'd be walking into. Since I was familiar with the history and role of the League, I did not need to perform exhaustive due diligence by talking with other people. Nor was it necessary to compile a lengthy list of pros and cons to satisfy myself that I had thought of everything. My head, heart, and gut were completely in sync.

When I got home that evening, I recounted to Marilyn what had happened and how I had told them that, if asked, I would serve. She had lived with my career choices for decades and shared my enthusiasm for the opportunity presented by the League. More cautious than I, however, she urged me not to make a hurried decision. I weighed her advice, which was always wise, but plunged ahead anyway. This could be a dream deferred come true, and I wasn't about to let it elude me.

Now that the League had initiated the courtship, I vowed to do my level best to consummate it. Having been given short shrift by WNET, I was determined to provide the search committee with the fullest possible picture of what I would bring to the position.

Charles and John started out by asking me for descriptive material on my career. In response, I sent them a lengthy letter detailing my major positions, including the scope of authority and responsibility. Enclosed with the letter were seven folders containing an assortment of my published articles, policy papers, speeches, and concept papers, along with brief histories of several key initiatives I had been instrumental in conceiving, such as the National Guard Youth ChalleNGe Corps, the Coalition of Community Foundations for Youth, and the National Commission on Teaching and America's Future.

Several days later, I submitted an even lengthier experience statement laying out what I had accomplished in my various jobs, even going back as far as law school. It also described the boards I served on and my personal interests. Finally, I supplied a list of nearly 150 professional contacts in the fields of government, philanthropy, communications, civil rights, economics, education, business, and law. My not-so-subliminal message was this: *Feel free to check me out with anyone, anywhere, and you will find that I am respected and wired, even if I'm not well known to the Urban League movement or the national news media.*

On top of these, I sent three additional memos: one on my leadership style, another on my management experience, and, lastly, a ten-page memorandum laying out my thoughts about the priorities and activities of the National Urban League, were I to be appointed president. In the latter memo, I fired every intellectual arrow in my quiver. I wrote about the social, economic, and political context in which African-Americans found ourselves, the threefold thrust that I thought should shape the work of the Urban League movement, and the specific roles of the National Urban League and its affiliate network.

This deluge clearly ran the risk of overkill. But I decided to chance it, figuring that Charles and John would read everything and hoping at least some members of the search committee would take the time to as well. I wanted it to be crystal-clear how enthusiastic I was about the presidency and how well prepared I was to take the helm. To hammer home this point, I never inquired during the courtship about compensation and benefits. It was the opportunity to serve the League I was after, not the material benefits. I subsequently learned from the chair of the board that I was the only finalist who was so single-minded, and that my solitary focus on the position instead of the perks made a favorable impression.

Then I entered a holding pattern again, awaiting further deliberations by the search committee and the final decision by the League's board of trustees. The board convened on May 23 and seemed to meet forever. As the day wore on, I sat forlornly in my office at Rockefeller, despairing that I had missed the brass ring again.

Late in the day, the phone call I had been waiting for my entire professional life finally came. I had been selected as the seventh president in the history of the National Urban League.

First, I called Marilyn, our daughters, and my mother to convey the glorious news. Then I dashed over to the board meeting and was formally introduced to the trustees. Though poker-faced customarily, I could not contain my glee about getting the job. I thought about my late father and how proud and overjoyed he would have been about my ascent to leadership of a national organization that had meant so much to our people. I also imagined how my late uncle Frank Jones would have reacted because he was major volunteer leader with the Urban League affiliate in Washington, and because he had once recommended me for the national board. Finally, my mind flashed back to that conversation with our daughter Traer in the kitchen seven years earlier, when I was in a funk after losing out on the presidency of WNET/Thirteen. This obviously was the "something more important" she predicted I was being saved for.

The next step after the board's decision was sitting for an official photograph to accompany the press release to be issued the following morning. Ironically, on the biggest day of my professional life, it was the lousiest formal picture I had ever taken. The stress, fatigue, and uncertainty of waiting it out all day showed in my face. What was worse, I had been so wrapped up in seeking the job that I had not bothered to visit a barbershop and get a proper trim in case I landed it. The combination made for a dreadful photo that was distributed nationwide to the news media and kept for future stories. What an inauspicious debut on the national stage! The shot greeted me in newspapers at every turn. Each week, it accompanied my weekly column, entitled "To Be Equal," which was syndicated nationally in black newspapers. Even the *Wall Street Journal* based a line drawing on it. Family and friends razzed me about the photo until we managed to persuade the media to use a replacement. When it comes to looks, Denzel Washington I'm not, so any improvement was most welcome.

For readers unfamiliar with the National Urban League, let me pause for a brief primer. Founded in 1910, it grew out of the Great Migration that swept the nation's cities beginning in the early twentieth century. When the League was created, ninety thousand Southern blacks had migrated to New York City, intent on escaping Jim Crow and improving their economic circumstances. Instead, they confronted a host of new urban problems, including a job market requiring sophisticated skills, deceitful employers who pushed young women into prostitution, poor health services, and overcrowded housing and schools. The League was organized to help these new arrivals overcome the problems of transitioning from rural to urban living. Black migrants faced similar problems elsewhere during the first half of the century, prompting the steady creation of Urban League affiliates in cities from coast to coast.

The primary constituency of the Urban League movement is African-Americans. Depending on local demographics, individual affiliates may also serve other groups, among them immigrants of African descent, Latinos, whites, Asian-Americans, and Native Americans. The Urban League's clientele runs the gamut from rough-hewn teenagers whom many employers won't hire to mothers eager to exit welfare, from displaced workers caught by downsizing to financially strapped senior citizens trying to supplement their Social Security checks. The heartbeat of the Urban League movement is the approximately one hundred professionally staffed affiliates, which carry out the day-to-day work of the League in cities across the country. In effect, the National Urban League is the mother ship of the movement. As such, it articulates the overall agenda and advances those goals in national policy circles and the media. The national office oversees movement-wide initiatives flowing from this agenda and sets the minimum qualifications to be an Urban League affiliate. The national office also provides technical assistance designed to help affiliates sustain themselves, reach their fullest potential, and cope with organizational challenges that occasionally crop up.

For decades, the local affiliates have operated effective job-training and placement programs aimed at helping the League's constituents earn good livelihoods that will put them on the road to self-reliance. Over the course of a quarter-century, affiliates funded through the League's Seniors in Community Service program helped retirees preserve their self-sufficiency and dignity by moving more than eleven thousand low-income seniors from subsidized to unsubsidized jobs.

Urban League affiliates have assisted ex-addicts and former inmates, the toughest sell to prospective employers, who would not hire them if they had their druthers. In the aftermath of the sweeping riots in South Central LA, the Los Angeles Urban League joined forces with Toyota to create a state-of-the-art training center to prepare local residents to work in all facets of automobile maintenance and repair. The center attracted such lavish praise that Prince Charles once toured it.

The League has a long tradition of combating housing discrimination. Over the years, providing affordable housing evolved into a programming mainstay. For instance, the Urban League of Greater Phoenix owned hundreds of units of rental housing at the turn of the twenty-first century and had ambitious plans to construct hundreds more. In the spirit of helping black families build nest eggs through home ownership, many local affiliates have helped first-time homebuyers shore up their credit ratings, understand the economics of home ownership, and secure mortgages.

Jobs and housing are longstanding program staples of the Urban League movement. Less pervasive but no less important has been the aid that a number of affiliates offer to entrepreneurs starting up businesses. Affiliate CEOs have used their clout to advocate for the inclusion of minority businesses in major local economic development initiatives such as airports, convention centers, and downtown revitalization projects.

In addition to providing direct services, the Urban League has long been a leading civil rights advocate on the national and local scenes. It has spearheaded voter registration and turnout drives, fought efforts to roll back the Voting Rights Act, and provided high-profile national and local leadership in combating police abuse of deadly force, racial profiling, and stop-and-frisk practices. The League advocates vigorously for equal educational opportunity, quality schools, and accountability. Throughout its history, the National Urban League and its affiliates have brought vigorous and principled advocacy, research, and policy analysis to bear on the primary problems confronting African-Americans, other minorities, and the poor in America. To my mind, what distinguishes it from other civil rights organizations is that the Urban League is the oldest and largest community-based movement devoted to empowering African-Americans to enter the economic and social mainstream.

Ill-informed critics occasionally accuse the Urban League of being a middle-class organization. The truth is that the movement focuses on equipping its constituents to enter the middle class. The League primarily serves low-income and working people who are striving day in and day out to improve their lives and gain entry to the economic mainstream. To a lesser degree, the League helps those who have already "made it" consolidate their gains, rise to higher plateaus of success, and, in the case of entrepreneurs, create economic institutions that generate jobs and wealth. Therefore, if helping low-income and working-class folk climb into the middle class equates with being a middle-class organization, I reckon Urban Leaguers would plead guilty as charged—and with gusto.

Within weeks of being appointed but before actually taking office, I embarked on a taxing, yet invaluable, get-acquainted tour of Urban League affiliates led by longtime veterans of the movement. One CEO I visited was Herman Ewing, the passionate, if prickly, head of the Memphis Urban League. During our conversation, I inquired what he thought the essential role of the Urban League was. In spare but eloquent prose, he said, "Our job is to help dependent people become independent." His succinct mission statement encapsulated the essence of the League's approach.

CHAPTER 16

TAKING THE REINS IN CONTENTIOUS TIMES

V enerable African-American organizations such as the National Urban League faced a complex political climate and a down-right hostile public policy environment when I took the helm in mid-1994. Some skeptics in the mid-1990s questioned the continued relevance of the League, as well as my suitability for the position of CEO. As an attorney and activist in the Northern antipoverty crusade, I was not well known to veteran leaders of the civil rights movement, based principally in the South. The perceived dichotomy between the two causes puzzled me because, as a direct-services organization spawned by the Great Migration, the Urban League, at least locally, tended primarily to the food, clothing, shelter, educational, and em-ployment needs of black people who lived above as well as below the Mason-Dixon line.

One particularly galling article that greeted my appointment was a cover story in *Emerge* magazine, the black community's equivalent of *Time* or *Newsweek* in those days. Its title was, "Is the National Urban League Dead?" As an alumnus of the *New York Times*, I understood that the press played by its own rules. Yet even in writing editorials articulating a distinct point of view, I customarily spoke to key players and knowledgeable observers in order to gain their perspective and present a full picture before reaching a conclusion. I felt blindsided in this case because the author never called to discuss my aspirations for the Urban League and the overall civil rights movement, let alone the qualifications and experience I felt I brought to both. The *Emerge* article made me all the more determined to prove that the League was indeed robust and relevant, and that I was right for the job.

The liberal tilt in federal legislative policy that the National Urban League and other civil rights groups traditionally supported was an anachronism by the mid-1990s. It was true that a Democrat, Bill Clinton, occupied the White House. The U.S. economy boomed on his watch, and black people unquestionably benefited with rising wages and lowered jobless rates. African-Americans haven't had it nearly as good economically since he left office.

Yet Bill Clinton proudly characterized himself as a "New Democrat" who espoused a "third way," whatever that meant. His agenda often mystified and troubled civil rights leaders. Once elected, the avowedly centrist president eschewed proclaiming an overtly "black" agenda, even an avowedly "urban" one. He joined with the Republicans who took over Congress in 1994 in "ending welfare as we know it" by imposing strict time limits on the receipt of public assistance. He never mounted a determined effort to improve the achievement levels of low-income and minority schoolchildren.

What's more, President Clinton waged an aggressive war against crime, which admittedly was wreaking havoc on black and inner-city communities. He supported tougher prison sentences and treating crack offenses more harshly than cocaine possession. States eagerly embraced tougher sentencing policies as well. These anticrime policies precipitated an alarming spike in black incarceration rates—especially among males—that persisted until recently, when the moral outrage, fundamental unfairness, and staggering cost combined to trigger a broad bipartisan pushback against mass incarceration.

To Clinton's credit, one of his closest outside advisers was Vernon Jordan, my National Urban League predecessor once removed. Plus, he appointed highly respected African-Americans including Ron Brown (another renowned National Urban League alumnus) and Rodney Slater to his cabinet and savvy political operatives such as Alexis Herman and Donna Brazile to senior posts on his White House team. But even though Clinton knew all the stanzas of "Lift Every Voice and Sing," liberal black leaders were not sure he was a "soul brother" ideologically.

To be fair, the president was obliged to expend considerable political capital on fending off the far right of the Republican Party, who were hell-bent on embarrassing him personally, crippling him politically, and impeaching him if possible, all the while aiming to radically reshape the policy landscape in this country. The GOP shocked the Democrats by seizing control of the House of Representatives in the fall of 1994 and proclaiming a new Contract with America as its legislative agenda. The National Urban League embraced nary one provision of the contract. Clearly, we were swimming upstream legislatively in Washington.

On another front, conservatives pursued a relentless and well-financed assault on affirmative action in college admissions and employment, a sacred cow in the eyes of civil rights groups. Opponents launched an endless salvo of hostile lawsuits, ballot initiatives, books, Op-Ed articles, radio commentaries, and TV diatribes. Every month, it seemed, conservative think tanks and publishers issued a new screed attacking the moral and constitutional basis of affirmative action, not to mention its effectiveness and fundamental fairness in a supposedly color-blind society. Conservatives trotted out angry whites as the symbolic victims of affirmative action. This battle became the policy wonks' equivalent of nuclear war.

President Bill Clinton at the National Urban League conference in 1997
National Urban League Archives

What's more, the black community was coping with the residue of the scorched-earth confirmation hearings for Clarence Thomas, the Rodney King beating, the Tawana Brawley scandal, and the O. J. Simpson trial. The media transformed each of these heart-wrenching episodes into metaphors for the African-American experience. The uproar put black leaders on the defensive as we endeavored to explain, for instance, why it wasn't right for cops to bludgeon Rodney King, even though he was a ne'er-do-well. As we worked to persuade politicians and the media that the criminal justice system really did discriminate against blacks, whether or not one thought justice was served in the O. J. case. As we tried to show why the Clarence Thomas/Anita Hill showdown may have been riveting soap opera but hardly typified relations between bosses and subordinates among blacks—or anyone else, for that matter.

Then there was the high-profile acrimony between blacks and Jews, who quite understandably were affronted by the inflammatory rhetoric of Nation of Islam minister Louis Farrakhan. It dominated the headlines, the editorial and Op-Ed pages, and the talk shows on radio and TV. Vitriol poured out from all sides and poisoned relations between these venerable allies in the civil rights cause.

The headline-grabbing controversies became prisms through which African-Americans were judged. They grossly distorted our reality and our contributions. Black organizations in 1994 when I took over the League struggled to get their bearings. The League's older sibling in the civil rights movement, the NAACP, was wrestling with financial problems and staff turmoil that the news media occasionally covered. Meanwhile, the National Urban League I inherited confronted transitional issues of our own. The press paid less attention to ours, which was fine by me because the lowered profile made it easier to reengineer the organization for the challenges that lay ahead.

The first orders of business were gathering a team of strong senior executives and preparing for the National Urban League's annual conference in Indianapolis, barely three weeks after I became president. Not unexpectedly, it took a little while to assemble the caliber of leadership team I wanted. Fortunately, I inherited a number of strong administrators and program managers who were a blend of savvy Urban League "lifers" and rising young stars. I also recruited talented new colleagues including Milton Little as executive vice president and chief operating officer, Gasby Greely as senior VP for communications,

Paul Wycisk as senior VP and chief financial officer, and Gena Davis-Watkins as VP for development.

The briefing visits and conversations with a broad cross-section of Urban Leaguers and outsiders enabled me to try out the programmatic priority I intended to champion as president—namely, the need for the Urban League movement to place heightened emphasis on the academic and social development of black youngsters.

The annual conference served as my coming-out party, where I met the movement's leaders from across the country. My keynote address would introduce me, along with my ideas and agenda, to a live audience of three thousand Urban Leaguers and who knew how many representatives of the news media, along with their print and broadcast audiences. As a newcomer to the national leadership stage, I had no inkling what kind of press coverage my address would generate. Our communications team worked assiduously to gin up coverage. We counted on reaching a national audience via C-SPAN but were not confident about other broadcast outlets and newspapers.

I would be less than candid if I didn't confess that, gearing up for that first conference, I was somewhat spooked by the ghost of Whitney Young and the living specters of Vernon Jordan and John "Jake" Jacob, former CEOs of the National Urban League. All three were towering figures in the movement and revered by many contemporary Urban Leaguers. As the former dean of the Atlanta School of Social Work, Whitney had trained many of the old-timers and brought them into the Urban League movement. The charismatic Vernon still cut a dashing figure on the national scene as Bill Clinton's highly publicized "best buddy" and as a fixture on the society pages of the *New York Times* and the *Washington Post*. Jake, a beloved lifer in the League, had steered the movement through perilous times politically and fiscally.

If this weren't pressure enough, it was hardly a secret that I'm no preacher, but merely a lapsed Unitarian not noted for emotionalism or histrionics. Therefore, a fire-and-brimstone keynote address simply wasn't in the cards. I would have made a mess of it had I tried. My forte was laying out facts, insights, and analysis, hopefully in an engrossing fashion, and then advocating concrete actions listeners could take to make conditions better. That was my style. The challenge was to become the best I could be at being me.

Throughout my career prior to the League, I wrote every speech I ever delivered. Never needed a speechwriter, never could afford one, and never wanted one, even if my organization could have afforded it. So, as was customary, I set about writing the keynote address myself. The League employed a veteran speechwriter when I joined. He was a terrific fellow and a graceful writer. But there was no way he could crawl inside my brain to figure out what I wanted to say. I eliminated the position and bought a laptop computer. This saved us some money and liberated me to write my own speeches, along with many of the League's subsequent position papers and Op-Ed articles.

Many friends marveled that I found the time and had the appetite to do all this writing, in addition to running the organization. I insisted because it compelled me to keep reading and reflecting on the issues faced by the Urban League movement and its constituents. Besides, I had never been comfortable speaking off the top of my head. Since I wasn't a stemwinding speaker, my speeches tilted heavily toward content. I punctuated them with lessons, quotations, and statistics from books and articles I had read. This kept me current. Plus, I did it to signal, however subliminally, to leaders of our movement that they, too, should stay up to speed on issues and research that affected our work.

I had given many a speech in my day and was reasonably confident in my ability to handle encounters with the media. Even so, Gasby Greely persuaded me to undergo media training, since I would be diving into the deep end of the pool, delivering speeches before thousands of people and being interviewed by seasoned, tough-minded members of the press corps. I questioned whether or not this was necessary but grudgingly agreed.

Were my colleagues ever right! I learned to use a teleprompter and rehearsed my speech, both of which were novel experiences for me. We practiced pauses, emphases, and pacing, all of which helped inject more energy into my delivery. Familiarity with the teleprompter liberated me to improvise, exhort, and gesticulate, if not quite preach. I increased eye contact with the audience and fed off the interaction.

In preparation for media interviews, I tried to overcome my propensity for verbose responses and struggled to learn to speak in sound bites. I also learned the laws of survival of canny politicians: *Going into an interview, decide what you are prepared to discuss and what you're not. Be wary of drifting into traps because you are infatuated with the sound of your voice or convinced of your powers of persuasion.* The media training fortified me for the grueling, yet energizing, communications challenges that lay ahead.

For the first year or two, I wrote every word I planned to say. The speeches were complete texts. This produced an unexpected bonus because newspapers occasionally ran them as Op-Ed articles or features, which was another way of extending their reach. What's more, the League published a compilation of them in a book entitled *Destination: The American Dream.*

But it eventually got dull—for listeners and for me—delivering these addresses with my eyes mostly glued to the page. In fact, just prior to my mounting the stage to deliver a written speech on one occasion, someone commented that it must be boring to deliver more or less the same prepared speech over and over. I assured him it wasn't. Then, as I droned on, I thought how stultifying it had become for me. That wasn't a helpful thought to have washing through my brain mid-speech because it showed.

Searching for a solution to my dilemma, I asked a cousin who once danced on Broadway in *The Lion King* and *Jelly's Last Jam* how she stayed interested in performing the same role night after night. She told me she injected an element of risk by improvising, doing roughly the same thing differently, instead of identically, every night.

I switched to circling key words and telling sequential stories that made my point, instead of strictly following the script. Using her simple tip made for livelier speeches that I enjoyed delivering repeatedly. There was a downside, though. An outline of key words was not publishable. So if a newspaper expressed interest, I ended up having to write out the entire speech after all. The extra work was a small price to pay for extended coverage.

In view of the fact that few of my speeches would make an oratorical highlight reel, I hoped the messages, insights, and strategies I espoused would have an afterlife. Often, I spotted people in the audience actually scribbling notes on program books or even napkins. Although they might not have been turned on by the preacher, they clearly were tuned into what I was preaching. This was gratification aplenty for me.

CHAPTER 17

MY SPEECH MAKES A SPLASH

Sunday, July 24, 1994, marked my debut on the national stage as the head of the National Urban League. In those days, the annual conference convened on Sunday evening with the president's keynote address as the featured attraction.

I began the keynote with a brief autobiographical sketch, harking back to my mother's activism in voting rights and school desegregation and describing the arc of my own career. The self-evident purpose was to acquaint the audience with my background. My subtler goal was to make the point that while I wasn't a veteran of the traditional civil rights movement, my family and I had for generations been active in our people's quest for freedom, equality, justice, and opportunity.

Then I segued to an analysis of the changing and challenging seas that African-Americans must be prepared to navigate. I noted that communism had crumbled and market economics reigned supreme, while immigrants and refugees streamed almost unchecked across national borders. To underscore my point in citing these phenomena, I warned, "This ruthlessly competitive world waits for no nation, no ethnic group and no individual. Should any competitor falter, there is always an emerging country, an enterprising people or an eager immigrant waiting in the wings or, more likely, already seizing the opportunity to fill the void. Technological change, rightsizing, industrial outmigration and structural unemployment are now familiar phrases throughout the developed world."

What no one had foreseen when the Supreme Court outlawed school segregation back in 1954, I continued, was that the manufacturing jobs that once enabled blue-collar workers to support their families and purchase their own homes would all but vanish from America's inner cities. The service jobs that often replaced them paid so miserably that the full-time employees who held them could not work their way out of poverty.

I recited these global and domestic trends because it was essential for black folk to place our circumstances in a larger context. Yes, racism was still abroad in the land. While it may have become subtler and somewhat less pervasive, it remained an undeniable reality in employment, housing, lending, and the like. Even so, I cautioned, "we must not let ourselves and, especially, our children fall into the paranoid trap of thinking that racism accounts for all that plagues us." The global realignment of work and wealth was, if anything, the bigger culprit.

Clearly, the civil rights movement had succeeded in placing those of us with solid educations, ample family support, personal drive, and a healthy dose of luck on the up escalator economically. Yet I reminded the audience that millions of our people remained stuck on the down escalator, headed nowhere. "Their dire circumstances must dwell in our consciences because of the tragic loss of human potential and the mounting drain on societal resources and compassion. It is the fate of those in greatest need that must be the primary focus of the Urban League movement."

Having set my overarching agenda for the movement, I then proposed three areas of concentration: (1) strengthening the education and development of our children in the inner city so they would have the academic and social skills to be successful; (2) enabling their families to become economically self-reliant; and (3) encouraging racial inclusion so our people could participate fully in mainstream society.

I argued that it would take concerted outside pressure from parents and community groups to prevail upon school systems to improve the education of inner-city children. I told the audience that I envisioned the Urban League mobilizing and equipping parents and community leaders to become sophisticated and insistent consumers of education for their children.

I continued that we also had to focus on what happened after school, when the social development of youngsters often occurred. When their values were shaped. When they learned to collaborate with others in teams. Yet this developmental infrastructure had atrophied because many parents had to work multiple jobs, school systems were too strapped financially to provide a rich array of extracurricular activities, settlement houses and youth services agencies were underfunded, and municipal parks-and-recreation departments were a shadow programmatically of their former selves.

I commented that inner-city gangs were omnipresent and preyed upon aimless young people who were eager to belong to something, anything. Politicians talked incessantly about taking back the streets from criminals. I told the audience that we should "take back our children from the streets and from the gangs, and the streets will take care of themselves."

I turned next to the second focus area—economic self-sufficiency for poor families. To break the cycle of neighborhood decay, despair, family breakup, and escalating violent crime, I argued, we had to go back to the source of the problem—namely, the growing inability of inner-city adults to find jobs that enabled their families to live in dignity with a decent standard of living.

Many politicians and economists, I observed, were in denial about the depth of this problem. Some blamed its victims, saying they didn't want to work, despite convincing evidence to the contrary. Others said high unemployment and low wages for low-skilled workers were the natural order of things in modern market economies, and that government ought not interfere. Still others argued there would be a happy ending when technology eventually replaced the vanished jobs with more highly skilled and highly paid new ones. I took sharp issue with these analyses. None of these scenarios held out much hope for inner-city people trapped in poverty because it was unrealistic to expect all of them to upgrade themselves overnight from laborers and welfare recipients to office workers and small entrepreneurs.

I went on to argue that traditional approaches such as providing job training, improving education, and encouraging entrepreneurship might not be enough to ensure employment for everyone who needed jobs. There was no alternative to government action if legitimate work was again to become the prevailing way of life in poor neighborhoods. I called upon government to create a new labor-intensive public enterprise to modernize the nation's infrastructure and perform other services valued by taxpayers. While the prevailing wisdom was that the private sector should create jobs, government had to step in when the private labor market came up short.

This brought me to my third and final focus area—helping our racially diverse society work more harmoniously. For all our suffering, I continued, we must not become so fixated on our problems that we ignored our commonality of interest with others. The problems that afflicted us, from inadequate schooling and alienated youngsters to chronic unemployment, cut across racial lines. If we were ever to deal with them on a scale remotely equal to their size, we must coalesce with people of other complexions who felt the same pain.

I then waded into the eye of the raging storm over black-Jewish relations. Many whites of good will had accompanied us on our long journey for racial, social, and economic justice. None had matched the Jewish community as long-distance runners in the civil rights movement. Just as we denounced misleading media stereotypes of African-Americans, it was morally repugnant to impugn an entire people, especially longstanding allies such as Jews, because of the unconscionable behavior of some of them. With our annual conference in 1994 coming on the heels of the birth of the new post-apartheid South Africa, I added, "If Nelson Mandela and F. W. de Klerk can bury the hatchets of hatred and oppression in the sand, instead of one another's heads, and get on with South Africa's future, then surely so can we."

Yet I also took issue with those who urged us to eschew any contact with Minister Farrakhan. Serious-minded African-Americans must be free to discuss the acute pain afflicting our community, I observed, even if that meant conferring with those with whom we vehemently disagreed on other issues. The time-honored role of the Urban League, I reminded the audience, was to build bridges not just between poverty and plenty but between peoples of all races and persuasions.

I concluded the keynote address by observing that the social compact between society and the individual needed strengthening on both sides. One side defined what people owed society—personal responsibility, the nurturing of children, the supporting of themselves and their families, and abiding by laws. The other side defined what society owed its citizens—the opportunity to be self-reliant and protection from anarchy at home and invasion from abroad. In recent decades, I said, important elements of both sides of the social compact had eroded due to the profound economic changes sweeping the developed world, including our own country.

We of the Urban League, I said, must work with our own in restoring personal responsibility and taking family obligations, child rearing, education, self-reliance, and citizenship seriously. But society must update and then uphold its end of the bargain. What use was talk of opportunity when poor people saw so little of it? The social compact must be revised so that self-reliance, with dignity and a decent standard of living, was an everyday reality instead of empty rhetoric.

The deluge of media coverage following my address astonished me. The only downer was that my father had not lived to share this experience and savor the coverage. He would have rocketed into orbit when he saw the interviews and articles.

The media attention began before I actually delivered the speech. We fed an advance copy to the *New York Times* in the hope that if it paid attention, other media might as well. On the morning of my speech, the *Sunday Times* ran a front-page article, written by Steven Holmes, headlined, "A Rights Leader Minimizes Racism as a Poverty Factor." The title was accompanied by two sub-headlines: "Cites New

Vice President Al Gore at the National Urban League conference in 1999
Official White House Photo

Economy as 'the Bigger Culprit' " and "The new head of the Urban League charts a course all his own."

Holmes wrote that, in tone and content, my speech marked a sharp distinction from other civil rights leaders. He cited my emphasis on racial inclusion, in contrast to the distance that other black leaders kept from whites. He also noted my focus on aiding the inner-city poor and the scarcity of my references to goals of primary interest to the black middle class. While I might have quibbled with the headline writer's use of "minimizes," the placement, length, and content of the article were truly thrilling.

The *Times* article probably tipped other media outlets that my speech later in the day would be worth covering. C-SPAN broadcast it live and repeated it for weeks on end.

The following morning, I was interviewed on NBC's *Today* show by Bryant Gumbel, who was known as a tough questioner. After a night of revelry, I faced an unconscionable wake-up call at four in the morning in order to appear on an early segment of the program. Since I'm not a coffee drinker, adrenaline kept my mind and body on edge. I summoned all of the media training I could remember. As best I recall, I was coherent and the interview went fine, although I vowed not to burn the candle at both ends in the future.

The *Wall Street Journal* weighed in a couple of days later with a major article entitled, "New Chief of Urban League Outlines Ambitious but Practical Plan for Cities."

Nationally syndicated columnists commented extensively on the speech as well. Within days, Bob Herbert of the *New York Times* wrote a column entitled, "Blacks' Problems, Seen Plain: Hugh Price of the National Urban League tells the truth, courageous and unadorned." He opened his column by saying, "The speech was delivered in Indianapolis without a lot of flamboyant rhetoric. It spoke the truth, unadorned, without crude appeals to prejudice. It was courageous, intelligent and important." Herbert continued, "In the overheated, oppressive, finger-pointing atmosphere in which much of our racial discourse is conducted, Mr. Price's speech was a welcome breeze. He was direct and unapologetic in his opposition to racism of any kind and to the fantasy of black separatism."

As Herbert noted, the essence of the speech was my recognition that the catastrophic circumstances enveloping so many African-Americans were in large part the result of changed economic conditions that were having a devastating effect on many whites as well. Blacks, possessing the least in the way of resources, were being hammered the worst, but no ethnic group was spared. Herbert concluded his column by writing,

> Hugh Price is of one of many African-Americans throughout the country who have long since rolled up their sleeves and gone to work in a serious way on what has become a hideous array of social and economic problems. They have the talent and the will to succeed but not nearly enough support. Needless to say, they don't get the same attention as Jew-baiters and celebrities in handcuffs. But they are the true leaders. They are the ones who will make things better for future generations.

William Raspberry, nationally syndicated columnist with the *Washington Post*, devoted two consecutive columns to my speech during the week after I delivered it. The first, published on Wednesday, July 27, was titled, "The Urban League Action Plan." He wrote,

> People who believe a problem can be solved tend to get busy solving it. Doubters spend their time making sure everybody knows it's someone else's fault. Hugh B. Price is a believer. The new president of the National Urban League used his keynote address . . . to take on some of the toughest problems facing black America—not to distribute blame but to talk, in plain language, about possible solutions.

Raspberry went on:

> It was an extraordinary speech, with food for virtually every mainstream philosophy: a little demand and a little self-blame, a little long-term development and a little here-and-now realism, a little integration and a little racial self-sufficiency, a little capitalism and a little economic planning.
>
> But for me, the heart of his remarks was his call upon black Americans to get busy on the problems nearest at hand: the rescue of our children, the restoration of our families and an end to our economic and social marginalization.

He wrapped up the first column this way:

> If you haven't been paying close attention, much of what Hugh Price said in that speech will sound fairly routine. It isn't. The current civil rights emphasis on racism has the ring of militancy, but offers

no solutions to the deadly problems infecting black communities. In many cases it is just another way of saying, "It's not my fault."

Hugh Price, who understands the futility of scapegoating, is giving white people something to do. That's smart. He's also giving me—a decently paid, seriously concerned member of the black middle class— something to do. That's *genius*.

Raspberry's second column concentrated on my analysis of the chronic employment woes of the underclass in inner cities. He was taken by my argument that the private job market appeared not to be up to the task of providing decent-paying jobs, and that government had to step in to provide work on public infrastructure projects:

> That was the point Hugh B. Price made in his remarkable maiden speech as president of the National Urban League. In case you were distracted by Price's warning that African Americans avoid "the para-noid trap of thinking that racism accounts for all that plagues us," or by his gutsy rebuke of Louis Farrakhan for his antisemitism, here's what else he had to say in that Indianapolis speech.

After quoting extensively from my speech and offering his analysis of the idea of creating labor-intensive infrastructure jobs, Raspberry concluded that "the specifics of the idea sketched by the Urban League chief ought to become the subject of serious debate in America. But on his general notion, I'm tempted to say: Price is right."

E. J. Dionne Jr., another syndicated columnist with the *Washington Post*, focused on my remarks about black-Jewish relations in a column titled, "Hugh Price's Radical Alternative to Farrakhan." He began by saying,

> It's easy to sound radical. Bluster, hatred and accusation usually do the trick. But messages cast in these terms are usually not radical at all. They don't challenge anybody to do anything except smolder in resentment. They don't lead to change. By contrast, ideas built on cool reason and the possibility of action often sound moderate. But they can be genuinely radical in their analysis of what's wrong and of what needs to be done.

Dionne went on:

> That is . . . what lies behind the important speech given on Sunday by Hugh Price, the new president of the Urban League, at the group's

Indianapolis convention. Price's address will rightly get a lot of praise for his denunciation of antisemitism, his call for cooperation across racial lines and his insistence that while racism remains an important problem, it cannot explain all that ails the African American community.

Dionne then turned to the heart of his commentary:

> But if the praise stops there, it will miss a central point of Price's speech and the genuinely radical message that underlies it. Price is challenging complacency by arguing that there is a deep disorder in the American economy that is leading it to fail a large class of Americans—including many African Americans but also many others. Price argues that "the global realignment of work and wealth" is a "bigger culprit" than racism.

He continued by remarking that I offered the unfashionable but compelling view that if a lack of jobs was the problem, the government should consider creating "a new, labor-intensive public enterprise to perform services valued by the taxpayers." He added, "To his great credit, Price is throwing down the gauntlet to both black separatism and white indifference. That takes courage, because neither side will really want to listen to all that he's saying."

Dionne dove even deeper into my speech with this observation:

> The real challenge to the way the system works comes from Price. On behalf of the poor and the unemployed of all races, he is asking for much farther-reaching change. That's what white Americans who may be cheering Price need to bear in mind. His is not a soft multiracialism, but a hard challenge. He is challenging well-off white Americans to make changes in an economy that is working well for them [but] is not working well for everybody. He is challenging well-off African Americans to a new engagement with the children of the inner city. He is challenging less affluent whites to see that the workings of the new economy give them a powerful shared interest with African Americans in social justice. And he is challenging the African American poor to fight the culture of violence and despair.

Not surprisingly, the speech attracted favorable coverage in Jewish newspapers such as *Forward* and publications served by the Jewish Telegraphic Agency. Thanks to syndicated news services including UPI and the Associated Press, significant articles about the speech appeared in newspapers across the country. Local columnists devoted their space to applauding or criticizing the speech. Many newspapers editorialized about it as well. For instance:

- *San Diego Union-Tribune*—"Self-Help for blacks: Urban League president reveals fresh thinking"
- *Ledger-Enquirer* (Columbus, Ga.)—"Urban League's chief hits all the right notes"
- *Los Angeles Times*—"Why the Price is Right"
- *Detroit Free Press*—"Urban League: Price offers a challenging vision in civil rights fight"
- *Charlotte Observer*—"Revive the compact: It is not just his members who should respond to Urban League chief's focus on children, jobs and racial harmony"
- *Fresno Bee*—"Hugh Price's Message: The new president of the National Urban League has a perspective that's both sensible and refreshing"

Some coverage came in an unexpected form. Several newspapers ran sizable excerpts from the speech without our even submitting it for their consideration. For example, the *Boston Globe* titled its excerpt, "Revising the social compact: The new head of the Urban League urges a new way of looking at our society."

Clarence Page, a nationally syndicated columnist for the *Chicago Tribune*, weighed in with a column entitled, "'Self help' signal at the Urban League." According to Page, "Mr. Price offered a strikingly clear answer to the question that Martin Luther King asked just before he died . . . : Where do we go from here?" Page continued, "By declaring racism to be something less than the worst problem facing African-Americans today, Mr. Price has been viewed with alarm, dismay, anger and skepticism simply for acknowledging what most black people know is true: that white racism is still our enemy, but that it is not always our worst enemy."

Page wrote that he had expected to hear some friends and colleagues accuse me of selling out, and that they had not disappointed him. He noted, "One close friend and colleague fumed that Mr. Price was serving 'ammunition to the enemy,' as if our enemies don't already know what's going on."

I could not predict where the flak would come from, but I fully expected some. Since I was knowingly wading into a contest of ideas and agendas, I did not take criticism of the speech personally.

DeWayne Wickham, a nationally syndicated columnist with *USA Today* whom I respected, took sharp issue with my speech in a column entitled, "Racism, not economics, top problem for blacks: New Urban League president is wrong and the statistics prove it." He wrote, "When it comes to things that [matter to] all African-Americans, Hugh Price thinks 'the global realignment of work and wealth' is a bigger culprit than racism. He's wrong. But Price, the new president of the National Urban League, can be forgiven for not knowing better. He comes to his job with an apparently good heart but no prior experience in the civil rights arena."

Wickham continued by arguing that my words gave absolution to bigots. He cited the stark and persistent disparities between blacks and whites in earnings, employment rates, home ownership, and net worth. Wickham closed by noting my promise to make the Urban League a force to be reckoned with. "That's a tall order," he wrote, before charging that the League had been absent from the civil rights struggle in recent years: "Rebuilding respect for the National Urban League within the civil rights community won't be easy. The organization must return to the battlefield it largely deserted after the death of Whitney Young. But first it's got to correctly identify the enemies we face."

Noted writer Joe Klein devoted his lengthy "Public Lives" column in the August 15 issue of *Newsweek* to my speech. The title—"A Tale of Two Cities: The problem isn't the absence of jobs, but the culture of poverty"—signaled his disagreement with much of my speech. He began by calling it solemn and honorable and praising me for telling some uncomfortable truths. Yet he took issue with my assertion that the paucity of jobs was the main problem in the inner city. Klein cited approvingly the observation of a sociologist about the pre-gentrified inner-city neighborhood of Fort Greene in Brooklyn—namely, that it was unlikely new jobs in such neighborhoods would go to local residents. "The people . . . are so isolated from the world of work, they don't know how to go about finding jobs," commented Jan Rosenberg of Long Island University in the column. Residents of poor neighborhoods were thus assumed to be unreliable. Klein argued,

The problem in the Fort Greene projects isn't the absence of jobs. It's the culture of poverty. It's the pattern of dependent, irresponsible, antisocial behavior that has its roots in the perverse incentives of the welfare system and the legacy of white racism, and the general, societal obsession with sex, materialism and violence and—yes—the departure of manufacturing jobs as well. It is complex and virulent; it has proved intractable.

Klein also criticized my proposal to mobilize the black middle class and provide after-school mentors. "All this may help," he wrote, "but mentors are not parents, and the absence of responsible parents, especially fathers, is the phenomenon at the heart of underclass poverty." Klein closed with some kind words, even as he criticized what he deemed the inaccuracy of my analysis and the inadequacy of my proposals:

> Hugh Price has made a start. His message overwhelms the despicable blather that has passed for leadership in the recent past. It doesn't reinforce hopelessness by suggesting that white racism is insurmountable—that no progress has, or can be, made. But it doesn't quite face the problem squarely, either: this isn't a poverty that will be cured merely by jobs or with surrogates. The children of the cities need parents.

Who could disagree with his final assertion? I opted not to play ping-pong with my critics by responding with letters explaining to Wickham, for example, that my views had been shaped by my experience on the ground in the Northern antipoverty movement, which focused mainly on black people. Or by asking Klein where on earth the parents were supposed to come from in neighborhoods bereft of both livelihoods and economically self-sufficient adults who were willing to form families and nurture their children. Mentors helped supplement, and in many cases substituted for, parents who were missing in action.

There weren't then—and still aren't—any facile solutions to these intractable problems. So I took comfort in an adage I learned in law school: "Reasonable people can differ."

Once the flood of follow-up interviews subsided, I climbed back down from the ego mountaintop and got to work on implementing the agenda I had optimistically and brashly articulated.

Writing this chapter prompted me to read the keynote speech for the first time in more than a decade. Like movies from another era, some speeches age gracefully, while others seem dated. I do not claim to be prescient. But I can say with a clear conscience that many of the themes I addressed in Indianapolis nearly a quarter-century ago resonate to this day. When it comes to overcoming racism and propelling black people into the social and economic mainstream, America remains a work in progress.

CHAPTER 18

SPREADING THE GOSPEL
OF ACHIEVEMENT

My inaugural keynote address signaled that the academic and social development of black youngsters would be the primary area where I hoped to make a mark on the Urban League movement and our community.

As soon as the annual conference ended, we went at the youth development issue with gusto. The passionate belief in its importance that I had cultivated in law school never subsided. The strategy we pursued was also shaped by my experience in the early 1990s as president of an African-American business and professional men's organization known as the Westchester Clubmen, located in the Westchester County suburbs north of New York City.

After years of supporting tutorial and scholarship programs for college-bound students, the club members were casting about for a way to help teenage boys struggling in school. We wanted to focus on youngsters who, given their current trajectory, were unlikely to do well enough in school to qualify for college or land a good job.

Initially, some of our members wanted the Westchester Clubmen themselves to serve as mentors. Citing my experience back in law school, I persuaded my colleagues instead to put up the money to hire youth workers and tutors who could be there with the boys five days a week after school. This would ensure that we met our commitment to the kids and minimized the risk of disappointing them because of conflicts in our schedules. The members could drop by the program from time to time and take them on excursions to museums and science parks.

The Westchester Clubmen's program, aptly known these days as "Higher Aims," was launched in 1992 and is still going strong. The last time I checked, three-quarters of the boys served had gone on to post-secondary education. What's more, the academic average for boys in the program was a solid B, one-third of them had made the honor roll, and some actually tutored other participants.

Over Memorial Day weekend some years ago, a woman approached me in a Barnes & Noble bookstore. She introduced herself as the mother of one of the original members of Higher Aims. I recalled that when I first got to know her son, he was bored to tears with school and seemed mildly belligerent. At one of our earliest encounters, he slouched, seemingly half-asleep, on the table where we sat. When I inquired how school was going, he mumbled a disinterested response. I pressed and asked what he was currently working on. He mentioned something about writing an editorial. When I told him I was once an editorial writer for the *New York Times*, one of his nearly closed eyes popped open. He rose in his chair and began to engage. Next thing I knew, he was talking energetically about his editorial topic, how the piece might flow, and what bottom-line position he planned to take.

Clearly, he was a bright young man. By engaging him and respecting his intelligence, I had uncorked his curiosity about what had struck him as a dreary school assignment, and for which he undoubtedly would have earned an equally dreary grade.

The young man's mother proudly told me he had just finished his third year of college and planned to become a physical therapist. Two years later, I ran into his teacher at a social event. She updated me with the news that he had completed his BA and was intent on securing a master's degree.

At a fundraising event in June 2004, the Westchester Clubmen honored this young man. He had shot up from a slender preadolescent boy of middling height to a strapping young man who towered over me and probably outweighed me by twenty pounds. In his acceptance remarks, he recounted the struggles that had nearly knocked him off course, including the loss of two buddies to a fatal auto accident and the killing of another close friend. Yet this resilient young man pressed forward and prevailed.

Children have so much talent and potential, if only we will invest in teasing it out of them. Such young people stand as affirmation of the fact that African-American boys can succeed academically when given encouragement, moral support, and the right dose of academic and social-emotional reinforcement. Their success is also a testament to the tremendous impact villagers who have made it can have on young people who wonder if they ever will.

Around the time we launched the League's youth development initiative, after-school programs were routinely derided in Congress as worthless expenditures of public money. I gave speeches all over the country citing the emerging evidence to the contrary. I questioned why politicians disparaged such programs for inner-city youngsters, while well-to-do suburban parents paid a small fortune to enroll their children in extracurricular clubs, after-school classes, and summer camps.

The League forged an alliance with the Advertising Council to mount a public service announcement (PSA) campaign on television and in print whose catch phrase was, "It's Time to Beat the Streets." It drummed home our message that youth development worked. In a major legislative victory, President Clinton and Congress appropriated federal funding for youth development programs. After-school programs had finally arrived inside the Washington Beltway.

Once the PSA campaign got rolling, we segued to a sharper, more aggressive focus on boosting the academic achievement of black youngsters. For years, the national office and affiliates had operated effective projects in this field such as alternative schools for pregnant teens and tutorial and scholarship programs for the college bound. The League had probably even spawned the first generation of urban charter schools a couple of decades earlier when it created street academies for youngsters who were not faring well in traditional schools. These programs benefited countless young people. Yet we were not throwing our full arsenal of capabilities—policy analysis, advocacy, community mobilization—at the challenge.

This arena struck me as ripe for the Urban League. By the mid-1990s, it was emerging as one of the paramount domestic challenges of our time. Why not piggyback on this momentum by making it the defining priority of our movement and positioning the Urban League as the go-to organization in the black community on public education? Instinct also told me that asserting leadership in this arena was an ideal way for the National Urban League and its affiliates to raise our profile, attract new funding and followers, and generate media attention. Many everyday people, even close relatives of Urban Leaguers, sometimes struggled to explain what the League stood for and did. This might help clarify our identity and agenda.

I never assumed, though, that the League would go solo or try to hog the show. Instead, I urged my colleagues to think of the League as "the hub of the wheel." As the hub, the Urban League possessed certain assets and capabilities. We understood the issue and were well versed in the research on what was amiss and how to improve it. We kept close tabs on legislation, government regulations, and appropriations affecting education and youth development. Obviously, we knew the target constituency and operated programs that were effective. Lastly, we possessed an enviable track record, largely unmatched in the black community, of collaborating across the board with political, government, union, business, and community leaders.

Those were the assets we could bring as the hub of the wheel. In my scheme, the spokes of the wheel were the array of organizations with sizable constituencies comprised of parents, grandparents, aunts and uncles, and other influential people in the black community. I had in mind sororities and fraternities, the Eastern Star, the Elks and Masons, black newspapers and talk-radio hosts, tenant associations, PTAs, and, of course, churches. These groups cared deeply about our children but were not necessarily steeped in what needed to be done in order to bolster their academic and social development. Solidly rooted in our community, they comprised its durable infrastructure, if you will.

The other attribute that drew me to these organizations was that they possessed tremendous influence but did not feel compelled to compete for the spotlight. I thought the world of the League's peer groups at the national level. But we all vied for money and media attention. On-the-job experience had taught me that sibling rivalries, however friendly, tended to complicate strategic collaborations. Often, these alliances were shallower, more opportunistic, and less strategic than they could and should have been. Thus, for this initiative, we decided to link the hub, namely the Urban League, to the spokes that connected most easily and were eager to roll together in the same direction.

Why was I fixated on identifying the League so prominently with promoting the academic and social development of black youngsters? The reasons leapt out from the unequivocal statistics about how poorly many of our children were faring, be it low academic achievement, school suspensions, retention, dropping out, arrest and incarceration rates, or unemployment. By the same token, the evidence of the benefits that flowed from education was compelling.

Take the National Assessment of Educational Progress (NAEP), in effect the national report card on how well youngsters were doing academically. In 1992, just two years prior to my inaugural keynote address, the NAEP reported that the majority of black fourth-graders could barely read. Sixty-eight percent of them registered at the Below Basic level—namely, two notches below grade level. As recently as 2013, half of our fourth-graders continued to read at Below Basic level, according to NAEP. Progress, yes, but nothing to crow about. That year, only 15 percent of our fourth-graders achieved the desired status of Proficient Readers, and far fewer—2 percent—reached the exalted status of Advanced Readers. Latino youngsters consistently read slightly better than black children, even though English wasn't the first language for many of them. By sharp contrast, the proportion of white fourth-graders reading at Below Basic level in 2013 was 21 percent. For Asian/Pacific youngsters, it was 20 percent.

Sadly, black children trail their white and Asian-American peers, whatever their socioeconomic status. Latino and Native American

Meeting the youngest achievers at the Los Angeles Urban League's "Doing the Right Thing" rally
Los Angeles Urban League

youngsters also lag, though not quite as badly as black children. The "achievement gap" afflicts virtually every school system with minority children. The gap is even more alarming—and stubborn—between suburban white youngsters and children of color from the kinds of low-income inner-city neighborhoods served by Urban League affiliates.

Complicating matters further is the disturbing ambivalence and outright indifference of too many African-American children toward academic achievement. From scholarly studies to newspaper accounts to anecdotes from parents and youngsters alike, the evidence of peer pressure not to achieve is profoundly disturbing and, worse still, counterproductive.

Academic failure simply isn't an option in the Information Age economy. This is especially true in the wake of the Great Recession, when educated people sliding down the employment totem pole compete for jobs usually held by the marginally educated.

Even in today's tough times, there's an indisputable correlation between educational attainment and economic status. Census data consistently shows that the better educated you are, the more money you are likely to earn and the less likely you are to be unemployed. For all the ups and downs in the economy, education remains the surest route to the American mainstream. Lousy education leads to economic apartheid. Education also equips young people for citizenship by enabling them to become lifelong learners and informed members of the body politic.

These were the primary reasons that prompted us to conceive of what we Urban Leaguers called the Campaign for African-American Achievement. It began back in March 1997 at the Shell Learning Center in Houston, where the National Urban League convened the Leadership Summit on Achievement and African-American Children. We brought together leaders of national African-American organizations, including the faith community, social and civic organizations, and professional associations. And that fall, the League linked arms with the Congress of National Black Churches to convene a summit in Florida for two hundred religious leaders.

The Achievement Campaign got under way in 1998, driven by three core strategies. The Urban League and its partners set out to

1. Spread the gospel that "Achievement Matters." The straightforward aim here was to mobilize our community to encourage

high achievement, to impress upon parents how important it was for their children to do well academically, and to overcome the ambivalent attitude toward achievement prevailing among many black children.

2. Transform parents into sophisticated consumers. The idea was to inform parents and caregivers of practical things they could do to boost the academic skills of their youngsters and keep track of how they were faring in school.

3. Create consumer demand for quality education. Our approach here was to encourage parents and community groups to work with their schools to boost children's academic performance, but also to apply pressure on educators if need be.

In this era before social media, we spread our achievement message using every means available, at every opportunity, and in every speech. I delivered keynote addresses at the National Press Club in Washington and before economic clubs in D.C., Detroit, and San Francisco, many of which were broadcast nationally via C-SPAN. Cumulatively, I spoke before thousands of attendees at annual Equal Opportunity Day dinners sponsored by local Urban Leagues. I spread our gospel all over television and radio on NBC, CBS, Fox, BET, CNN, NPR, and local commercial radio and television stations. C-SPAN telecast many of our policy forums focused on education and youth development.

What's more, I published Op-Ed articles in local newspapers about the imperative of achievement and the goals of our campaign. I also cultivated nationally syndicated newspaper columnists, which paid dividends when they then devoted their columns to our cause. Bob Herbert of the *New York Times* and Bill Raspberry of the *Washington Post* were especially drawn to our message and generous in their coverage.

We informed the affiliates that our writings and speeches were movement property and encouraged them to adapt this material for use in Op-Eds and speeches in their own communities. Our affiliates lined up a wide array of local collaborators, including sororities and fraternities, churches, school systems, public housing authorities, and even billboard companies and transportation agencies. Many of these groups had scarcely paid attention to the achievement gap in the past. In addition to the dozens of black groups that signed on, the National Urban League enlisted an imposing roster of national partners, among them corporations such as State Farm and Met Life and organizations including the Educational Testing Service, Scholastic, the National Newspaper Publishers Association, the Education Trust, Kaplan Tutorial Service, the National Education Association, and Magic Johnson Theatres, to name just a few.

Thanks to an advertising campaign in African-American newspapers financed by State Farm, black parents, caregivers, and groups began seeing the campaign's message. In Seattle, municipal buses carried placards bearing the local Urban League's catchy slogan—"The bar has been raised: Get over it! Achievement Matters." We also trumpeted the message through public service announcements in movie houses, spots on radio, and coverage on television.

To get parents engaged, local Urban Leagues staged education summits, some of which drew as many as a thousand people. These summits familiarized parents and community leaders with the educational challenges facing our young people, acquainted them with supportive public policies and successful interventions, and helped mobilize them to get involved.

To neutralize negative peer pressure and start transmitting pro-achievement signals to children, we designated September as Achievement Month. On the third Saturday of the month, affiliates across the country staged block parties, achievement rallies, and street festivals to celebrate youngsters for "Doing the Right Thing"—namely, striving to excel in school. In contrast to the ceaseless media coverage of black people committing murder and mayhem, we used these events to secure favorable coverage of black youngsters. Each year, these events drew upwards of sixty thousand young people and parents. The mother of all events occurred in Gary, Indiana, where the Urban League and its campaign partners sponsored a back-to-school parade for ten thousand students, right through downtown.

The capper when it came to recognizing academic achievement was the National Achievers Society. Here's how I learned about it. A few months after I took the helm of the League, Don Bowen, head of our affiliate in Broward County, Florida, invited me to witness a recognition ceremony for black students who were doing well in school, after which I would be inducted as an honorary member of something called the McKnight Achievers Society.

I was blown away by the experience! There in this black church in Fort Lauderdale that Saturday were several hundred schoolchildren, every one of whom had earned a B average or better in school.

Hundreds more proud parents, siblings, and grandparents filled the pews. The youngsters were inducted into the McKnight Achievers Society in a ceremony that was equal parts solemn and celebratory. Each inductee proudly came forward to receive a handsome jacket. Then they uttered the oath in unison. When they were done, it was my turn to join their ranks. After the ceremony, folks milled around at the reception for more than an hour, snapping pictures and eating snacks. When it came to preaching the gospel of achievement, the church was chock-full of true believers that day.

I returned from Fort Lauderdale determined to learn more about this powerful idea and to figure out a way to incorporate it into our work. The McKnight Achievers Society dated to the mid-1980s, when Dr. Israel Tribble, then head of the Florida Education Fund, conceived of it as a community-based vehicle for recognizing high achievers and encouraging achievement by black children. Over the next decade, Urban League affiliates in Florida had collaborated with Tribble in inducting academic stars who had earned GPAs of 3.0 or better. The organization provided these young people with encouragement and, frankly, protective cover from peers who scorned achievement.

The Campaign for African-American Achievement embraced this idea as one of its centerpieces and took it national. With Tribble's approval, we rebranded it the National Achievers Society. We scored a publicity coup when we enlisted General Colin Powell, the recently retired chairman of the Joint Chiefs of Staff, to help launch the national version by keynoting the first induction ceremony in the spring of 1998 at Metropolitan Baptist Church in Washington.

I had gotten to know General Powell after he retired as head of the Joint Chiefs and founded America's Promise. I admired him and considered him a class act and an exemplary role model for our children. Amusingly enough, people used to come up to me and ask if I was General Powell, especially in the days when we both wore aviator-style glasses. Don't get me started on how many white folk think all blacks look alike. Anyway, I would pause before confessing I wasn't. But I'd go on to say I would be delighted to play Powell's double, provided he cut me in on his speaker fee.

The inaugural induction ceremony for our National Achievers Society took place on April 17, 1998, in Washington. Nationally, thirty-two Urban League affiliates staged ceremonies inducting more than two thousand youths between the ages of five and seventeen. At the D.C. event, thirty-five inductees received designer jackets fashioned by Karl Kani, one of the hottest designers in the eyes of young people. Echoing the military's training philosophy, Powell told the inductees, "There is nothing in this society you can't have. There is no job you can't have or profession you can't excel in. But you are going to have to work for it." Noting that he had seen considerable progress since growing up fifty years earlier, he warned the adults in the audience, "It will all be irrelevant if we can't bring up this new generation of youngsters to believe in themselves."

I vividly recall the induction ceremony for the local chapter of the National Achievers Society staged by the San Diego Urban League one Saturday afternoon in December 2001 at Bayview Baptist Church. The church was packed with eighteen hundred well-wishers. In fact, some people had to sit up front in the pews customarily occupied by the choir.

Arrayed before us were 350 inductees, all of whom had earned B averages or better, and half of whom were boys. Judge Joe Brown, the television personality, was the keynote speaker. Together, the inductees recited the NAS Litany: "I am excellent. I am excellent. I am excellent. My mind is a pearl. I can do anything. Anything that my mind can conceive, I can achieve. Anything that my mind can conceive and my heart can believe, I can achieve. I am excellent. I am excellent. I am excellent. I am a National Achiever!"

Between assembling the youngsters and the audience, staging the ceremony, and holding the reception afterward, the festivities lasted close to three hours. In other words, this was no hit-and-run event. The *San Diego Voice & Viewpoint*, the local African-American newspaper, provided enthusiastic and extensive coverage, devoting a dozen pages to stories and photos of the inductees and their families.

I was struck that nary one of those inductees disparaged achievement as "acting white." They all eagerly stepped forward to be anointed as achievers and proudly wore the jackets available only to NAS members. Many young people I talked with there and at other ceremonies around the country in effect asked what had taken grownups so long to find them, recognize them, and provide them with the protective cover of a like-minded peer group.

The philosophy of the Urban League in Gary, Indiana, was the more honorees, the merrier. To reach and motivate the maximum number of students each year, it recognized every youngster from grades four through twelve who earned a 3.0 GPA (or the equivalent in the early grades). It inducted them the first time they earned those grades and every year thereafter when they did as well. In 1998 alone, the local League recognized two thousand students. And it drew nominees not just from Gary but from all fifteen school districts in the vicinity. At the end of the school year, the League also honored the top twenty-five achievers from each of the high schools in these districts.

The NAS induction ceremony in Gary was held at Westside High School on the first Saturday of June each year. The League looked to the teachers to get their inductees and parents to turn out for the event. Since induction into NAS was serious business, the girls and boys were instructed to wear a white blouse and dark skirt or a white shirt and dark slacks, respectively.

At the ceremony, the youngsters sat with their school contingents. Parents received packets containing a T-shirt, a medallion, a certificate, and an NAS pin. To keep the costs manageable, the League got the mayor of Gary to pay for the pins and persuaded a local printer to provide the program books for free. As should be no surprise, given its size, the annual induction in Gary attracted media attention from local newspapers and TV stations.

Public recognition unquestionably made a favorable impression on the inductees. As JaToya Jones, a high school freshman in Gary, remarked, "I was unaware of the amount of students coming here tonight. It's great that the Urban League is doing it because it builds the students' self-esteem and makes us want to work harder in our studies." Amber Demerson Lewis, a high school senior, echoed this sentiment: "I didn't know people were watching me and seeing that I was doing well in school. It made me feel really honored for people to recognize me."

The National Achievers Society struck a responsive chord in communities around the country. By the time I left the League, roughly thirty thousand youngsters had been inducted, counting the ten thousand or so McKnight Achievers who were "grandfathered" into the national unit. Churches and school systems in communities without Urban League affiliates inquired how to start chapters of the NAS.

In speeches around the country, I often said that what we did with the NAS was create, in effect, a national achievement "gang" that kids were clamoring to join. It gave youngsters who wanted to do the right thing something constructive to compete for. Our gang had its unique rituals and regalia, its own credo and colors. The exclusive jacket students received couldn't be purchased at a sporting-goods store. It was what appeared on the youngsters' report cards that counted, not how much was in their wallets. Excellent grades were the only currency that mattered. Local newspapers, especially the African-American ones, displayed the students' photos prominently. These achievers were the toast of their towns. They knew it and understood the reason why— because they had taken the gospel of achievement to heart.

Much as I gloried in what the NAS represented, I was convinced communities could go even farther in recognizing achievers. I once suggested to a mayor of New York that the city should stage a parade down Fifth Avenue for all the schoolchildren who earned B averages or, better yet, for all the youngsters who passed the state reading exam. If cities could host St. Patrick's Day parades, West Indian Day parades, Gay Pride parades, and parades for the World Series champs, I argued, why not Achievement Day parades down the main street of every town in America? Think of the powerful message this would send to America's children that "Achievement Matters."

The Achievement Campaign orchestrated by the National Urban League served as a tantalizing real-world example of the benefits when communities bestirred themselves to motivate youngsters to achieve. The League put achievement and literacy on the radar screens of schoolchildren and their families. Put differently, we gave them credibility in the eyes of kids.

The Academy for Educational Development evaluated the Achievement Campaign. In a telling observation about our impact, AED noted in its evaluation that

> the most striking finding is that the Campaign fills a long unmet need for recognition on the part of young African Americans who excel academically. In contrast to peers who may be celebrated for their athletic prowess, "smart" youth have often been the butt of jokes and ridicule and their treatment at the hands of their peers has further reinforced the myth that it is not "cool" to be smart.

AED continued:

> NAS (National Achievers Society), Achievement Month and Doing the Right Thing Celebrations partially remediate this situation by saluting young people for their academic efforts. The impact of this

cannot be underestimated. Focus group respondents actually marveled at the turn of events whereby their peers were seeking them out to find out how "to get one of those jackets."

The young people reached by the Achievement Campaign cited a number of benefits, notably a clearer sense of what it meant to achieve. As AED reported,

> In the materialistic culture in which all of these youth live, many acknowledged that their peers and even they, themselves, defined achievement in strictly material terms, focusing on short-term gain. However, participation in the Campaign has helped to change these perceptions. Coupled with this clearer understanding of achievement is also a clearer sense of how academic achievement and future success are linked. Young people report that exposure to the Campaign is implanting and reinforcing the message that regardless of the career path they choose to pursue, academic achievement will make it easier.

One focus group respondent put it succinctly: "A rapper that knows how to read and write stands a better chance of holding on to his loot than one who can't."

The AED evaluators wrote glowingly of the League's community-based honor society:

> The National Achievers Society helped to establish a common bond among young people in the same community but not necessarily of the same background. Within the same focus groups, participants often hailed from disparate backgrounds. However, the quest to achieve united them. They spoke of the positive peer influence that they exerted on each other as one of the benefits of the Campaign. They also mentioned how collectively they are changing the often negative perception of African American youth in their communities.

AED also praised Urban League affiliates for helping the non-achievers in their communities:

> Many of the affiliates . . . have started Believers groups for individuals whose GPA is not sufficiently high to allow them membership in the Achievers Society. The youth in question and their parents and teachers note that this is very important because in some cases these youth have felt marginalized as all of the attention is focused on youth who are excelling. The Believers groups promote the philosophy that

the community believes that these young people, with extra effort, can become tomorrow's Achievers. The establishment of the Believers' groups has gone a long way to dispelling the notion that the NAS is an exclusionary group.

The youngsters reached by the Achievement Campaign recognized the assistance they received with practical problems as another dividend. They and their parents cited the information they received about college applications, scholarships, tutoring, and job placement as particularly helpful. This assistance extended to nonacademic concerns such as money and time management, even dress and grooming.

Once the Achievement Campaign got rolling, we turned our attention to early literacy. This was because whether we were parents, grandparents, pastors, or mentors, we had to see to it that every youngster learned to read and write, reason and compute, and navigate the internet. The reason, as Sherlock Holmes used to say, was elementary. If our children could read well, they could study the African diaspora and Western civilization. They could absorb the teachings of the Bible and savor Toni Morrison, William Shakespeare, and Langston Hughes. If they couldn't read, all they would ever learn was what they saw on screens and heard on the streets.

If youngsters are behind in reading when they exit elementary school, they'll struggle to catch up. How will they handle the reading load in social studies, the writing assignments in history, and the word problems in algebra? How will they meet the stiff high school graduation standards being imposed by the states? In all probability, they won't perform well on college entrance exams or on qualifying tests required by employers. Whatever the fate of affirmative action, young people must be competitive academically to land in the pool of qualified applicants.

This explains why the Urban League and its allies in the Achievement Campaign embarked on encouraging and equipping parents and caregivers to help children become good readers. We teamed with Scholastic, the world's largest publisher of children's books and magazines, to create a guide for parents on helping their children become good readers. It was called *Read and Rise: Preparing Our Children for A Lifetime of Success.* The content was derived from guidelines developed by the International Reading Association and the National Association for the Education of Young Children. In addition to the print version, it was available on the National Urban League and Scholastic websites.

By 2002, we had distributed nearly a quarter-million copies of *Read and Rise* via our affiliates and Scholastic's network of contacts. Scholastic emailed it to more than two hundred thousand teachers and reading specialists and nearly one thousand librarians nationwide. The New York Urban League placed fifteen thousand copies in the back-to-school packets children took home when school opened in the fall. Urban League affiliates in D.C. and Knoxville handed them out at barbershops and beauty parlors. The mayor of Eugene, Oregon, arranged for new mothers to receive copies when they checked out of the hospital. The Urban League in Gary, Indiana, persuaded a local billboard company to create *Read and Rise* billboards overlooking major highways around town. One member of Congress distributed *Read and Rise* to ten thousand families in public housing in his district.

Our partners in the Achievement Campaign pitched in as well. The National Newspaper Publishers Association, reaching a weekly readership of more than two million, featured excerpts from the guide in black newspapers for an entire month, in conjunction with a special series of stories on early literacy. The AKA sorority, fraternities including the Omegas and the Alphas, the National Black Child Development Institute, and the National Alliance of Black School Educators distributed the guide to their chapters and members.

Congressmen Edolphus Towns and Major Owens invited my colleagues and me to join them at an ecumenical *Read and Rise* Breakfast convened for 150 ministers at Berean Missionary Baptist Church in Brooklyn. When it came my turn to speak, I exhorted the pastors to see to it that all the children in their congregations became proficient readers. We pledged to work with them. Toward that end, Scholastic and the League produced a supplementary guide entitled, *What the Faith-Based Community Can Do to Improve Early Literacy.*

Although this breakfast event did not ignite the hoped-for involvement, I still dream about the impact churches could have if they embraced the literacy challenge. If every member of the clergy around the country, from storefront preachers and parish priests to ministers of mega-churches, declared they would see to it that every child in their flock was going to become a proficient reader, and if the ministers then mobilized the church elders and members to make it happen, there is no doubt in my mind that the percentage of black fourth-graders who can barely read would plunge—and quickly at that. In the heyday of the civil rights movement, our religious leaders showed the world they had the power to inspire and orchestrate dramatic societal change. They should use it today to liberate our people through literacy.

The Achievement Campaign and the high-profile advocacy role I played in K-12 education policy landed me on the radar screen of George W. Bush, then governor of Texas. In 1999, the League staged the regional meeting of our Southern affiliates in Austin, Texas. Word reached me through Herman Lessard, CEO of our affiliate there, that Governor Bush wanted to meet me. I leapt at the chance because he was known for caring about education. Plus, who knew how the 2000 presidential election would turn out?

We met one on one in the governor's office for about an hour. For the first fifteen minutes, we swapped baseball stories. He once owned part of the Texas Rangers, so we hit it off there. Then the conversation turned to education. Bush was familiar with my writings, as well as the League's initiatives on education. I sensed from the enthusiasm and conviction in his voice that this was a visceral concern for him. That he genuinely wanted to boost the reading proficiency and achievement levels of minority children. And that if he ever reached the White House, it would become a priority for his presidency.

My next contact with Bush on the topic of education came shortly after the 2000 election but prior to his inauguration. The president-elect convened a group of corporate CEOs and civic leaders at Blair House, across the street from the White House. There, he elaborated on his legislative plan for K-12 education reform. He exhibited impressive knowledge of the issues and research and had assembled on his team some of the nation's foremost experts on reading.

Liberal pundits and politicians were fond of denigrating Bush as an intellectual lightweight. While we were polar opposites ideologically on most issues, I left those early conversations about education with an unexpectedly favorable impression of him. It struck me that, when he cared enough to immerse himself in an issue, he exhibited a sophisticated command of it. Also, he displayed a laudable determination to focus on a limited set of big objectives, instead of dabbling in lots of modest initiatives that would scarcely move the needle even if they worked.

I emerged from these encounters thinking that, like Ronald Reagan, George W. Bush could well become a more formidable president than skeptics reckoned. To my dismay, he subsequently staged a preemptive war against Iraq based on erroneous intelligence and false pretenses, imprudently slashed taxes for the wealthy, plunged the balanced federal budget inherited from President Clinton into crippling deficits, and otherwise drove domestic policy rightward.

As the League's Achievement Campaign gained momentum, I resorted to another time-honored technique of spreading the gospel of achievement. I decided to write a book, entitled, fittingly enough, *Achievement Matters: Getting Your Child the Best Education Possible.* The idea came to me as I visited a bookstore in Chicago. I was browsing the selection of recently released nonfiction when I spotted a book co-authored by the Jesse Jacksons, father and son, about investing in the stock market. I thought that if they could write a book about investing, then surely I could do one about boosting academic achievement.

Over the next several months, I huddled with my colleagues and drafted a preliminary description of what I wanted to cover. Tom Dortch, a friend who headed 100 Black Men, a civic organization devoted to mentoring, educating, and empowering black youngsters, referred me to the agent and writer he had worked with on his book about mentoring young people. One spring day in 2001 at the agent's office, we interviewed publishers who had indicated preliminary interest. We then picked the one, Kensington, that expressed genuine passion for the book, presented the most imaginative marketing strategy, and offered a decent-enough advance to enable me to hire a talented writer, Carla Fine.

At my behest, Carla interviewed many young participants and parents in the League's programs, especially the National Achievers Society. She read books and reports I unloaded on her, along with other material she dug out on her own. Over the summer of 2001, Carla prepared preliminary drafts of the chapters and sent them to me. Now, it was my turn to take over the writing process. I rewrote every chapter, inserting anecdotes and personal stories, observations and tips, and generally ensuring that it read and sounded like me.

I relayed the completed chapters to my editor as I went along and submitted the conclusion by Thanksgiving, pretty close to the original due date. The publisher quickly approved the manuscript with minor requests for edits here and amplifications there. Needing only eight months to progress from interviews with prospective publishers to final approval by the editor, the book moved from conception to birth like a child who could not wait to exit the womb.

Achievement Matters hit the bookstores in late August 2002. Like a first-time father, I was so thrilled that I visited every bookstore in sight just to sneak a peek at it stacked among the new releases. Several times a day for weeks on end, I logged onto the Amazon and Barnes & Noble websites to read the reviews and follow the oscillating sales rankings.

The publisher dispatched me on an arduous book tour that was loads of fun nonetheless. I worked the early drive-time radio and television circuit, struggling each morning to rid the sleep from my voice and eyes. Typically, I closed out the day with an appearance at a bookstore, sometimes to audiences of thirty to fifty but more often before much smaller gatherings. In between, I visited newspapers, conducted long interviews on local NPR stations, lunched with columnists, the works. Much to my delight and appreciation, some Urban League affiliates pitched in by staging book signings, by getting corporate sponsors to buy books for me to autograph at fundraising dinners, and by sponsoring assemblies in schools, where I promoted the book and its underlying messages.

As I explained at these appearances, I wrote *Achievement Matters* for parents and caregivers who wanted to help their children perform well in school. The practical tips in the book tapped many sources, among them the insights and lessons of the Achievement Campaign. I drew on the experiences and advice of academically successful youngsters and parents involved in the National Achievers Society, on the League's role in running educational and youth development programs, and on the advice of the organization's young trustees and members of our young professionals' organization. The book also cited useful lessons from researchers and from successful academic enrichment and after-school programs around the country.

I had fun with young people when I described my other major source for the book. You should have seen the looks on their faces when I told them I was a retired kid. They obviously thought this was impossible, and that they'd never get so old!

Many memories linger long after the book tour. Two stick most prominently in my mind. I recall the early-morning drive-time shows on urban radio stations that appealed to hip-hop audiences—namely, teenagers as well as young parents. On the air, the radio personalities would rap away in their distinctive lingo, which was fine by me. In my day, I certainly wasn't above "dishing it" with my buddies. Some mornings on the book tour, I was so sleep-deprived that I would loosen up and get right into it, as best I could. But when we took a station break, the rapping paused as well. On many an occasion, the on-air hipsters started talking to me about what they had read in the *New York Times* that morning—how terrible it was that so many people lacked health insurance, how urgent it was for parents to get involved in their children's education, what they thought about school vouchers, and so forth. Then, the moment we resumed talking on the air, it was back to rapping. In other words, these radio personalities were completely bilingual. To their audiences, they spoke the lingo of the streets. Off the air, they knew it would get them nowhere in the world beyond the streets. This exasperated me because they knew better, yet they were rapping our young people down a road to nowhere. We owe it to our youngsters to show them which way is up and what it takes to get there.

The other encounters that deeply upset me were the times I spent with parents at bookstores in the heart of the black community. Almost every time, I would get a question something like this: "Mr. Price, it's all I can do to provide my children with food, clothing, and shelter. Why can't I just trust the teachers?"

Translated, their comments meant any of several things—"I don't have time to get involved in the schools," or "I don't have enough energy left at the end of the day to get involved," or "I don't have the knowledge or self-confidence," or "The teachers are the pros, let them handle it," or, worse yet, "I don't care to get involved."

Typically, I replied by citing several reasons why they should not just trust their children's teachers. What if the teacher didn't believe their child could achieve? What if the teacher was inexperienced and in over his head? What if the teacher didn't know what he was doing? What if the teacher misdiagnosed their youngster and placed her in classes way below her appropriate academic level? Worse still, what if the teacher wrongly assigned their son to special education because she did not know how to handle him or wanted him—and his lowly reading scores—out of her class so her students' performance on state-mandated tests would look better? Or what if the school was all screwed up and they didn't know it? What if the teacher needed them to get their child to knuckle down and stop acting out in class?

Study after study has shown that, whether in suburban schools or inner-city ones, whether in public or private or parochial ones, parent involvement is key to children's success. I realize that most parents work hard. They have little energy left when they get home. I understand. But we don't have time not to make time. We must stop playing hooky from our children's education and start taking charge of making sure they achieve. When it comes to seeing that teachers and principals give our children the education they need and deserve, parents should get involved and stay on the case. They must "trust but verify."

In 2008, our Achievement Campaign inspired a second book. Titled *Mobilizing the Community to Help Students Succeed*, it focused on the critical importance of getting community groups and churches engaged in encouraging youngsters to achieve and celebrating them when they did. This book drew heavily on the kinds of motivational activities that Urban League affiliates and their local partners mounted. Examples included the local National Achievers Society chapters, the designation of September as Achievement Month, back-to-school rallies, literacy Olympiads and book-reading competitions, annual recognition lunches and receptions for high achievers, school assemblies celebrating youngsters who "Do the Right Thing," mass "readathons," and even SAT awareness rallies.

Public schools have come under withering criticism over the years, for understandable reasons. Parents, advocates, and policymakers have grown impatient with the yawning achievement gap dividing low-income and working-class youngsters from their well-to-do peers, between black and Latino children on the one hand and white and Asian-American students on the other. This chasm makes an utter mockery of the ideal of universal access to the American Dream. And to be crassly pragmatic about it, this situation undermines the future productivity of our economy and the strength of our national defense, both of which rely on educated workers, especially minority youth, who gradually will become the majority of the adult U.S. labor force.

Regrettably, this impatience has also triggered an orgy of tougher academic standards and incessant testing. Waves of reform have washed up on the shores of public schools, from mayoral control and Common Core standards to school vouchers and choice. Teachers' unions and politicians have battled over merit pay, tenure, and accountability. Meanwhile, dissatisfied parents cast about for alternatives such as charter schools and small public schools. The bottom line is that children already struggling in school are told to jump higher academically, while educators thrash about for strategies and support to enable them to do so.

Instead of providing—and paying for—public schools that actually educate all youngsters to their fullest potential, we still tolerate institutionalized elitism. The ablest teachers routinely take higher-paying jobs in the suburbs. Inner-city schools often must cope with obsolete buildings, woefully outdated books, and well-intentioned but inexperienced teachers. Youngsters take less challenging courses than they can handle and write far less than they should. The upshot is that only a comparative handful of black youngsters receive the best that public education has to offer, and the rest are stuck with third-rate education or worse. The education apartheid I witnessed in the mid-twentieth century persists and has probably worsened in the twenty-first.

Since the Achievement Campaign was the centerpiece of my administration, I cannot claim to be entirely objective about what we accomplished. Looking back, I believe the Urban League helped spawn a grassroots achievement movement that gradually gained momentum in cities around the country. I take immense pride in the accomplishment.

While I cannot prove a connection, I am convinced our campaign stoked black parents' interest in how their children were faring, how the public schools were performing, and what options, including charter schools and small public schools, were available if they believed their children were being given short shrift. The pressure for transparency and accountability was ratcheted up at the local, state, and national levels, driven by increased parental interest, awareness, and engagement.

I firmly believe our Achievement Campaign helped fuel this phenomenon within the black community and urban school districts. The jury remains out on whether or not the heightened awareness and activism will ultimately translate into more widespread, robust, and enduring academic gains for our children.

CHAPTER 19

THE CRIMINAL INJUSTICE SYSTEM

T he issue aside from education that captured the most attention when I headed the National Urban League was the criminal "injustice" system. It remains one of the realms of American life where Jim Crow still runs amok, decades after the Supreme Court outlawed racial segregation. During my tenure at the League, racism ran the gamut from the seemingly unjustified police killings of unarmed black civilians to rampant stopping and frisking on New York City streets and widespread racial profiling on highways.

Actually, in the 1990s, racial profiling was but the tip of the iceberg. In my travels around the country, black police officers confided to me that there often were two sets of rules on the streets. White kids from affluent suburbs who did something stupid or were caught with a tiny amount of cocaine were hauled back home to their parents. Kids of color, they told me, typically went straight to the lockup.

Racial discrimination reared its ugly head elsewhere in the criminal justice system. Back in 2000, a study by the Justice Policy Institute found that, in California, black and Latino teenagers were much more likely to be locked up—and for longer—than white teens who committed the same crimes. According to Eric Lotke of the institute, African-Americans constituted 12 percent of the nation's population and 13 percent of its drug users. Yet we were 57 percent of the inmates incarcerated in state prisons for drug crimes. Whites, at 69 percent of the population, comprised 68 percent of the country's drug users. But according to the study, they were only 23 percent of those imprisoned for drug crimes. An analysis by the *Miami Herald* of eight hundred thousand felony cases in Florida revealed that twice as many white drug offenders as black were allowed to take special pleas without incurring criminal records.

Discriminatory treatment did not end there. Under California's regressive "three strikes" law, the ratio of black felons to white felons getting slammed with severe sentences was twelve to one. What's more ridiculous—and wasteful—was that nearly two-thirds of those sentenced had committed nonviolent offenses. According to another study, by an outfit called Building Blocks for Youth, black youngsters who had run afoul of the law but never before been incarcerated were forty-eight times more likely to land behind bars than whites with similar records.

The tragic result of the way drug laws were enforced under the purported "war against crime" was mass incarceration of nonviolent minority offenders. In New York State, for instance, first-time offenders convicted of possessing as little as four ounces of heroin or cocaine could draw stiffer prison sentences than murderers and rapists. That was absurd.

On my watch, the National Urban League joined other groups in urging an overhaul of the drug-sentencing laws that consigned minor offenders to years behind bars. Fortunately, policymakers of both major parties seem finally to be coming to their senses. Persuaded by mounting evidence of the inhumanity and futility of mass incarceration, and pressured to trim government spending in the wake of the Great Recession, states as well as the federal government are scaling back their prison populations and modifying their wasteful sentencing policies.

The most draconian example of Jim Crow at work in the criminal "injustice" system is capital punishment. Studies show that minorities draw the short straw more often than whites. It is barbaric for government to execute someone who isn't a mortal enemy. The inmates on death row may not be angels. But they are children of God. This is why repealing capital punishment—or at least imposing a nationwide moratorium on executions—is warranted on moral grounds alone. The only exception I might make is for the mythical Jim Crow, who I would happily strap in the electric chair myself. There is a pragmatic reason as well. In all too many cases, bona fide doubts exist about the competence of the defense attorneys and the reliability of the evidence. Subsequent examinations of DNA evidence have exonerated some people convicted of capital offenses.

Such disturbing cases set me to thinking afresh some years ago about the appropriate burden of proof under the law. In civil cases, where essentially all that's at stake is the defendant's money or property, a plaintiff must prove the claim against the defendant by "a preponderance of the evidence." That's sort of like saying you need at least a 51–49 split in favor of the plaintiff. In criminal cases, where one's liberty is at risk, the rule is "beyond a reasonable doubt." This burden of proof applies whether the charge is shoplifting or serial murder. Whether the punishment is community service or the electric chair. I believe this traditional standard is far too lax when a person's life is at stake. Politicians know full well that some innocent people are being executed. Yet most of them lack the courage to say what error rate they find acceptable.

In my keynote address before the National Urban League's annual conference in 2000, I challenged America's politicians to muster the courage to repeal capital punishment altogether or at least to enact a tougher burden of proof in capital cases. I proposed requiring judges and juries to find the defendant guilty "beyond any doubt whatsoever." If those who passed judgment weren't convinced to that degree by the evidence, then they would have the option of finding the defendant guilty beyond a reasonable doubt. Under those circumstances, the punishment would be anything short of execution. But the government could execute someone only if there was a finding of guilt beyond any doubt whatsoever.

This idea went nowhere at the time. Then, in the spring of 2004, I noticed an obscure article about a study in Massachusetts urging the state to do something similar. As with the quasi-military youth corps, unorthodox ideas often must marinate before they attract adherents.

Yogi Berra, the Hall of Fame catcher and renowned quipster, once said, "It's déjà vu all over again." I thought about his truism when, thirty years after the New Haven riots, I resumed dealing with the tensions between police and the black community in the mid-1990s. The issues were so important and so emotional that the National Urban League had to take them on, as our affiliates from Los Angeles to Pittsburgh to New York to St. Petersburg were smack in the midst of the fight against racial profiling and brutality by local police.

As a former criminal defense lawyer, I had long ago shed any illusions about the criminal justice system and those who broke the law. Certain offenders deserved harsh punishment because they were one-person crime waves who wreaked havoc on society and on our children, families, and communities.

That said, the criminal justice system was wreaking its own form of havoc. I'm talking about unwarranted use of deadly force when an officer's life clearly was not in danger, about inexcusable brutality and rampant racial profiling, and about pervasive, indiscriminate stopping and frisking of black folk who had done little or nothing wrong. I know police work is dangerous. The overwhelming majority of officers are good people who do a great job. I also realize that some young people lose their cool when stopped by an officer and place themselves needlessly at risk. The police deserve our gratitude and support.

Yet when the politicians and police declared war on crime a generation ago, they all too often declared war on innocent people and petty offenders along with the bad actors. Some police departments went way overboard with racial profiling and, fortunately, were caught red-handed. When I ran the League, I recall a black police officer reported being stopped in a Philadelphia suburb by a white officer who said his inspection sticker was placed "abnormally high" on the car's windshield!

Such police practices shredded the civil liberties of ordinary citizens whose only suspicious trait was the dark pigmentation of their skin. Whose only offense was living in the inner city or driving lawfully where they supposedly did not belong. These practices made a mockery of due process, of the constitutional protection against unreasonable search and seizure.

In the 1990s, New York City was the epicenter of mounting police-community tension as anger over baseless police brutality and killings, racial profiling, and widespread abuse of civil liberties erupted. Mayor Rudy Giuliani's in-your-face attitude toward minorities encouraged police officers to overreach.

In August 1997, a policeman with a nightstick sodomized Abner Louima, a thirty-year-old Haitian immigrant who had been taken into police custody, while other officers pinned the victim down in the bathroom of a precinct house. Eighteen months later, an unarmed African immigrant named Amadou Diallo was slain in a fusillade of forty-one shots fired at point-blank range by four policemen. Searching for a rape suspect, they had approached Diallo outside his apartment and opened fire when he reached for what turned out to be his wallet. There also was rampant stopping and frisking of youngsters who supposedly looked suspicious, even though they were not accused of doing anything wrong.

At the height of the tension over these incidents, Ed Lewis, co-founder of *Essence* magazine, convened a small group of civic and business leaders in New York to discuss what to do about the escalation in police brutality. The Reverend Al Sharpton, the irrepressible activist, was already staging marches. In a show of solidarity, I marched across the Brooklyn Bridge in one of Sharpton's many protest rallies. In the crowd, I spotted a black friend who probably made millions of dollars as a high-ranking executive with a Fortune 500 corporation. When I asked why he, too, was marching, he replied, "Because I have four sons."

I told those who assembled in Ed's office that the National Urban League intended to try to smoke out President Clinton, who was lying low on this issue. For the life of me, I could not figure out why Clinton, who otherwise was empathetic toward blacks, would sidestep an issue that roiled our community so deeply. We needed his leadership on this one because the Justice Department could compel mayors and police chiefs to cease and desist the racial profiling and excessive use of deadly force.

Working the policy front nationally and locally was right up the Urban League's alley. We staged press conferences at the National Press Club featuring local Urban League directors, accompanied by the grief-stricken parents of victims who had been wrongfully killed or severely beaten by police.

The National Urban League joined other minority groups in calling for an audience with the president. When I had sat next to him in White House meetings on other subjects, I would slip him newspaper clips about the latest atrocity. Typically, Clinton would shake his head sympathetically and make a notation on the article. But still nothing happened.

I ratcheted up the public pressure on President Clinton by sending him a lengthy open letter on February 17, 1999. To guard against the letter's getting lost in the bowels of the White House, the League purchased space to run it prominently in the *New York Times*. We also published it as my weekly "To Be Equal" column, carried in black newspapers nationwide. We kept up the drumbeat by devoting several of my weekly radio commentaries to the topic.

THE CRIMINAL INJUSTICE SYSTEM 209

Mind you, this problem was reaching a crescendo just as Clinton launched his high-profile initiative on race, known as "One America." In the letter, I cautioned that his vision of "One America" would never materialize without resolving this issue. Furthermore, I implored the president to "exert every means of leadership at your disposal to address the festering issue of police abuse of minorities that is undermining the very goals you espouse."

Recalling a lesson from my former consulting partner Joel Cogen that he who proposed an agenda helped set it, I urged Clinton to take the following concrete steps:

- Show the nation unequivocally that you care. If, perish the thought, there's another unjustified fatality at the hands of police someday, you or the First Lady could attend the funeral of the victim.

- Utilize your bully pulpit to draw national attention to this crisis and urge that elected officials, law enforcement officials and community leaders work together to devise genuinely effective solutions.

- Convene a White House summit to place the national spotlight on this problem and to press the key stakeholders—mayors, police chiefs, civil rights and community groups, young people and others—to find constructive answers.

- Instruct the Attorney General to prosecute vigorously all egregious abuses of civil rights, such as the wanton slayings of Amadou Diallo in New York City and Deron Grimmitt in Pittsburgh, and to investigate any practices of racial profiling and harassment.

- Instruct the Justice Department to conduct public hearings around the country to ferret out evidence about the patterns of police misconduct, excessive use of force and abuse of civil liberties.

- Direct the Justice Department to convene a task force to devise guidelines for state and local law enforcement agencies that employ tactics like New York's elite street crimes unit. The guidelines could cover such issues as the need for careful training and psychological screening and mandated use of in-car police video cameras to monitor, record, and thus influence police behavior.

The point of the guidelines is to prevent the offensive practices and protect civil liberties without undermining effective law enforcement.

- Instruct the Justice Department to be aggressively supportive of language to track racial disparities in the juvenile crime legislation.
- Request that the U.S. Commission on Civil Rights conduct its own inquiry into the recurring patterns of police/community tension around the country and identify the law enforcement practices contributing to those conflicts.

I concluded my open letter to President Clinton by indicating that I knew he did not view his initiative for "One America" as an empty gesture, since he considered improved race relations a centerpiece of his legacy. I then cautioned that "in order for your initiative to be taken with the full measure of seriousness that you rightly seek, there is no way to sidestep the searing issue of police misconduct and abuse. There simply cannot be One America if law enforcement officials have license to split America apart."

President Clinton wrote back a week later expressing appreciation for my thoughtful letter and recommendations. He acknowledged that I was due to meet with Deputy Attorney General Eric Holder (my former Columbia Law School student who would rise to attorney general under President Obama). Clinton also indicated that he had asked Charles Ruff, the White House counsel, to follow up with me personally.

Meanwhile, we came up with another tactic to keep the pressure on Clinton. Earlier that month, it had dawned on me that the best way to capture his attention might be for the National Urban League to convene the mother of all press conferences—what I affectionately called our "strange bedfellows" press conference. It would feature many of the high-profile black leaders that the news media loved covering. To make the event even more irresistible, we invited an array of leaders of other ethnic groups to show that blacks weren't the only people beset by problems with the police.

Did it ever work! On the morning of February 25, a superstar cast of leaders gathered at my invitation in the National Press Club in Washington. The place overflowed with African-American luminaries—Kweisi Mfume of the NAACP, the Reverend Jesse Jackson of Operation Push, Dr. Dorothy Height of the National Council of Negro

Women, the Reverend Al Sharpton of the National Action Network, noted attorney Johnnie Cochran, Wade Henderson of the Leadership Conference on Civil Rights, Elaine Jones of the NAACP Legal Defense and Educational Fund, comedian Dick Gregory, James Clyburn and John Conyers of the Congressional Black Caucus, and Sandy Cloud of the National Conference of Christians and Jews. The array of leaders from other ethnic groups was equally eye-catching. They included Raul Yzaguirre of the National Council of La Raza, Abe Foxman of the Anti-Defamation League, Karen Narasaki of the National Asian Pacific American Legal Consortium, and Fred Rotondaro of the National Italian-American Foundation. In the spirit of piling on, we also invited parents of victims in the most recent police brutality cases. As you can imagine, the parents' impassioned remarks were the most riveting of all.

The press came out in force. C-SPAN replayed the event for days on end. It made the evening network television news and captured headlines in countless newspapers the following day. I also heard that the press conference actually was piped into the White House.

Joining other prominent political and civil rights leaders
at National Urban League press conference in 1999
to protest police brutality and racial profiling
© by Jason Miccolo Johnson

The upshot of February 25 was that a broad assemblage of leaders from across the racial spectrum served public notice that President Clinton had to deal with this issue. To his credit, he finally heard us loud and clear. The Saturday following our press conference, he invited many of us to the White House to witness his weekly radio address to the nation, in which he decried police brutality and abuse. Clinton then hosted a meeting with many of us. Afterward, his staff confirmed that I should connect with Charles Ruff, the White House counsel who was Clinton's point person on this issue, as well as lead counsel in defending him in the congressional impeachment proceedings.

Several days later, I visited Ruff at the White House. As I sat in his office, I spotted photos of Satchel Paige and Larry Doby on the wall by his desk. When I inquired why they were there, I discovered to my delight that he shared my passion for baseball—and specifically for the Cleveland Indians of the late 1940s and early 1950s. We swapped baseball stories for several minutes. Then we got down to the pressing business of police brutality and abuse.

As I probed to understand President Clinton's reticence about this issue, Ruff finally helped me see the light with an observation that astonished me. The president made no bones about attacking crime, Ruff observed. He was determined to be in front of the wave of popular opinion on this issue and not let Republicans portray him as soft on crime, as they did to so many Democrats. Ruff went on to say it was the Clinton administration's view that everyday blacks were equally intolerant of crime. After all, he opined, black people were the predominant victims of urban crime, so we were more anxious than anyone else for something to be done about it. How could I quarrel with that assertion?

Then came the show-stopper. Ruff said it was the Clinton administration's judgment that the African-American community would accept some weakening of civil liberties in exchange for increased safety. I was flabbergasted that this was the administration's view, and that he would come right out and admit it. I disagreed vehemently. I insisted that we wanted both, and that civil liberties and safety were not mutually exclusive. What's more, I argued, the police needed cooperation from the community in order to fight crime. Fomenting tension was not the smartest way to persuade our community that the cops were on our side.

While we agreed to disagree about where the black community stood on this tradeoff, the Clinton administration, to its credit, took concrete steps to alleviate the police-community tension. Drawing on my letter, Attorney General Janet Reno convened a conference on June 9 and 10, 1999, entitled, "Strengthening Police-Community Relationships." It brought law enforcement officials from around the country together with civil rights, civil liberties, and community leaders to understand more deeply the causes of mutual distrust and to lay the foundation for tangible improvements in policy and practice.

President Clinton addressed the conference and, with me seated next to him, chaired a round-table discussion. He issued a directive for federal enforcement agencies to collect and report data on the race, ethnicity, and gender of the people they stopped and searched. The agencies were instructed to report their findings one year later and to make recommendations on how to ensure greater fairness in federal law enforcement processes. Clinton also announced support for legislation introduced by Congressman Conyers to conduct a nationwide study on the nature and number of traffic stops by state and local enforcement agencies.

I discovered at this conference that there was abundant ignorance to go around. One situation that angered the advocates among us was the intimidating practice by policemen of placing their hand on the butt of their pistol when approaching a car they had pulled over. A related concern was the number of times unarmed drivers stopped by police ended up getting shot, seemingly without justification. Yet from the law enforcement officials, we learned that these were the most dangerous types of encounters for officers because they could be taken by surprise by armed drivers. This revelation cooled our rhetoric in such cases, especially when, right around the time of these meetings, former black activist H. Rap Brown was charged with killing a policeman in precisely the same circumstances.

The Justice Department began cracking down on renegade police units such as the Rampart Division in LA, which had virtually taken the law into its own hands. Police officers who engaged in racial profiling were prosecuted in New Jersey. These get-tough measures sent a signal to the law enforcement community to cut out the abuses. In cities including Boston, local police forged close relations with community groups that enabled them to work together on identifying bad actors or one-man crime waves. This example provided encouragement that, when it came to police-community relations, collaboration worked better than alienation. The tension between minorities and police gradually subsided in much of the country, as egregious offenders were prosecuted and, under pressure from the Justice Department, police embraced new policies and practices that curbed the worst instincts of cops—at least for a spell.

Sadly, police killings of unarmed African-Americans, mostly males, and the resultant mistrust, tensions, uprisings, and protests continue to this day. As long as racism persists in the criminal justice system, there's always the risk Yogi was correct—that it will be déjà vu all over and over and over again.

Yet after a half-century of observing and combating police misconduct, I am cautiously optimistic that durable progress may finally be made. The advent of smart phones with sophisticated cameras enables onlookers to record police encounters with civilians and to refute or affirm officialdom's rendition of what transpired. Transmission of these riveting images on television and social media will enable the American people to view what transpired and understand that most, if not all, black protests are well founded. Social media also facilitates mass impromptu mobilization by organizers seeking justice and progress. In my day, we lacked these forceful tools of proof and persuasion.

Confronted by embarrassing images and relentless political pressure, many police leaders, prosecutors, mayors, and federal officials, from the president to the attorney general, realize there is no ducking or downplaying this issue any longer. Police chiefs across the country increasingly acknowledge that they must strengthen the selection and training of officers and reform policy and practice when it comes to using deadly force and keeping interactions with nonviolent civilians from escalating.

Measures like these will not solve the shortcomings of capitalism, much less cure the chronic poverty and deficient education that afflict so many low-income and minority communities. But I hope that the determined and energetic organizers of such modern movements as Black Lives Matter will concentrate on making concrete advances in police policy and practices.

Tangible victories matter in the struggle for social justice. Overreaching by aiming to reform the entire social order will lead only to frustration and further alienation. Since deadly police-civilian confrontations ignite riots and demonstrations, reducing or avoiding them will render communities calmer and safer. In a world rife with seemingly intractable problems, measurable gains strike me as welcome progress that might finally prove Yogi wrong.

My revelatory experiences with the Black Coalition can serve as a cautionary tale for the organizers of Black Lives Matter. They need to be vigilant about making certain their allies and members truly are on their side. Leaderless mass movements are especially vulnerable to infiltrators whose purpose is to distract and discredit.

The ambush killings by black men of police officers in Dallas and Baton Rouge in 2016 brought to mind another risk facing contemporary movements such as Black Lives Matter. When I headed the Black Coalition in the mid-1960s, a handful of brothers who were riled up over some police outrage or another occasionally would threaten to grab their guns and "off some pigs." Fortunately, we managed to talk sense into the hotheads. These days, profoundly disturbed murderers who have no affiliation with the movement can take revenge on the police. This risks undercutting the public perception and forward motion of the movement. Navigating the turbulence following these traumatic events requires resilience, resolve, and political deftness by the leaders and activists in this loosely organized movement.

CHAPTER 20

AFFIRMATIVE ACTION AND OTHER FIGHTS

ndless skirmishes over affirmative action kept me busy during my Urban League tenure. Our spirited defense of diversity and inclusion was informed by research and reality, starting with personal experience. I often cite my admission history at Yale Law School when defending affirmative action and debating the uses and misuses of standardized entrance exams. Yale undoubtedly admitted me ahead of hundreds and perhaps thousands of applicants with stronger paper credentials and especially with loftier LSAT scores. I have no doubt Yale's commitment to inclusion tilted the decision in my favor. Keep in mind that this predated affirmative action as we have come to know it.

Let the record show that I did not shine academically in law school. Perhaps those dreadful LSAT scores accurately forecasted my academic performance there. But consider this. I ended up finishing toward the top of the bottom sixth of my class, which was nothing to brag about. Yet viewed another way, this meant close to one-sixth of our class ranked below me. Knowing how large and accomplished Yale's applicant pool was, I would wager that many, maybe even most, of those below me had better LSAT scores than I did.

While that's sinking in, remember that I was married from the middle of the first year onward. Our eldest daughter was born midway through my second year. My parents paid my tuition, but otherwise we did not rely on Marilyn's family or mine for day-to-day expenses. To help make ends meet, I worked ten to fifteen hours per week during my first year. During my second and third years, I ratcheted it up to twenty to thirty hours per week. This was on top of the heavy class assignments in law school. Time spent earning money was time not spent preparing for class or thoroughly completing homework assignments.

Since graduation, I have pursued an unorthodox career path that I would like to think has made Yale proud and brought a satisfied smile to the late dean Runyon's face. The highest award that the Yale Law School Association, the alumni association, bestows on esteemed alumni is the Award of Merit. Luminaries including President Bill Clinton, Cyrus Vance, Hillary Clinton, Eleanor Holmes Norton, and Supreme Court justices Sonya Sotomayor, Clarence Thomas, and Samuel Alito have received it. In 1998, the association selected me to receive the Award of Merit, horrific LSAT scores, unimpressive grades, and lowly class ranking notwithstanding. Numerous classmates have told me I am one of the stars of our class and of the law school itself. Several years later, I received an honorary degree from the university as well.

As proud as I am of these accomplishments, I recount this tale not to toot my own horn. Rather, my life experience illustrates the perils of judging talent and potential through slavish reliance on standardized test scores and grades. These modes of assessment tell admissions officers some—but by no means all—of what they need to know about an applicant's ability to handle the work. But there's much more than that to judging talent and potential.

Ideological conservatives routinely claim that affirmative action undermines merit. Rubbish. When I entered Amherst in 1959, highly selective colleges and universities quietly practiced affirmative action—for white students. Instead of basing admission decisions on paper credentials alone, they picked flexibly from a broad pool of qualified applicants to ensure that entering classes included a cross-section of white students from across the country—the East Coast, the South, the Rockies, and the West—as well as from public, parochial, and prep schools.

That's the way the system works to this day. When it comes to white applicants, selective schools resist picking strictly by the numbers. In February 2003, the *Wall Street Journal* reported in a revealing front-page article that Duke University admitted a wide array of white students with weaker scores and grades over applicants with stronger paper credentials. The applicants so favored included children of alumni, residents of North and South Carolina, children of wealthy parents who weren't alumni but were hot donor prospects, and, yes, athletes for its sports teams.

I ask conservatives who despise affirmative action to explain something to me. If it's fair for selective schools to admit these white applicants over other, say, white and Asian aspirants with stronger paper credentials, in the interest of geographic inclusiveness, athletic competitiveness, and endowment growth, why, then, is it unfair to give qualified black, Latino, and Native American applicants extra weight in the interest of promoting inclusion and diversity?

I just don't get why this causes such indigestion. I suspect rank racism is lurking beneath much of the opposition. At a minimum, it is downright hypocritical for the foes of affirmative action to condone the admission of whites in this way, yet condemn the admission of blacks and Latinos under similar circumstances.

As president of the National Urban League, I debated many strident foes of affirmative action on Fox's *O'Reilly Factor*, CNN's *Crossfire*, and other TV talk shows that more resembled verbal food fights than civil debates. My opponents usually hyperventilated when I argued that admissions officers ought not to pick applicants strictly by test scores and grades. "Mr. Price, why should a white kid with superior SAT scores be rejected," they virtually screamed at me, "while a black kid with lower scores gets admitted? That's patently unfair."

It isn't unfair because test scores and grades do not tell admissions officers everything they need to know about a given applicant's talent and potential, let alone what he or she is likely to accomplish professionally down the road. At the risk of turning a personal anecdote into a generalization, I cite my Yale experience as illustrative of why admissions officers should weigh a variety of factors beyond test scores in deciding whom to admit. It is not a simple matter to judge who may possess what former Massachusetts governor William Weld aptly called the "grit and determination" to succeed.

Many Rhodes Scholars and Phi Beta Kappas go on to accomplish extraordinary things. Others never quite measure up. Some squander their education and ability. Test scores do not differentiate the lifetime learners and hard-chargers from those who go brain dead and throw in the towel years after graduation. Nor do standardized exam scores and grades necessarily capture incandescent creativity in the arts or the delicate touch of a gifted physician.

My argument should not be construed as anti-intellectual, although opponents of affirmative action probably will do so anyway. Quite the contrary! Colleges and universities should evaluate applicants using assessments, instincts, and experiences that gauge talent and potential in all their robustness, variety, and nuance. On this very point, the medical school at the University of California at Davis once gave special consideration to white and minority applicants who lacked stellar scores on entrance exams but who had served, for instance, in the Peace Corps or as nurses. Interestingly enough, their eventual careers as physicians were virtually indistinguishable from classmates with more impressive paper credentials.

For six years, I served on the board of the Educational Testing Service, which designed and administered the SAT for the College Board. I learned that students with a rather broad range of SAT scores were quite capable of handling the work at the most demanding colleges and universities in this country. It did not mean they all ended up as Rhodes Scholars or magna cum laude graduates. Of course, it is important for admissions officers to try to project who will excel academically. Yet the truth is that how graduates fare in their professional lives over the long haul matters immensely to those institutions—and to society at large—as well.

Marching in 2000 to protest the Confederate flag
at the State Capitol in Columbia, South Carolina
National Urban League Archives

When I headed the National Urban League, we became alarmed by the excessive reliance on college entrance exam scores in admissions decisions and the diminished weight placed on more qualitative attributes that contributed to leadership and success after college. This trend, coupled with the relentless legal assault on affirmative action, blocked many eminently qualified black and Latino students who in prior years would have gained admission to top universities. Most of them surely would have graduated and then gone on to successful careers and leadership positions in their professions and communities.

At my behest, the League's Institute for Opportunity and Equality commissioned the noted survey research firm DYG, Inc., to survey top executives in Fortune 1000 companies. We wanted to learn what the captains of American industry considered the key attributes of leadership and success in the world of business. How did the characteristics they valued the most align with those captured by college entrance exams?

The findings were fascinating. The business leaders interviewed by DYG stressed the following attributes as key to success in corporate America: character, integrity, ability to overcome obstacles, determination, drive, ambition, and willingness to take risks. They also cited problem solving, the will to succeed, and the ability to motivate as critical characteristics. In fact, a majority of them believed colleges and universities should place less emphasis on SAT scores in admissions decisions.

The private sector isn't the only realm of American life where these attributes matter. They are also associated with leadership and success in public life and the nonprofit world. These lessons about how corporate leaders view merit, talent, and potential have important implications for college admissions. After all, if Fortune 1000 executives say these qualitative attributes matter, then surely college admissions officers should be free to consider them as well.

Affirmative action is more than a set of tools for promoting diversity. It is a philosophy of inclusion aimed at fostering broad participation in the most robustly diverse society on earth and at keeping us from backsliding into tokenism and exclusion.

Cynics say affirmative action is divisive. But imagine how fractious our country would be if minorities today were shut out of mainstream schools, as they were in the mid-1960s and earlier. Remember how few black classmates I had at Amherst and how few black undergraduates there were on other ostensibly integrated campuses. Remember that the doors of many Southern universities were completely closed to African-Americans.

For years, the tandem of conservative legal advocates abetted by sympathetic justices on the Supreme Court threw one roadblock after another in the way of affirmative action. Yet in a telling reflection of the deeply ingrained and irreversible value of diversity, college and university officials have continued to extol the virtues of inclusion and to devise creative methods for advancing it that hopefully will survive judicial scrutiny.

Nor is higher education alone in espousing this core value of twenty-first-century America. Over the years, leaders from other sectors of American society have weighed in with amicus curiae briefs in Supreme Court cases by arguing that diversity is a compelling state interest. Former secretaries of defense William Cohen and William Perry, four former chairmen of the Joint Chiefs of Staff, and Norman Schwarzkopf, commander of U.S. forces in the first Gulf War, endorsed a friend-of-the-court brief contending that the military needed a diverse officer corps in order to effectively lead the increasingly diverse ranks of enlisted men. Race should be among the factors used in determining who gets to go to the universities and military academies that funnel future officers into the military.

More than sixty Fortune 500 corporations also filed briefs in favor of affirmative action. The marquee corporate names included General Motors, American Airlines, Boeing, Johnson & Johnson, and Coca-Cola, to cite just a few. They argued that "diversity creates stronger companies," which boosts the productivity and global competitiveness of the U.S. economy. Other powerful allies included the United Auto Workers and the American Bar Association.

Demographic Imperative + Moral Imperative + Educational Imperative + Economic Imperative + Military Imperative = Compelling State Interest. That equation works for me, and it should for America.

Some opposition to affirmative action reflects a principled concern that race is a constitutionally suspect classification and should be weighed only in situations that constitute a compelling state interest. Of course, the high court's articulation of what constitutes a compelling state interest has evolved with the increasingly conservative tilt of its membership. Other opponents of affirmative action are not so high minded. They are simply jockeying for advantage in the allocation of opportunities and determined to improve their odds by undermining any advantages of their competitors.

While affirmative action has not and cannot cure all that ails black people or America, it unquestionably has been a win-win for both. Detractors claim it doesn't work. That is pure baloney because the data convincingly show that it does. *The Shape of the River*, the definitive study by William Bowen and Derek Bok, documented the abundant benefits of affirmative action to society. It pushed open doors to opportunity that had long been closed and has kept them ajar for roughly two generations. The composition of college and university student bodies, as well as corporate and municipal work forces, is vastly more diverse today than prior to affirmative action. The black middle class has grown exponentially since its inception, as blacks have moved into the management ranks of corporations, government, and the nonprofit sector.

One of the shibboleths advanced by opponents is that blacks were progressing just fine prior to affirmative action. But the facts don't lie. Consider the stunning gains in black enrollment at historically white colleges and universities during the heyday before the relentless legal assaults. In 1960, prior to affirmative action, only 146,000 black students—a little less than half of all black students in higher education—attended predominantly white schools. By the mid-1990s—after three decades of affirmative action—the number attending these institutions had soared to 1.3 million, constituting nearly 90 percent of all blacks in colleges and universities.

Starting with the presidency of the United States, few, if any, glass ceilings remain today. African-American CEOs have run Fortune 500 corporations including Time Warner, American Express, Maytag, Merrill Lynch, Aetna, Xerox, Merck, McDonald's, TIAA (twice), and Carnival Cruise Lines. Blacks have also served as U.S. secretary of state and presidents of such august colleges and universities as Michigan State, Smith, Brown, and Rensselaer Polytechnic Institute. We've had Pulitzer Prize winners, astronauts, billionaires, presidents of major foundations, governors, and senators, not to mention hip hop artists and impresarios who are vertically and horizontally integrated mini-conglomerates. African-American managers are commonplace in companies of all sizes. This contrasts sharply with the pre–affirmative action era, when blacks seldom rose above clerk, secretary, or messenger in white institutions.

On the entrepreneurial side of the economic equation, African-Americans now own franchises and dealerships. Whereas we once were shut out entirely, black-owned businesses have gained a share of airport construction, downtown development, and neighborhood revitalization. As a direct result of affirmative action, our firms have pushed beyond inner-city neighborhoods and ethnic markets and into the mainstream economy.

These gains, coupled with the growth in black public sector employment, helped fuel the dramatic growth of the African-American middle class. Before affirmative action, the ratio of African-Americans who considered themselves middle class rose from 12 percent in 1949 to 15 percent by 1966–68, a jump of 25 percent. Following affirmative action, the ratio soared to 41 percent by 1996. Sadly, middle-class families of all races, especially African-Americans, have been ravaged by the Great Recession and structural economic shifts.

Some critics say affirmative action bypasses the poor and benefits only minorities who have already made it. While more certainly must be done to help those mired in poverty, it is fallacious to argue that affirmative action helps only the privileged few. After all, where did that mushrooming black middle class come from? Obviously, these talented folks did not all descend from the miniscule black upper class. They ascended from more modest circumstances, thanks to their ability and drive—and thanks as well to the determination of universities and employers to include them.

Affirmative action—or inclusion, as it's called these days—has demonstrated impressive staying power despite heavily financed attacks by right-wing ideologues, conservative blacks, and angry whites, among many others. Ballot initiatives in states such as California have thwarted the use of affirmative action in public universities. Even more destructive to the cause, the Supreme Court and lower-level federal courts have steadily chipped away at affirmative action and forced institutions that espouse inclusion to be more creative about their criteria without running afoul of the courts.

I believe affirmative action endures in practice, if less now in name, because it is actually two concepts, not one. First, it's a philosophy of inclusion that has taken blessedly deep root in America, the most diverse and open society in the history of humankind. The institutions that constitute our nation and make it tick cannot as a practical matter function without diverse work forces, student bodies, and leadership ranks. Opponents of affirmative action cannot prevail on this philosophical plane because exclusion is so contrary to the nation's self-concept and self-interest. Secondly, affirmative action is a set of tools created to accomplish inclusion. That's what the litigation is all about as opponents attempt to cripple its application or persuade courts to outlaw it outright.

Happily, the naysayers finally hit a wall with the Supreme Court in the 2016 case of *Fisher v. University of Texas*. The court ruled that colleges and universities can indeed consider race as one among many factors in creating diverse student bodies. The landmark decision is considered reversal-proof because the majority opinion was written, quite unexpectedly, by Justice Anthony Kennedy, who had never before approved an affirmative action plan for higher education.

When all is said and done, either you support sharing the American Dream with all Americans or you don't. That's the line in the sand in this debate. If you strip away all the disputes, the fundamental question facing our nation is this: will we do our level best to ensure that all Americans—including able young people of color—get to share in the American Dream, or will we leave inclusion to chance?

No society as robustly diverse as ours can survive if opportunity isn't widely shared. This was the way the gates of opportunity were rigged circa 1960, prompting the push for affirmative action in the first place. Reverting to exclusion and tokenism is a surefire formula for even more wrenching social schisms in the twenty-first century. America tried inclusion by chance in previous eras and found it wanting. We must stay the course in our commitment to inclusion by design. Our nation's fate hinges on it. For as A. Bartlett Giamatti, the late president of Yale University, once put it so compellingly, universities—and presumably all such institutions—should be tributaries to society, not sanctuaries from it.

Although the Great Recession wreaked widespread economic havoc on our community, African-Americans today remain solidly ensconced in the middle class as executives and managers, physicians and attorneys, venture capitalists and bankers, educators and entrepreneurs, nurses and executive assistants. This is the impressive and undeniable legacy of *Brown* and the demonstrably effective engine of integration that it inspired—affirmative action.

We fought other policy battles and tackled other contentious issues during my tenure at the Urban League. My overture to the Jewish community in my inaugural keynote address prompted a response in kind from its leadership. At the national and affiliate levels, we held many quiet meetings with leaders of the Anti-Defamation League, the American Jewish Committee, and other groups aimed at thawing the chilly relationship between blacks and Jews and fortifying collaborative efforts on behalf of equality and justice. When black churches in the South were torched by arsonists, the ADL and the Urban League teamed up to help rebuild them, the funds coming primarily from the Jewish community. Upon learning of the shocking assassination of peace-minded Israeli prime minister Yitzak Rabin on November 4, 1995, I headed immediately to the ADL headquarters in New York City to sit quietly with other mourners.

At the urging of Jewish leaders, I addressed a massive rally in support of Israel on the grounds of the Capitol in Washington. When they invited me, I told the leaders that in addition to expressing my stalwart support of Israel's right to exist, I intended to call for the creation of an independent Palestinian state, which must pledge to live in peace with Israel. The leaders hesitated, but when I did not bend,

President George W. Bush
at the National Urban League conference in 2001
National Urban League Archives

they accepted my proviso. When I expressed those dual sentiments in my remarks, some in the crowd booed me, not surprisingly. I am convinced that such public utterances and collaborative initiatives, including Abe Foxman's participation in the League's high-profile press conference to protest police abuse and pressure President Clinton to address this wrenching issue, contributed to de-escalating the hostile rhetoric and warming the relationship between the African-American and Jewish communities.

To fortify our policy and advocacy work, we enlisted William Spriggs, a PhD in economics, to head the National Urban League Center for Opportunity and Equality, our policy operation, based in Washington. I fondly called him "our card-carrying economist." With my economic education limited to an introductory college course, I could go only two sentences deep in a discussion of economic policy. I happily shared the media stage with Bill, a respected scholar and policy expert who was capable of going toe to toe with conservative economists on the federal budget, fiscal policy, and Social Security reform on TV programs such as the *MacNeil/Lehrer NewsHour* on PBS.

The League parted company with President Clinton on welfare reform. While we understood the impulse to impose time limits on the receipt of public assistance, we felt strongly that this should be accompanied by public jobs in the event able-bodied recipients could not find work after their benefits expired. We worried about what would become of them if the economy tanked and unemployment rates surged. During the late-1990s economic boom following the enactment of welfare reform, many ex-recipients found their way into the labor market and welfare rolls shrank dramatically—and former critics of welfare reform such as the Urban League were sometimes derided as "Chicken Littles."

It took a decade for our worst fears to materialize. The Great Recession forced the federal government and states to extend benefits and provide jobs and training in order to forestall worse economic carnage for poor families. Yet some heartless, penny-pinching states refused to do so, leaving vulnerable families and children with no safety net whatsoever.

As the internet became ubiquitous, the League aggressively took up the cause of closing "the digital divide." Black families lagged in computer ownership and internet use, while their public schools and libraries were slower than counterparts in more advantaged communities to get wired. One of our young tech wizards, B. Keith Fulton, spear-headed our advocacy efforts by writing articles, staging policy forums, testifying before the Federal Communications Commission, and supporting the agency's ultimately successful attempt to establish its E-Rate program, which provides discounted rates for wiring public schools and libraries in needy urban and rural communities. While progress did not occur overnight, we counted the League's digital divide campaign as an unqualified advocacy victory.

When conservative writer Charles Murray disparaged the intelligence of black people in his outrageous 1994 book, *The Bell Curve*, the National Urban League mobilized to protest the accuracy of his argument and its implications for societal cohesion. We staged a policy forum featuring noted science historian Stephen Jay Gould and other scholars, who attacked Murray's research and conclusions. C-SPAN broadcast the forum repeatedly. I kept up the drumbeat of criticism in my weekly newspaper column. The League's efforts, along with those of other critics, contributed to discrediting both the book and its author, at least on this issue.

The National Urban League certainly did not prevail in all of these policy battles. For some, we flew solo. On others such as affirmative action and welfare reform, we collaborated with simpatico civil rights and social justice organizations. Fighting the good policy fight was energizing and rewarding. Looking back on the experience, my liberal arts and legal educations, along with my experience as a legal services lawyer, urban affairs consultant, program evaluator, editorial writer, and media and foundation executive, cumulatively equipped me for combat. For a wonk like me, leading the League in these policy wars was indeed a dream come true.

CHAPTER 21

FRINGE BENEFITS

L eading the National Urban League provided a treasure trove of vivid memories. I flew incessantly, carried aloft by everything from jumbo jets and Gulfstream corporate jets to—much to my consternation—helicopters and tiny planes that struck me as slightly elongated crop dusters. Once, on a shuttle flight from New York to D.C., I heard a hellacious thunderclap, everything went to white light outside the windows, and the airplane wobbled like it had hit the mother of all potholes in the sky. After an interminable pause, the pilot came on the intercom to announce that we had been hit by lightning but were okay and would have no problem landing. I knew from this incident what it meant to be terrified—and probably could have written a freshman English essay worthy of an A, even from Professor Baird.

When I visited affiliates, I was driven to and from airports in all manner of vehicles. Never one to stand on ceremony, I did not insist on limo services. My rides ranged from a well-worn pickup truck driven by a young staffer to a prom-sized stretch limo the bilious color of Pepto-Bismol. A state trooper once took me to the Pittsburgh airport in a police cruiser. I rode in the front seat straddling an antiriot rifle that seemed the size of a bazooka.

During our annual conferences, my staff arranged for police escorts to squire me around town from venue to venue. New York City provided the biggest charge, as squad cars with sirens screaming shoved traffic aside and barreled through stoplights. My mother got a huge kick out of those trips, chuckling with glee as the Big Apple made way for us. An unnerving but necessary aspect of the annual conferences was the armed guards provided by local police departments, who accompanied me everywhere and stayed in a hotel room adjacent to mine. They also briefed me on the most expeditious escape routes from the convention halls where I delivered the keynote addresses. I tried not to think about why these precautions were prudent.

Occasional invitations to social events at the White House went with the job. Early on, Marilyn and I attended a party there. It began with a small concert and then segued into a dancing party in both wings of the White House. Vice President Al Gore and his wife, Tipper, led the merriment on the dance floor. Around ten-thirty that evening, I noticed a group of four or five people clustered around President Clinton, who was talking animatedly, as was his wont. I motioned to my wife that the leader of the free world was standing nearby chatting with a small audience, and that we should go join them. Clinton continued talking, regaling us with his frustrations about press coverage. He kept talking and talking and talking. Mrs. Clinton approached the group around midnight and told her husband she was turning in. He talked some more until finally calling it quits around twelve-thirty. We and the other members of his exclusive audience then wandered out of the White House, dazed and marveling at what we had just experienced.

My most memorable encounter with Clinton stemmed from an invitation to accompany him and his entourage on several segments of a multistate tour to promote his New Markets Tax Credit initiative, aimed at stimulating economic development in struggling urban and rural communities. The tour included several flights on Air Force One. I traveled along with cabinet officials, White House staff, and other guests in the area behind the president's quarters. The press corps occupied the cramped rear section of the airplane. As best I could tell from a tour of the president's office and sleeping quarters, the real Air Force One bore a close resemblance to the mockup in the movie thriller of the same name starring Harrison Ford.

During the flights, Clinton occasionally strolled back to our area to chat with his staff and guests. He relaxed by plopping down on the arms of the chairs. While he interacted mostly with his colleagues, we sometimes got a word in edgewise. I actually ate a couple of meals on board. Since Mrs. Clinton wasn't along to keep an eagle eye on the menu, the fare would not have been endorsed by *Prevention* magazine. One evening, we ate pork chops smothered in gravy. Dessert was French apple pie—which, for the uninitiated, is apple pie covered with butter cream icing. It had been one of my favorite sweets in junior high, and I had not eaten it since—until, of all places, aboard Air Force One.

I watched Bill Clinton, the penultimate natural politician, in action on the trip. The Reverend Jesse Jackson accompanied us on one of the segments. Before disembarking from the presidential helicopters in rural Arkansas, Jesse whispered to me, "Now, you're going to see real political genius in action." Coming from Jesse, that was quite a concession. Clinton disembarked first and immediately began working the rope line of well-wishers. Jesse quickly exited and joined right in, working the line as though he were vice president. It was fascinating and hilarious to witness two political forces of nature plying their craft. I retain treasured mementos of the trip to this day, including the menu, the itinerary, and a small container of presidential M&M's.

Our ideological differences notwithstanding, President George W. Bush was every bit as sociable as President Clinton. While he was still governor of Texas, the National Urban League staged a meeting in Austin for our affiliates in the Southern region. Bush hosted a reception for us at the Governor's Mansion. Since Mrs. Bush was away and he had nowhere else to go that evening, he circulated and socialized

Meeting Fidel Castro in Havana
during Time *Newstour in 1995*
© 2016 David Burnett/Contact Press Images

easily among the Urban Leaguers. We had a terrific night and paid no attention to the passage of time. In fact, I told Bush we were having such a good time that he'd have to put us out when he tired of us. He got a kick out of that comment, perhaps because it brought back memories of hanging out in college.

I attended an education meeting in Washington convened by Bush shortly after he was elected in 2000 and just prior to his taking office. During one of the breaks, he mentioned that he would enjoy having Marilyn and me come to the White House to watch movies with him and Mrs. Bush. It never happened because the Iraq War and ideological wars intruded.

I have General Colin Powell to thank for the scariest speaking experience of my life. In April 1997, he organized a national summit on volunteerism, held in Philadelphia. Officially labeled the Presidents' Summit for America's Future, it featured all of the living presidents except for Ronald Reagan, who was stricken with Alzheimer's disease. The orgy of media coverage did wonders to promote Colin's pet cause of mentoring young people. With his unmatched cachet and credibility, he lifted youth development way up the totem pole of public policy

Muhammad Ali at the League's Equal Opportunity Day dinner in 1997
National Urban League Archives

priorities and schooled the skeptical national news media on the issue, compelling them to cover it.

Knowing this meshed perfectly with the League's youth agenda, Colin generously arranged for me to be one of the speakers at the huge plenary session on Sunday. Somehow, I overlooked the instructions that I should come to Philly in the morning for a rehearsal session and to arrange for my remarks to be entered into the teleprompter all the speakers would use. I arrived at the convention center that afternoon, only to learn it was too late to stick my five minutes' worth of comments in the machine. *No problem*, I told myself. I'd just carry my notes, scribbled on yellow legal-sized paper, out to the podium and place them out of sight from the audience. But when I glanced out on the stage, I discovered to my chagrin that the lectern was made of transparent Plexiglas. No way I'd let the audience see my unsightly yellow papers. I had to go cold turkey without notes.

When I inquired where I was slotted, I learned it was between the comedian Sinbad and the singer Michael Bolton. *That's just great*, I thought. *Who'll want to listen to this deadpan speaker drone on about youth development just after a jokester and in front of a crooner?* Well, that's the hand I'd been dealt, so I had to play it.

Oprah Winfrey at the League's Equal Opportunity Day dinner in 2002
National Urban League Archives

When the time came to go on the stage, I walked out warily confident but really nervous. Then I noticed the house lights were up. I could see everything. It looked like five thousand people were out there waiting for the next act. In the first row, I saw, clear as day, President and Mrs. Clinton, President and Mrs. Ford, President and Mrs. George H. W. Bush, President and Mrs. Carter, and First Lady Reagan. They all peered intently at me. To add to my misery, there next to these current and former leaders of the free world were General and Mrs. Powell. He gazed at me with this look that said, *I arranged this slot for you, little brother. Don't screw it up.*

There I stood with no notes before all these reigning and erstwhile leaders. Fortunately, the words came out without a hitch, and my voice did not betray me. But the rest of my body was quaking. My knees knocked the way they had when I first gazed out from a precipice into the Grand Canyon. Happily, there wasn't a puddle of pee around my shoes.

In the fall of 1995, Reg Brack, the CEO of *Time* magazine and chair of the League's board of directors, invited me to participate in the *Time* Newstour, which he was orchestrating. It was an around-the-world tour in eight and a half days to such exotic destinations as Havana, Moscow, Bangalore, Hanoi, and Hong Kong. Reg shepherded several dozen corporate CEOs around the globe. Johnetta Cole, the effervescent president of Spelman College at the time, and I were the only nonprofit executives on the trip.

The Million Man March took place while we were abroad. During one of the lengthy flights between destinations, Jonetta and I struck up a conversation with several senior editors of *Time*, including Norm Pearlstine, editor in chief of *Time* Inc. The topic was what the magazine should make of the Million Man March in the issue that would come out right after the event. I argued there were two ways to view the march—one obvious but the other, I submitted, vastly more interesting. The obvious tack was to concentrate on Minister Louis Farrakhan—namely, what made him tick, what he was after, what it would mean for him in the aftermath of the event. The other approach, I argued, was considerably more important in the long run, yet few news organizations were likely to take it. The question worth concentrating on was why so many African-American males from all walks of life were likely to be drawn to the event. What were they seeking by coming to the Washington Mall and bringing their sons? What were they hoping to say by joining hundreds of thousands of other blacks in bearing witness that day?

This angle really intrigued the *Time* editors. The edition they published in the aftermath of the march clearly reflected it. The cover story in archrival *Newsweek* featured a stark black-and-white photo of Farrakhan, his face half in shadow, half in light. Inside, much of the copy focused on him. *Time* took the opposite tack—namely, the one Johnetta and I had advocated. It devoted the cover story of the October 30, 1995, issue to the march. On the cover was a vivid color photo of several black fathers and sons, dressed in suits and to all appearances middle class. The title of the cover story was, "We, Too, Sing America." It went on to say, "African American men marched in search of hope, strength and one another. Meet some who went, hear what it means to them."

Thus, that impromptu conversation at forty thousand feet paid off for *Time*, for black folk, and presumably for the march's organizers. It surely was a more indelible contribution to the overarching goal of the march than any brief speech I could have delivered on the Mall. The editors of *Time* signaled their gratitude for the suggestion by incorporating several quotes from me in the stories.

Senator Hillary Clinton at the National Urban League conference in 2000
National Urban League Archives

Those conversations on the *Time* Newstour flights put me on a first-name basis with the editors. I tapped this relationship two years later when I approached them with another idea. Several months before our 1997 annual conference in Philadelphia, I contacted Norm and John Huey, the executive editor of *Fortune*, with the suggestion that they key off our conference theme, "Economic Power: the Next Civil Rights Frontier," and do some stories about the rapid ascent of blacks into the highest echelons of corporate America. The editors liked the idea. Leaving nothing to chance, I followed up quickly with a memorandum to them outlining the kinds of articles I would consider, were I an editor of *Fortune*. From there, it was in their hands. A brother and good friend named Roy Johnson, a senior editor there, took charge of the issue.

This conversation produced the historic best-selling issue of *Fortune* for August 4, 1997, which featured a cover story called "The New Black Power" and contained over forty pages of accompanying copy. The editors generously acknowledged the League's contribution to the issue by including a story about us. The issue broke new, exciting ground in the magazine's coverage of blacks in the business world and, for good measure, in the media's coverage of the National Urban League. In subsequent years, *Fortune* produced an annual issue on the status of blacks in corporate America, ranking companies according to their records on diversity.

CHAPTER 22
REFLECTIONS ON LEADERSHIP

When I headed the National Urban League, nothing annoyed me more than people who asked to my face, not
to mention in letters and columns, "Where are the black
leaders today? Why don't we see them and hear from them?" Or, even
more aggravating, people who said, "Today's crop doesn't measure up
to the towering leaders of yesteryear."

Comments like these really smart when you're traveling nearly every week and half the weekends, giving speeches, publishing Op-Ed
articles, holding press conferences, cultivating newspaper coverage by
syndicated columnists, and appearing on every TV and radio program
that will let you get your point across, all the while raising money,
supporting affiliates, and exhorting busy or beleaguered people to get
deeply involved in their children's education.

I became intrigued by the nature of leadership and by leaders, since
I was now one. After all, I had come of age professionally yearning to be
a leader on the national stage. I had met, known, observed, interacted
with, and learned from many leaders, from national politicians and noted civil rights figures to CEOs of Fortune 500 companies. So I set about
analyzing what type of leader I was when I took office and what kind I
had the potential to become. In the near term, I needed to raise my profile. Over the long term, my aim was to broaden and deepen my impact
and, vastly more important, that of the Urban League movement.

Martin Luther King is widely cited as the exemplar of black leadership, and deservedly so. He was our Moses, who braved unimaginable

perils to part the waters between segregation and integration and herald the dawn of a new America. I shudder to think what our country would be like today had he never been born or had he chosen a different line of work.

Incandescently charismatic leaders such as Martin, like Gandhi and Mandela, are accidents of history. They are born, not bred, almost destined for greatness in spite of themselves. There's no graduate school of leadership that promising young people can attend where they take advanced courses in greatness, personal bravery, transcendent vision, and near-saintliness.

Some gifted leaders are beneficent descendants of Machiavelli who have a gut instinct for human and organizational behavior. We pray that transcendent, inspirational leaders mean well. Those so blessed achieve astounding breakthroughs that lift the spirits and brighten the lives of humankind. But some are evil incarnate. Think of Hitler, Idi Amin, Saddam Hussein, and Stalin. Authentic evildoers leave death and destruction in their wake. Whatever side of the moral line they fall on, charismatic leaders of this caliber stand astride the world stage to be followed and celebrated, or else condemned and contained.

People under siege who wait hopefully for their next messiah steadily lose ground to those who rely on themselves and on ambitious mortals in leadership positions—people who grind out progress day in and day out, year after year. That's how most ethnic groups get ahead. Why should it be any different for African-Americans?

There are many types of leaders, although when it comes to black folk and those who presume to anoint our leaders, the focus usually trains on only one type. The best known, the ones who garner most of the attention, are charismatic leaders. However, those luminaries around whom the media flock aren't the only species of leader who help advance causes. Heads of grassroots organizations, sororities, fraternities, and groups such as Eastern Star and the Masons matter enormously as well because of the sway they potentially hold over their members. The same goes for pastors, of course.

The least-appreciated kind of leader is the type no movement worth its salt can do without. It is what might be called the catalytic leader. This person melds compelling ideas with potent constituencies, points them in the right direction, and persistently nudges them toward the goal line. This is a subtle, Svengali style of leadership that's seldom appreciated for its indispensability and impact. Bayard Rustin, the organizing genius behind the 1963 March on Washington, fit this mold, as does Ernesto Cortes, the fabled community organizer with the Industrial Areas Foundation.

Grassroots activists occasionally rise unexpectedly to spark potent movements. These previously unsung, impromptu leaders may even make historic contributions. A case in point was Gardner Bishop, the black barber in D.C. who launched the months-long boycott that helped topple school segregation in the nation's capital.

Those who hold elective office constitute another category of leaders. Adam Clayton Powell, the flamboyant congressman from Harlem, pioneered the use of political power by exploiting his leverage and longevity in Congress to shape antipoverty legislation and shepherd it to final enactment. His successor, Charles Rangel, wielded considerable clout for years in Congress. Whether serving as the prickly conscience of their legislative bodies or as the highest elected officials in their jurisdictions, African-American politicians are a critically important leadership cohort on the contemporary scene.

In 2008, Barack Obama shattered the mold by rocketing in just a few years from obscurity as an Illinois state senator to the presidency of the United States, then winning reelection in 2012. Even though his election has not calmed America's racial turmoil, Obama's stunning victory turned a corner in our nation's history. Actually, had General Colin Powell gone for the gold in 1996, I suspect he could have been elected president, provided he managed to win the Republican nomination. While President Clinton struggled politically, Powell was at the peak of his popularity in the wake of Operation Desert Storm, the successful first Gulf War.

In courts of law, activist attorneys and visionary jurists can engineer profound changes in the legal system and thus society. When he served as dean of Howard University's law school, Charles Houston took pride in training his students to become superb lawyers and social engineers who used the Constitution and statutes to help African-Americans achieve their place in the nation and to make sure the system guaranteed justice and freedom for everyone. His mantra was that "any lawyer that was not a social engineer was a parasite on society." As chief justice of the Supreme Court, Earl Warren orchestrated a unanimous decision in 1954 that altered the course of American history. The Warren court proclaimed in *Brown v. Board of Education* that "in the field of public education the doctrine of 'separate but equal' has no place," and furthermore that "separate educational facilities are inherently unequal." *Brown* set the stage for similar rulings in voting rights, public accommodations, employment, and housing. But as has been proven in recent years, jurists of contrary ideological persuasions are capable of turning back the clock on issues such as voting rights, school integration, and affirmative action that are vital to the interests of African-Americans.

Another category of leaders who matter enormously constitute what I call idea people. By this, I mean those intellectuals and visionaries whose writings and insights shape the understandings, perceptions, ideas, agendas, and actions of others, especially other types of leaders. Intellectual leaders seldom claim an official constituency whom they can cajole or mobilize. Few ever head organizations because that does not play to their strengths. Plus, it intrudes too much on their primary work of researching and reflecting, synthesizing and analyzing, writing and proselytizing on behalf of their ideas.

Some idea people think so far ahead of their times that they pass from the scene before others catch up with them. This is why it's vitally important that they leave a written record of their work for future generations to examine and digest. Frequently, they take intellectual risks and conceptual leaps that expose them to criticism, even ridicule, from those who cannot fathom where they are headed. Occasionally, they are dead wrong in their analyses or prescriptions.

Leaders share many—but certainly not all of the same—attributes, and to varying degrees. Oftentimes, exercising leadership is akin to an out-of-body experience, requiring perspective and reflection even in the midst of the fray. Effective leaders try not to delude themselves or live inside the proverbial bubble. They surround themselves with strong, smart colleagues who are not afraid to dissent. They also listen to constituents and customers on the front lines. I once heard it said that the smartest organizations listen closely to three categories of employees: those who interface with customers and constituents, their youngest workers, and their most recent hires. Some savvy CEOs travel incessantly to visit company operations and employees, mine universities for new research and ideas, and interact with policymakers.

Leaders often rely on intuition, are fearless, and are prone to leaps of faith. They dare to be right and are willing to be wrong. This positions them ahead of the pack, the competition, and the opposition.

240 HUGH B. PRICE

The best of them know what they don't know and where to turn for advice and answers.

Wise leaders read extensively to be certain they are au courant with research, policy, and even ideological screeds, whether generated by those who share their world view or quite the contrary. Many are conscientious students of history and current events. I often learned from experts and advocates who operated outside my comfort zone. At a minimum, I read to keep an eagle eye on what they were saying, so I would be equipped to debate them and hopefully rebut their arguments.

I have never met a leader who was not astute, book smart, street smart, or all three. Leaders possess a capacity to explain as well as inspire. Joel Cogen, my former business partner, once told me that if I could not explain something so my reasonably intelligent aunt got it right away, then it was not clear in my own mind, and I needed to clarify my thoughts. Leaders know how to "perform" the role, as President Reagan demonstrated so effectively. I consistently marvel at how leaders typically outwork everyone else. They are "all in." Even when they are ostensibly off duty and at rest, the furnace is always on, the mind churning.

Impact is the ultimate barometer of leadership. Press clippings aren't the measure of a leader—although admittedly it is fun to send piles of them to one's parents. Much of what leaders do amounts to busywork, albeit useful and sometimes necessary busywork. Some things leaders claim as accomplishments are ephemeral. They feel important and feed one's sense of self-actualization for the time being, but all traces of them soon evaporate like dew on a summer's day.

The accomplishments that impress me most are those with staying power. Movements that generate opportunity and thwart injustice, that engage and empower the previously disengaged and powerless. Voter registration and get-out-the-vote campaigns on behalf of candidates who support our people's and our country's best interests, and against those who do not. Organizations that fight for the enactment of progressive legislation and regulations while relentlessly battling regressive measures. Lawsuits and legal briefs that generate court decrees that demolish barriers to the American mainstream. New laws that fundamentally alter the rules of the game so that those who have traditionally been left out are finally allowed to succeed. Solid and sustainable programs that enable people to get a leg up on life by landing a good job, purchasing a home, or starting a successful business.

Other achievements falling into this category include initiatives that turn youngsters on to learning and then stand them in good stead as citizens and providers for the rest of their lives. Rejuvenated communities that instill a sense of belonging and hope. Durable business enterprises that create livelihoods, sustain families, and generate wealth that fuels philanthropy and finances political engagement. Program interventions that rekindle optimism and cultivate the potential of people society has written off, such as school dropouts, ex-offenders, and welfare moms.

These accomplishments and others like them improve the well-being of humankind. They are the bottom line for judging if leaders live up to the label. Some accomplishments are miniscule but valuable nonetheless. Others are incremental, still others monumental. They all matter because they constitute the building blocks of progress.

Where do I fit on this continuum of leadership styles? The Charisma Kid I'm not—that much I know about myself. I have never met a charismatic leader who wasn't a natural. They have ham aplenty in them. The truth is, I am innately shy. I worked hard at learning and then practicing the people skills expected of the president of the National Urban League. When I entered a roomful of relative strangers, I never lit it up due to the neon glow of my presence. Instead, I took a deep breath and dutifully plunged ahead. I became reasonably comfortable with the role and the responsibilities that went with it, although working a crowd as a speaker or a schmoozer would never top any list of how I prefer spending my time.

Howard Gardner, renowned professor at the Harvard Graduate School of Education and the author of *Multiple Intelligences*, argued that there are seven types of intelligence. Some people, he said, excel at one. Others exhibit several to varying degrees. That's me when it comes to leadership. Mix a smidgen of this with a dash of that and a pinch of the other, stir the ingredients together, let them simmer for several decades, and, presto, you've got leadership Hugh Price–style.

I am probably a combination of catalytic, organizational, and idea leadership. The catalytic variety is exemplified, for instance, by my role in spawning the National Guard Youth ChalleNGe Corps, the Campaign for African-American Achievement, the National Commission on Teaching and America's Future, and the Coalition of Community Foundations for Youth. These examples—especially the first two—also illustrate my propensity to propagate ideas and even, to borrow a delightful word coined by the Reverend James Forbes of Riverside Church in New York City, to "tangibilitate" my novel ideas on occasion. My articles, speeches, and position papers further illustrate this style of leadership. Moreover, I have run and rejuvenated organizations including the National Urban League and the national production division at WNET/Thirteen. Those organizations' good works serve as the most powerful affirmation of my legacy as a leader.

The plain but unappreciated truth is it takes all manner of leaders to move people forward. I refer to those awash in celebrity as well as the anonymous local leaders who do the grunt work of mobilizing the troops and advancing agendas on the ground. Black Lives Matter and the minimum wage movement are examples of consequential modern movements with no symbolic or dominant leader.

No pro football quarterback I know of has ever won a game, let alone a championship, single-handedly. Victory requires head coaches, assistant coaches, blocking backs, tight ends, tackles, safeties, and so forth, all propelling the team forward by pulling their weight according to the game plan. When it comes to twenty-first-century leadership in the black community, a synchronized division of labor among many kinds of leaders is a smarter bet than pining for the next messiah to part the waters.

Much as clothes make the man, the media anoints the leader. At least this was a game the press loved playing with African-Americans during my Urban League years. We constantly read of black notables referred to as civil rights leaders. Other ethnic groups were not similarly burdened to nearly the same extent. Who were the Latino leaders, the Asian-American leaders, the Native American leaders, the Arab-American leaders, and indeed the white leaders who bore this label? The mainstream press wasn't the only segment of the media in the anointing business. Black-owned magazines, newspapers, and TV and radio stations played it to the hilt by meting out coverage and deciding who would appear and with what frequency in their pages and on their airwaves.

To be sure, the game has changed significantly in the era of YouTube and social media, which have diffused and democratized coverage. Social movements such as Black Lives Matter are not organized by or around a recognizable national leader. Indeed, they are so localized that they seem leaderless. Passionate and compelling spokespeople—be they parents, attorneys, or workers—emerge from the local scene to express their grievances and advance their cases. The capacity of social media to help mobilize pop-up protests lends credence and political power to their causes. These movements have gained traction with a spontaneity and rapidity that was unimaginable in my day. To some extent, this amounts to a natural changing of the guard between generations of leaders, but the transition is more profound, fueled by the media revolution itself.

I operated in a media environment that seems prehistoric by contemporary standards. As president of the National Urban League, I enjoyed modest celebrity and received substantial press coverage from time to time. Early on, when I was something of a novelty, attention came easily. This lulled me into thinking I wouldn't have to work hard to attract the press. Yet the coverage soon cooled off, and we had to hustle for the remainder of my tenure. We received generous coverage from nationally syndicated newspaper columnists, who often found our work and my writings a useful point of departure for their own commentaries. Yet with each passing year, we labored harder and harder, and ever more imaginatively, to generate whatever media coverage we received.

During one of the periodic dry spells when we couldn't scare up coverage no matter what we tried, I sought out several print reporters and editors at national newspapers and newsmagazines for an off-the-record chat. When I asked why the League's policy pronouncements and program initiatives weren't deemed newsworthy, their candid responses stunned me. One reporter told me point blank, "Basically, if there isn't any soap opera going on inside an organization, we aren't interested." Another responded, "If you aren't operating way out there on one ideological extreme or the other, we could care less what you have to say." From a third insider, I heard, "If your programs aren't fronted by a celebrity, readers won't read the articles, so we won't bother to write them." Finally, a senior editor disavowed any interest in what organizations such as the League had to say. Sending him press releases, he advised, was a waste of paper.

These frank conversations made the reasons for skimpy media coverage perfectly clear—and quite disheartening. To compound the problem, the escalating competition among media outlets meant they were resorting increasingly to what was called "enterprise journalism." Instead of covering and keying off what bona fide organizations said or did, some newspapers were conjuring up their own story ideas and angles, then deploying reporters to research and write them. If your organization happened to fit snugly into one of these stories, or if your leader was called for a pithy quote, you got covered. Otherwise, you might never even know the story was in the works until you read it in the paper. Enterprise journalism crowded out coverage of other events and utterances that editors believed did not serve their journalistic agendas.

Radio emerged during the 1990s as one of the most effective and efficient means to reach mass audiences and especially African-American audiences. The morning drive-time talk shows, whether nationally syndicated or local, enjoyed vast and fiercely loyal followings. Plus, the programming was enriched by news services that distributed stories and interviews for broadcast. NPR was quite receptive and reliably sought out my colleagues and me for interviews. At the outset of my tenure, radio ranked as a stepchild in our media strategy. By the end, it stood on equal footing with every other form, and even became the avenue of choice, depending on what we were pitching.

Television was a different story entirely. BET, the cable channel focused on African-Americans, stayed interested in the League throughout my tenure. For all the brickbats hurled at BET, some of which were deserved, I never joined the chorus of detractors. Of course, it served the League's interest to stay on BET's good side. But a higher order of pragmatism explained my position. Whatever its shortcomings, BET was the only television network whose news and public affairs programs, such as *Lead Story*, consistently displayed genuine interest in black issues and organizations. It was the only network that routinely invited my colleagues and me, as well as leaders of other black groups, to appear on the air to comment on some policy issue or outrage. It was the only network dedicated to black issues that produced lengthy-enough interview segments to allow guests to speak in complete sentences. And it was the only network that called upon us as readily as we called upon it.

C-SPAN was extremely generous as well, within the strictures of the way it operated. We craved C-SPAN coverage of our press conferences and policy symposia, as well as my keynote speeches and other sessions at the League's annual conferences. Although its ratings were miniscule in any given time slot, the network ran its programs repeatedly, day and night for months on end, presumably until the master tape wore out. After an appearance on C-SPAN, I sometimes heard about it within an hour from Colin Powell, or several weeks later from an airport baggage handler who had watched a recent rebroadcast in the middle of the night before heading to work.

I frequently appeared on Fox News, even though the network and I generally held polar opposite views. Friends used to sympathize with me for having to go mano a mano with conservative anchors such as Bill O'Reilly and Sean Hannity on Fox, Pat Buchanan on CNN, and Alan Keyes on MSNBC. I debated Ward Connerly, an avowed foe of affirmative action, so often that we joked about creating our own point-counterpoint talk show on TV.

Friends and even producers of these shows who felt sorry for me overlooked the fact that I was trained as an attorney. Lawyers enjoy verbal combat. Besides, I felt strongly that advocates like me must not allow our adversaries a free ride with nationwide audiences. I strapped on my armor, grabbed my verbal lance, strode brazenly into the opponents' arenas, and did ideological battle. The truth was, I enjoyed the on-air combat.

Occasionally, a conservative talk-show host pulled a bait-and-switch by inviting me on to discuss some generic issue, only to open the show with a scathing commentary on what some other leader supposedly had done or said. The host would try to lure me into joining the chorus of criticism. But I never bit, routinely responding that I wasn't that leader's spokesperson, nor had I any clue what he or she had done that prompted the question. These standoffs produced moments when I remained utterly silent, which the hosts hated, until they realized I wasn't going to play their game. Silence was anathema to those talk shows, so I simply waited quietly until the anchor was obliged to move on to a different topic.

Twice, the League teamed up with the Advertising Council to create public service announcements that spread our messages on television and radio. Thanks to our partnering with State Farm, the "Achievement Matters" message appeared in ads in black newspapers around the country. Our affiliates unleashed their own creativity. My book *Achievement Matters* and the accompanying tour, which lasted nearly five months, spread our gospel of achievement, along with the League's brand, to newspapers, television and radio programs, and bookstores across America. We even placed articles in tiny shopping newspapers that were hungry for editorial copy and reached millions of consumers each week.

The democratization of the media may pose challenges to traditional organizations, but it unquestionably is a boon to the causes they espouse. When conservatives gleefully needled the news media about its purported liberal bias, my reaction from firsthand experience at the helm of a venerable and respected liberal organization was, "That's BS." Adversity made us inventive and enterprising. It weaned us from dependence on traditional media and forced us to mine the possibilities of new technology and social media.

CHAPTER 23

DENOUEMENT OF AN ADVENTURESOME CAREER

By the fall of 2002, as my ninth year at the helm of the National Urban League approached, I realized I was a spent rocket. I've always believed that leaders of organizations such as the League should go flat out as long as they can but then pass the baton before they stumble, get winded, or wear out their welcomes. Glancing at my schedule, I was reminded that for nearly nine years I had spent the better part of four weeks out of five and two weekends out of five on the road, doing the League's bidding and business. I was never a relaxed flier to begin with. Incessant air travel, especially following 9/11, had taken a physical and psychic toll, thanks to the interminable lines, flight delays, and anxiety over whether terrorists would strike the airlines again.

I felt I'd had a good run and realized much of what I had hoped to contribute in accepting the position. Of course, there was much unfinished business. It is seldom possible to achieve closure on big causes like improving children's education or combatting police-community tensions.

That November, I announced to the National Urban League board, staff, and affiliates and the news media that while there was never a good time to leave the job of a lifetime, the time for me had come. I would pass the reins to a new generation of leader with new ideas, fresh energy, and more contemporary skills. To remain vital and relevant, organizations must periodically regenerate themselves with infusions of leadership and ideas. As I approached the age of sixty-two, I explained, I was determined to recalibrate the balance between my personal and professional lives. What's more, I wanted to explore whether or not I had one more significant professional move ahead.

Thanks to a chance encounter at JFK International Airport with a former Rockefeller colleague, I had discovered prior to my resignation that the foundation offered a unique fellowship to its former trustees and executives (plus their spouses or significant others) at its spectacular conference center in Bellagio on Lake Como in Italy. The role, either solo or shared with one's partner, entailed serving as titular host(s) of the center, greeting arriving scholars and artists who would spend a month there, presiding at their pre-dinner presentations, taking them on tours of picturesque towns, and working on a project of one's choosing. I dashed home to tell Marilyn that I had the perfect exit plan.

My last day with the League was Friday, April 11, 2003. The following Monday, we flew to Milan and drove on to Bellagio for the start of an idyllic—and productive—two-and-a-half-month stay in paradise. Bellagio is a jewel of a town. In April and May, the shores of Lake Como are festooned with blooming rhododendron and azalea bushes rising to a height of two or three stories. I devoted the mornings to beginning work on this memoir. During the afternoons, we socialized with the guests, led them on tours, and kibitzed in conferences on all manner of topics. After dinner, we joined guests in making gelato runs into town and ranking the desserts.

One night, we accompanied hundreds of townspeople and tourists in celebrating a local feast by carrying torches and marching a couple of miles along the lake to a nearby town. We came upon a street festival with group dancing in the square. The musical beat sounded vaguely familiar. When we strolled over to watch the dancers, we discovered they were primarily women doing the Electric Slide, which was the craze in the black community back home.

Our sojourn in paradise ended in late June. Once back home, I turned my attention to deciding on my next professional move. At the top of my list was running a national foundation. Between the board members, the staff colleagues, and the donor community, I had always enjoyed the stimulating intellectual environment of foundation life, not to mention the creativity and flexibility made possible by giving away other people's money. I had a major caveat, though. At my age, I was determined to stay on the eastern seaboard, which was home to most of our family and close friends. We had no appetite for starting afresh in a new region of the country. While I fielded some tentative inquiries about foundation opportunities elsewhere, no leadership positions that met my criteria materialized.

I interviewed for the presidency of a prestigious college. However, the fit did not feel right, especially since the sector would be entirely new to me and I questioned if I had enough runway ahead of me to learn what the job entailed, to earn the confidence of the faculty and board, and to make an impact that would be fulfilling. What's more, I was still spoiled by the high-profile nature of my National Urban League role and was not sure I could adapt to the less-public nature of the position, which, of necessity, stressed administration, student and parent relations, and, of course, endless fundraising.

Another possibility was a senior position with a major corporation. I received one nibble, but the portfolio felt too limited. Fortunately, I was in a financial position to be picky and patient, thanks to my membership on three Fortune 500 corporate boards—namely, Verizon, MetLife, and Sears.

The opportunity that ultimately materialized was one I least expected. When an enterprising young associate, Nat Piggee with the law firm of Piper Rudnick, read about my resignation, he recommended to the managing partners that they approach me about joining the firm. We held an exploratory conversation before my wife and I departed for Italy. The discussion focused on my playing a client development role, capitalizing on the corporate CEOs and general counsel I had gotten to know through the League. Since I wanted to mull the conversation, we agreed that neither they nor I were in any rush and that we would reconnect once I returned from Bellagio.

I joined Piper Rudnick in the summer of 2003. I was curious about being part of a large, bustling law firm and was attracted by the fact that many of the attorneys were extremely personable. The downside, though, was that I had not practiced law since 1968. It made no sense whatsoever for me or prospective clients that I should try to resume functioning as an attorney. I enjoyed some success linking the firm's lawyers with prospective clients and actually helped land a whopper. Meanwhile, the firm expanded from nine hundred to twenty-seven hundred attorneys, thanks to two mega-mergers, and morphed into the global firm now known as DLA Piper. However, it eventually became clear why law firm life had never been my forte—especially in this instance, since I could not actually practice. So two years after my arrival, the firm and I parted company amicably.

Newly idle at age sixty-four except for the boards, I wondered if I was now out of the game entirely. I felt ready to ratchet up my love of photography into a more consuming hobby. But a chance encounter with Isabel Sawhill, a distinguished economist at the Brookings Institution and a grantee from my Rockefeller days, rescued me from premature idleness. "Belle" inquired what I was up to, and I replied that, aside from the boards, my professional dance card was mostly empty. She suggested that we chat about linking up with Brookings. Given Brookings's sterling reputation as the nation's oldest and largest think tank, I readily agreed.

Brookings and I struck up a relationship that suited me just fine. I became a nonresident senior fellow. I kid people that this meant I was an old guy who lived out of town. We agreed that I would spend one week per month at Brookings in Washington. Since much of Brookings operates on so-called soft money or grants, it could pay me only if I managed to raise money. Thanks to those corporate boards, I had no pressing need for compensation. Brookings met my two most important needs—coverage of expenses for my monthly visits and provision of a full-time research assistant, who turned out to be Oliver Sloman, a bright young graduate of Williams College.

Brookings kept my synapses firing. I rekindled my interest in the lessons to be learned from military approaches to education and training that might help youngsters struggling in school. With Oliver's able help, I cranked out position papers and made presentations at various conferences and symposia in D.C.

I hatched and wrote another book while at Brookings. Inspired by the National Urban League's Campaign for African-American Achievement, it was entitled, *Mobilizing the Community to Help Students Succeed.* It delved into the research about why communities matter in promoting achievement and laid out lessons from the League's campaign and other ideas for stoking student interest in school. The Association for Supervision and Curriculum Development, an organization of school principals, administrators, teachers, and advocates, published the book in 2008 and distributed it to its hundred thousand members around the world. This was a ten-strike in terms of reach and readership.

I frequently sat in on the steady stream of forums and speeches by prominent policymakers that Brookings staged almost daily. Other think tanks, advocacy groups, and government agencies sponsored forums as well. I was in policy-wonk heaven.

During my three years in this part-time, nonresident role at Brookings, I occasionally received queries asking if I was interested in making a run at a full-time position. I interviewed for one intriguing post but quickly came to realize I no longer had the appetite for learning a new organizational culture, running or reorganizing anything, raising money, downsizing anyone, or performing the other roles that invariably went with leading an organization.

Besides, I had discovered something else about myself. Having led an organization of consequence and, I thought, done it rather well, I no longer wished to compete for anything and risk being rejected. I doubted my ego could handle it at this age. If someone wanted me to consider doing something, the drill now was to chat to determine the degree of mutual interest. If it was a go, then we'd seal the deal, no waiting around to see who else surfaced and how the search turned out. I realized this was arrogant of me. But I was too old and experienced to be told no thanks.

Come 2007, I was enjoying my Brookings position when another chance encounter triggered what turned into the capstone of my professional career. At a reception in New York City to celebrate the seventy-fifth anniversary of the Russell Sage Foundation, I ran into longtime friend and noted scholar Katherine Newman, whose research and writing we had supported during my Rockefeller years. Katherine was a tenured professor in the Woodrow Wilson School at Princeton University. She inquired what I was doing, and I mentioned the board service plus the part-time Brookings relationship, adding that these commitments consumed roughly half of my time. Katherine then asked if I would be interested in teaching at the Woodrow Wilson School.

The idea intrigued me because, after all, Princeton was Princeton and because I had always enjoyed teaching, albeit never on a full-time basis. Early in my career, I had taught an occasional seminar at Yale College, Yale Law School, and Columbia Law School. Ironically, I never got the geography right. When I taught at Columbia in New York, we lived in New Haven. I began law school at Yale while we were in New Haven but continued even after we moved to Westchester County, just north of New York.

I visited the Princeton campus to meet with Katherine and the acting dean of WWS. I also delivered a guest lecture that sort of served as an audition, although their minds and mine were close to made up. Since I had delivered many a speech, press conference, and presentation in my time, the audition was stress-free.

We sealed the deal when I accepted a full-time, endowed visiting professorship. The five-year appointment began in the fall of 2008. The position appealed for many reasons. The school administrators made it crystal-clear that my role was to teach, mentor, and minister to the needs of the students. And as an endowed visiting professor, I needn't worry about raising money for the position, serving on committees, or publishing for tenure.

I taught public policy seminars to undergraduate and graduate students in the Woodrow Wilson School. As might be expected, they were all exceptionally bright. Several were off-the-charts brilliant. Two of my students were named Rhodes Scholars, one won a German Marshall Fellowship, and several more were near misses, for reasons that eluded me. In an attempt to console them, I told these disappointed students that it was the programs' loss, not theirs. One of the gratifying, yet privately amusing, aspects of having students compete for these coveted fellowships was that many asked me to write letters of recommendation. I pondered what I could possibly write that would help them land a prize I never had the academic chops to win.

I never had a Princeton student I didn't like. They were so bright and conscientious that I had to challenge and even surprise them in order to keep them intellectually stimulated and engaged. I frequently utilized unorthodox formats in class, such as simulated C-SPAN policy forums, press conferences, and legislative testimony, which required them to make presentations that their classmates then critiqued. These young people relished taking charge of their own learning. While I did encounter rare procrastinators (usually for some emotional reason), I never had any slackers, who would not have been able to survive the rigors at Princeton anyway.

Students often visited my office to discuss issues raised in the seminars, prospective term paper topics, post-graduate education, career aspirations, family issues, whatever. When I was in college and law school, I was too reticent and intimidated by my professors to seek out meetings with them. My Princeton students brimmed with self-confidence. In fact, during my first week there, a young woman who was a senior requested a meeting. When she arrived, she sat down, opened her laptop, and blithely asked, "So, how was your summer?" *No shrinking violets here*, I thought.

Once again, I flunked geography when it came to teaching. I faced an hour-and-a-half drive each way between New Rochelle and Princeton. I typically stayed there from Monday through Thursday. Marilyn came down occasionally to stretch it into a weekend, when we'd enjoy dinner with local friends or a play at the McCarter Theatre. I confess that the evenings were quiet and lonely at times. For most of my five years there, I lived in a university-owned efficiency apartment that might charitably be called "sparsely decorated." "Man cave" would be more apt.

As a visiting professor who was seldom around on weekends, I never really got into the flow of faculty social life. I made several friends among WWS administrators and visiting faculty and occasionally dined out with them. To stay busy most weeknights, I took advantage of the stimulating array of lectures and presentations by luminaries including novelist Toni Morrison, economist Alan Blinder, and Isabel Wilkerson, Pulitzer Prize–winning author of *The Warmth of Other Suns*. As an avid film buff, I saw many a movie at the quaint Garden Theatre in town. By Thursday, I was eager to complete my seminar(s) and student meetings and head home.

The beginning of my teaching career at Princeton bordered on madcap. I had to get acclimated to the commute, the rhythms of yet another new career, the workload of creating and then teaching three new courses, and the final stages of traveling the eastern seaboard with my latest book. While I remained affiliated with Brookings, my involvement tapered off substantially and essentially petered out by the end of my Princeton stint in 2013.

Ironically, my Princeton career was bookended by two books. Promoting *Mobilizing the Community to Help Students Succeed* consumed some of my time and energy at the outset. And two years prior to the end of my tenure, I embarked on researching and writing a book about my pet idea of utilizing military education and training methods, as exemplified by the Youth ChalleNGe program, to help youngsters failing in school. By the end of my appointment, I had completed the draft manuscript and begun to shop it to publishers.

Regrettably, no one bit. Since the book was fully baked, I decided it was coming out of the oven, as it were, even if I had to self-publish it.

I ended up going this route, working with a boutique self-publishing firm known, fittingly enough, as Small Batch Books. Thus was born *Strugglers Into Strivers: What the Military Can Teach Us About How Young People Learn and Grow*, published in the fall of 2014. Since I underwent major back surgery barely a month before it came out, much of my post-operative energy and thoughts focused on self-marketing it. I reveled in the fact that John Merrow, the education correspondent for the *PBS NewsHour*, rated *Strugglers Into Strivers* one of the dozen most important education books of 2014.

By mid-2013, Marilyn and I had decided it was time to retire for real. We were in our early seventies, several years past the customary Social Security retirement age. As much as I enjoyed teaching at Princeton and especially interacting with the wonderful students, being away from her and from home for most of the year had gradually gotten old. So that summer, we both entered a state of semi-, supposed, sort-of retirement. And when I turned seventy-two, I "aged off" the corporate boards.

Marilyn and I remain quite busy with immensely enjoyable civic and social groups and nonprofit boards. I continued for a while on the board of Georgetown University, which was a fascinating experience. Where else would the agenda for meetings run the gamut from the expected business of a great university to the future of Big East basketball and the implications of Pope Benedict's surprising decision to relinquish the papacy? I reluctantly stepped down from Georgetown when I became chair of the board of a wonderfully creative nonprofit film and education center, the Jacob Burns Film Center in nearby Pleasantville, New York. Still, I remained determined to avoid volunteer overload, which can destroy any semblance of true retirement. Besides, I was intent on protecting enough time to resume writing this memoir.

Thus, we remain true to "retirement" on our terms. We relish our expanded time together and with our daughters and their spouses. We see more of siblings, in-laws, nieces, nephews, and their kids, socialize with dear friends, partake of the incomparable intellectual, entertainment, and cultural bounty of New York City and environs, devour books instead of having the web devour us, enjoy the beauty and tranquility of the Berkshires, and travel enough to remain curious about the world. After a hiatus dating back to junior high, I have even resumed playing cards with a garrulous group of fellows affectionately known as the Whist Brothers. At our monthly gatherings, we play bid whist, relax, eat, and spiritedly talk politics.

Needless to say, I was astonished and overjoyed when Barack Obama was elected president. I am impressed by his accomplishments, intellect, resilience, and grace in the face of virulent political opposition, vicious racist attacks on his character, the scourge of terrorism, and the unnerving instability in the world. I do not pine for the supposedly halcyon days of yesteryear. But as may be true of many who are aging, the world to me seems increasingly unhinged and incomprehensible. Despite being a *New York Times* alumnus and a lifelong public policy junkie, I vacillate these days between avidly following the news and avoiding it altogether because I cannot stomach it.

I pray that our daughters, their spouses, and our extended families, as well as my Princeton students and all future generations, will mobilize to take charge of the turbulent world they are inheriting, that they will force the elders who control politics today to stand down, for they have made enough of a mess of things. It is time to stand down from hate, from spewing venom against gay and transgender children of God, against ethnic groups and faiths other than one's own, against political opponents and sports rivals. It is high time to replace destructive strife with unstinting devotion to the well-being of everyday people and the fragile earth that we—the most privileged of species—inhabit.

ACKNOWLEDGMENTS

Throughout the inexorable march of African-Americans toward our nation's social, economic, and political mainstream, we have been propelled forward by the vision, resolve, and sacrifices of those who pointed the way and then actually paved it. As is evident from this memoir, I've been the beneficiary of such nurturing and guidance from my beloved wife, my daughters, and their spouses, as well as my ancestors, parents, brother, teachers, close friends, colleagues, and mentors. Many are cited in my memoir, although those who shaped me and my journey are far too numerous to mention.

I owe a debt of gratitude to several individuals who took enormous leaps of faith in me that I might not have dared to take myself: Charles Runyon of Yale Law School; Mitchell Sviridoff of the Ford Foundation; Max Frankel of the *New York Times*; and Jay Iselin of WNET/ Thirteen, the PBS station in New York City. National Urban League board chair Reg Brack, along with Bernard Watson, Charles Hamilton, and the other directors, took a chance on a comparatively low-profile foundation executive as the next head of the legendary organization, thus fulfilling my dream of holding the job of a lifetime. To the extent my tenure was productive and successful, it was in substantial part attributable to the passion and professionalism of my Urban League colleagues in the national organization and the local affiliates across the country.

Numerous role models who served our people with brilliance, dignity, and compassion inspired me as I came of age professionally. I wanted to grow up to be like them. I speak of Charles Hamilton Houston, Whitney Young, Robert Weaver, Dorothy Height, Thurgood Marshall, Judge Constance Baker Motley, E. Frederic Morrow, Vernon Jordan, John Jacob, Clifton Wharton, Marian Wright Edelman,

Dr. James Comer, Eleanor Holmes Norton, and Franklin Thomas, among others.

Portions of my memoir were adapted from previous books and articles. When it came to ancestral research, I mostly rode the coattails of my mother, Charlotte Schuster Price, and her sister, Violet Royster, and cousin Winifred Norman, along with Professor Asa Davis of Amherst College and Merrill Beach, the town historian of Trumbull, Connecticut. Regrettably, none are alive for me to thank personally for their considerable contributions to this book.

I am deeply grateful to Sybil Haydel Morial, the author of *Witness to Change* and mother of Marc Morial, my esteemed successor as president of the National Urban League, for introducing me to her publisher, John F. Blair. The enthusiastic embrace of my book by Blair's president, Carolyn Sakowski, spurred me to complete it after years of proceeding by fits and starts. The deft workmanship of Steve Kirk, Blair's editor in chief, made my manuscript more focused and reader friendly. Their colleagues in publicity and marketing have been enormously supportive as well.

Lastly, I thank the Rockefeller Foundation for allowing me to spend sustained time at its magnificent Bellagio Center on Lake Como in Italy. The idyllic, yet intellectually stimulating, atmosphere enabled me to reflect on my life, research my lineage, and begin writing what would become *This African-American Life*.

REFERENCES

Abdul-Jabbar, Kareem. *Black Profiles in Courage: A Legacy of African-American Achievement.* New York: William Morrow, 1996.

Beach, E. Merrill. *From Valley Forge to Freedom: A Story of a Black Patriot.* Chester, Conn.: Pequot Press, 1975.

Buckley, Gail. *American Patriots: The Story of Blacks in the Military from the Revolution to Desert Storm.* New York: Random House, 2001.

Burnham, Phillip. "Selling Poor Steven: The Struggles and Torments of a Forgotten Class in Antebellum America: Black Slaveowners." *American Legacy* (Summer 2003), 44–54.

Carlson, Tucker. "Washington's Lost Black Aristocracy." *City Journal.* Autumn 1996. www.city-journal.org/html/washington's-lost-black-aristocracy-12024.html.

Cultural Tourism DC. 2016. http://www.culturaltourismdc.org. Accessed Spring 2003. This website includes brief histories of Freedmen's Hospital, the Howard University Hospital/Griffith Stadium site, the U Street/Shaw neighborhoods, and the Brookland neighborhood.

Davis, Asa J. "The George Latimer Case: A Benchmark in the Struggle for Freedom." Nov. 21, 2005. http://edison.rutgers.edu/Latimer/glatcase.htm. Accessed Fall 2005.

Edwards, Bill. "Eleanor 'Dora' Nora Goldberg Bayes Gressing Norworth Clarke Gordon Friedland." http://www.ragpiano.com/perform/nbayes.shtml. Accessed Fall 2015.

Freedman, Marc. *The Kindness of Strangers: Adult Mentors, Urban Youth, and the New Volunteerism.* San Francisco: Jossey-Bass, 1993.

Gac, Scott. "Slave or Free? White or Black? The Representation of George Latimer." *New England Quarterly* 88 (March 2015): 73–103.

Jacobellis, William. *Sports Photo Album.* New York: David McKay, 1951.

Jones, R. Frank. *Trials of a Pioneer.* American Urological Association and Hoffman-LaRoche, 1981. Paper presented at Forum on the History of Urology, Washington Meeting of the American Urological Association, May 22, 1978.

Kabaservice, Geoffrey. *The Guardians: Kingman Brewster, His Circle and the Rise of the Liberal Establishment.* New York: Henry Holt, 2004.

Kibler, M. Alison. "Nora Bayes." *Jewish Women's Archive.* March 1, 2009. http://jwa.org/encyclopedia/article/bayes-nora. Accessed Fall 2015.

Kluger, Richard. *Simple Justice: The History of* Brown v. Board of Education *and Black America's Struggle for Equality.* New York: Alfred A. Knopf, 1976.

Lesko, Kathleen Menzie, Valerie Babb, and Carroll R. Gibbs. *Black Georgetown Remembered: A History of Its Black Community from the Founding of "The Town of George" in 1751 to the Present Day.* Washington, D.C.: Georgetown University Press, 1991.

Lindsay, Drew. "The Court Decision That Changed Everything." *Washingtonian* (May 2004): 52–67.

Mackall, Henry C. "Robert Gunnell of Langley: An Emancipated Slave." *Fairfax County Stories.* 2007. http://fairfaxstories.sharepoint. com/Pages/JamestownEssaysAuthors.aspx.

Madden, Bill. *1954: The Year Willie Mays and the First Generation of Black Superstars Changed Major League Forever.* Boston: Da Capo Press, 2014.

McNeil, Genna Rae. *Groundwork: Charles Hamilton Houston and the Struggle for Civil Rights.* Philadelphia: University of Pennsylvania Press, 1984.

Myers, Walter Dean. *Now Is Your Time! The African-American Struggle for Freedom*. New York: Harper Trophy Books, 1992.

Norman, Winifred Latimer, and Lily Paterson. *Lewis Latimer*. New York: Chelsea House Press, 1994.

Price, Hugh B. *Achievement Matters: Getting Your Child the Best Education Possible*. New York: Kensington, 2002.

———. "Jackie and Me." *Washingtonian* (August 2005): 35–40.

———. "Looking ahead in South Africa." *Amherst*, 43 (Summer 1991): 22–23, 35.

———. *Mobilizing the Community to Help Students Succeed*. Alexandria, Va.: ASCD, 2008.

———. "The Search for Nero Hawley: A Family Seeks a Tangible Link to a Black Patriot Ancestor." *American Legacy* (Fall 2008): 16–23.

———. *Strugglers Into Strivers: What the Military Can Teach Us About How Young People Learn and Grow*. Amherst, Mass.: Small Batch Books, 2014.

Snyder, Brad. *Beyond the Shadow of the Senators: The Untold Story of the Homestead Grays and the Integration of Baseball*. New York: McGraw-Hill, 2003.

Sugrue, Thomas J. *Sweet Land of Liberty: The Forgotten Struggle for Civil Rights in the North*. New York: Random House, 2008.

Turner, Glennette Tilley. *Lewis Howard Latimer*. Englewood Cliffs, N.J.: Silver Burdett Press, 1991.

"Washington, D.C.: A National Register of Historic Places Travel Itinerary." *National Park Service*. http://www.cr.nps.gov/nr/travel/wash. Accessed Spring 2003. This web page includes brief histories of the Greater U Street Historic District and the LeDroit Park Historic District.

INDEX